Jonathan Clements is the author of many books on East Asian history, including biographies of Empress Wu, Admiral Tōgō, the statesman Prince Saionji and Coxinga, the Japanese-born 'pirate king'. His acclaimed collection of poetry translations, *The Moon in the Pines*, is published in paperback as *Zen Haiku*. He divides his time between London, England and Jyväskylä, Finland. His website is www.muramasaindustries.com

D0964904

Titles available in the *Brief History* series

A BRIEF HISTORY OF

THE SAMURAI

The Way of Japan's Elite Warriors

JONATHAN CLEMENTS

ROBINSON   RUNNING PRESS
PHILADELPHIA · LONDON

Constable & Robinson Ltd
3 The Lanchesters
162 Fulham Palace Road
London W6 9ER
www.constablerobinson.com

First published in the UK by Robinson,
an imprint of Constable & Robinson Ltd, 2010

A copy of the British Library Cataloguing in Publication
data is available from the British Library

UK ISBN: 978-1-84529-947-7

1 3 5 7 9 10 8 6 4 2

First published in the United States in 2010
by Running Press Book Publishers

9 8 7 6 5 4 3 2 1

Digit on the right indicates the number of this printing

US Library of Congress Control Number: 2009935109
US ISBN 978-0-7624-3850-1

Running Press Book Publishers
2300 Chestnut Street
Philadelphia, PA 19103-4371

Visit us on the web!

www.runningpress.com

Typeset by TW Typesetting, Plymouth, Devon
Printed and bound in the EU

For
Dominic Clements

CONTENTS

ACKNOWLEDGEMENTS

I would like to thank my commissioning editor Leo Hollis and all at Constable & Robinson, my agent Chelsey Fox of Fox & Howard, Sharon Gosling, Adam Newell, Ellis Tinios, Alex and Reiko McLaren, Jaqueline Mitchell, Tamamuro Motoko, Stephen Turnbull and the staff of the library at the London School of Oriental and African Studies. And, as ever, my wife Kati, who celebrated this book's completion by fighting for four days at a temple on Shikoku: 'fit to confront a demon or a god, she was worth a thousand warriors.' (*Heike Monogatari*, IX: 4)

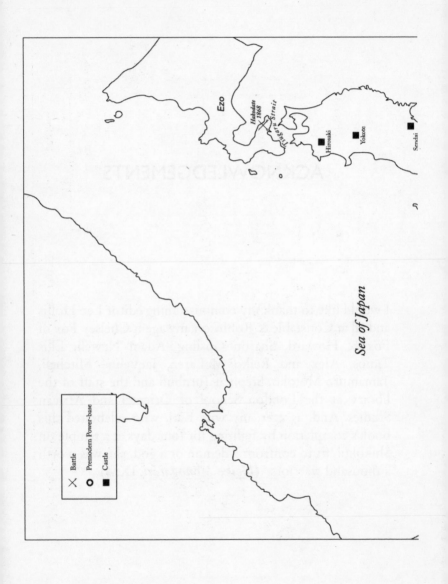

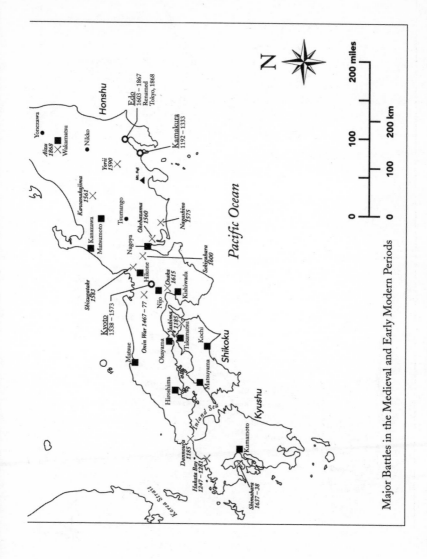

Major Battles in the Medieval and Early Modern Periods

Honshu

Yonezawa

Aizu
1868
Wakamatsu ✕

● Niiko

Yori
1590 ✕

Mt. Fuji ▲

Edo
1603–1867
Renamed
Tokyo, 1868

Kamakura
1192–1333

Kawanakajima
1561 ✕

Kanazawa ■
Matsumoto ■

Tsumango ●

Nagoya ■

Okehazama
1560 ✕

Nagashino
1575 ✕

Pacific Ocean

Shizugatake 1583 ✕

Hikone ○

Sekigahara
1600

Matsue ■

Kyoto
1338–1573

Onin War 1467–77 ✕

Nijo ■

Osaka
1615 ■

Kishiwada ■

Yashima
1185 ✕

Okayama ■
Hiroshima ■

Takamatsu ■
Matsuyama ■

Kochi ■

Shikoku

Dannoura
1185 ✕

Inland Sea

Kumamoto ■

Hakata Bay
1247–1281 ✕

Shimabara
1637–38 ✕

Kyushu

Korea Strait

N

0   100   200 km
0   200 miles

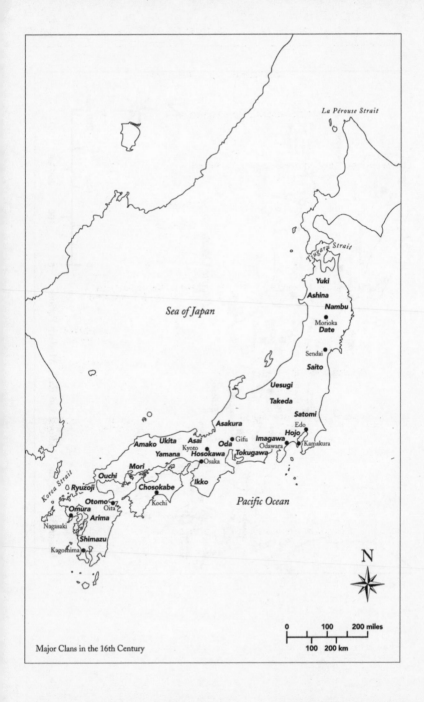

Major Clans in the 16th Century

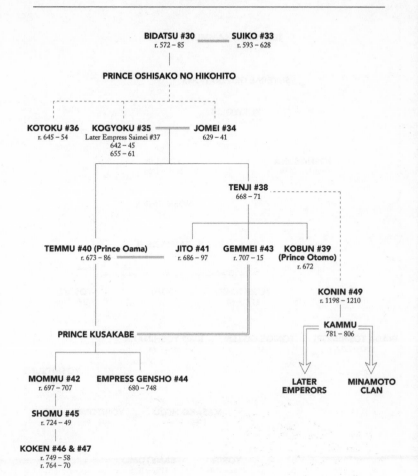

Emperors of Japan in the 6th and 7th centuries

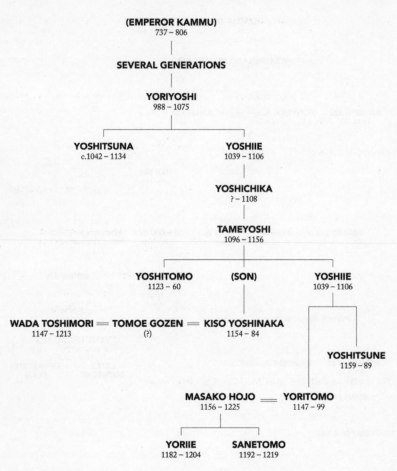

(EMPEROR KAMMU)
737 – 806

|

SEVERAL GENERATIONS

|

YORIYOSHI
988 – 1075

YOSHITSUNA   **YOSHIIE**
c.1042 – 1134   1039 – 1106

YOSHICHIKA
? – 1108

TAMEYOSHI
1096 – 1156

YOSHITOMO   **(SON)**   **YOSHIIE**
1123 – 60   1039 – 1106

WADA TOSHIMORI ═ **TOMOE GOZEN** ═ **KISO YOSHINAKA**
1147 – 1213   (?)   1154 – 84

YOSHITSUNE
1159 – 89

MASAKO HOJO ═══ **YORITOMO**
1156 – 1225   1147 – 99

YORIIE   **SANETOMO**
1182 – 1204   1192 – 1219

The Minamato

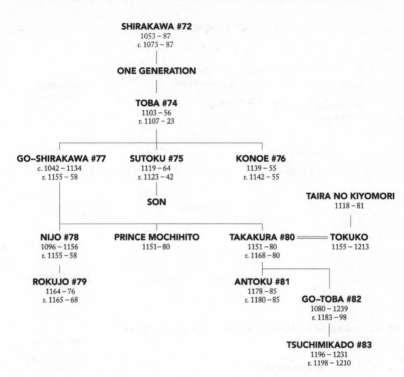

The Emperors of Japan in the 12th Century

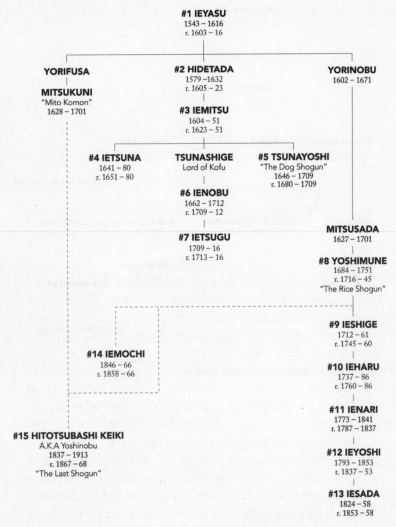

The Tokugawa Shogunate

INTRODUCTION

The samurai were the warrior caste of medieval Japan, a class of powerful mounted soldiers who rose to power as retainers of feudal lords and the military arm of the imperial court, before establishing a new national order. Like the Vikings of Scandinavia they were initially men with nothing to lose, who won land at the point of a sword. Like the knights of Crusader Europe, they went on to export their military prowess in a handful of foreign expeditions. But contrary to a common modern misconception, the samurai were not a solely 'Japanese' creation. Throughout Japanese history, the great unspoken influences are China and its Korean vassal kingdom, presented variously as a threat to be fought off, a source of culture and precedent, a source of refugee aristocrats and wealth, or trade. It was the 'Chinese' Emperor, or rather China's Mongol conqueror, Khubilai Khan, who inadvertently united the samurai in their finest hour – the spirited defence of Japan in the thirteenth century. It was the prospect of conquering China that led the samurai in their ill-fated invasion of Korea in the late sixteenth century. But a millennium earlier, the first samurai were also created in reaction to a military system borrowed from China, which foundered when exported to Japanese terrain. Their image owes much of its origin to frontier wars in what is now considered to be Japanese territory, but at the time was distinctly foreign. However, despite periodic contacts abroad to define and redefine their self-image, the bulk of the battles of the samurai over a 700-year period were fought among themselves. Held up to modern readers as a quintessential element of the soul of Japan, their system was brought crashing down by the onset of modernity itself.

The word *samurai* literally means henchman or retainer. The earliest use of the word comes attached to low-ranking civil servants in old-time Japan – a warrior class that began as a brawling rabble in the early Middle Ages, before the knightly class began to win favour, its own feudal domains and with them, a yearning for high culture. As the life of a successful warrior garnered spoils and wealth, the trappings of these military men became more ostentatious. So, too, did their personal battle with the nature of loyalty itself. Throughout the history of the samurai, the question of loyalty is a constant, incessant refrain. Loyalty to *whom* – this or that pretender, this or that general? Loyalty to *what* – the imperial institution, its martial representative, the status quo, or even the *idea* of a new order, if only the current order could be overturned?

An ethos of suicidal constancy and fearlessness created a quasi-religious worship of battle itself, with the samurai as vainglorious actors in deadly displays of valour. Early samurai battles, at least in so far as accounts of them have survived, have a ritual, theatrical quality, as champions ride out to recite their names and lineage; it was important for one's kills to be counted and one's performance to be noted.

Samurai would often wear personal flags to make it clear who it was that was winning heads on a battlefield, and many had distinctive armour, richly decorated, with deliberately eye-catching helmet decorations, including devil's horns, a crescent moon or a demon's head. In the later period, some old warriors lamented the anonymity of the crowded modern battlefield, and the unsightly, dishonourable egalitarianism afforded to unskilled musketeers who could point and shoot after mere days of training, instead of a lifetime studying archery and the sword.

A samurai was supposedly a perfect soldier, keeping to a draconian martial code that was set down much later as *Bushidō* – the 'way of the warrior'. Honour, bravery and prowess in battle were valued above life itself. One of the most famous samurai was Kusunoki Masashige – a statue of him on a horse has a prominent position outside today's Imperial Palace in Tōkyō. Ordered into a battle he knew he could not win, he still led the charge, and died proclaiming that he wished he had seven lives to give for his country. He later became an unofficial emblem of the *kamikaze* pilots in the Second World War.

Most notoriously, samurai were expected to choose death over dishonour. In order to prove that they were not afraid, samurai suicides followed the practice of *seppuku* – cutting open the belly, more vulgarly known as *hara kiri*. This was regarded as the most excruciating and unpleasant death known to man, and was a kind of voluntary torture undergone by samurai determined to prove their purity of purpose.

Certain samurai eventually came to dominate the emperors they were supposed to serve. Many would use an old military rank to justify this, claiming that the emperor had made them *shōgun* – a supreme general with orders to suppress unrest, particularly to protect

Japan from barbarian incursions. From the Middle Ages until the late nineteenth century, Japan was effectively under the control of the samurai class, and imperial decrees merely ratified the decisions taken by the most dominant warlord. Samurai continued to fight among themselves, often claiming to be loyal to an emperor who had received the wrong advice from his closest retainers. Such an attitude turned the emperors into pawns of whichever warlord had the best access to them.

A series of civil wars came to an end in the sixteenth century, with several prominent samurai generals seizing control of the country in the Emperor's name. The final and most enduring victors were the Tokugawa family, who would supply the shōgun for the ensuing 250 years.

The sheer size and scope of the samurai world makes it impossible to cover in its entirety. Every town has its local hero; every prefecture has its school trips to battlefields that the education board deem to be important. Samurai history has its undeniable high points, those leaders among the agglutinative, multi-word designations who had somehow gained a single, stark name in popular accounts: Yoshitsune, Nobunaga, Hideyoshi, Ieyasu. For the historian, however, there is the inevitable need to be concise, to cast aside moments, periods or figures in the interests of clarity. There are books about the samurai that confine all mention of the seven-year Korea campaign to a footnote, books that start long after the Thirty-Eight Years War, or finish centuries before the Meiji Restoration. Even the precise end of the samurai era is debatable. Its last battle was arguably fought in 1638, where a pocket of veterans, many of them Christian, led an ill-fated revolt in the south against the third Tokugawa Shōgun. The rebellion was ruthlessly crushed, the men and their families massacred, sending a clear message to the rest of Japan. In the Shōgun's own words: 'There will be no more wars.' Japan was decreed closed to outsiders, shutting out the pervasive foreign influences of Christianity and foreigners.

For the next 200 years, Japan was a prosperous but fearful police state – the samurai were 10 per cent of the entire population, and were kept at that level by strict sumptuary rules. The lower classes struggled to support a warrior elite with no more wars left to fight, and the samurai themselves declined into bureaucracy, brigandage and sometimes poverty. Some died in vendettas over the increasingly intricate laws of propriety and conduct. Others, their livelihood lost with the death or dishonour of their lord, became masterless, wandering toughs (*rōnin*) or sneaked abroad to fight in foreign wars. Some even took a step that would have been unthinkable to their ancestors, renouncing their samurai status to become merchants or farmers.

Most of our stories of the samurai come from this period. Even tales of older deeds and battles were often set down in their modern forms during the era of decline, by authors attempting to recreate or remember the glory days, or by playwrights forced to tell old stories as a mask for banned reportage of current events. Our knowledge of the samurai era is often refracted by these demands, told with anachronistic trappings, or viewed through rose-coloured spectacles, from books, woodblock prints and plays.

Nor is this issue confined to the modern age. The great era of the *gunkimono* or military chronicles was the fifteenth century, 100 years removed from the events that they described. The great era for tales of the bloody unification of the country was the eighteenth century, once again, at least a century after the fact. We should regard such sources with the suspicion we might apply to a Viking saga, and ask ourselves who was writing, who was reading, what was lost and what was added before such tales were set down for posterity.

Anachronism is an intriguing part of the samurai experience. For more than 200 years, the Japanese entered a consensual time warp, returning to a world of castle towns, swordsmen and archers, giving up the gun and maintaining artillery at seventeen-century levels of technology. While the Industrial Revolution got underway elsewhere, Japan remained curiously preoccupied with the concerns of the warrior elite that had united it. After centuries of conflict, it might be said that the hard-won victory of the samurai was so bloody, so brutal and so entire, that they were left dazed and unprepared for peace itself.

There are many problems that beset the writer (and reader) of a general samurai history. Sometimes it seems as if every tiny hamlet on a mountainside has a connection to a great warrior or famous incident. For the historian who must be brief, there are often heartbreaking decisions about the anecdotes, testimonies and descriptions that must be left out. There is also a difficult balance to strike between precision and complexity. Academics are strongly discouraged from drawing direct parallels with Western institutions or time periods – while terms such as knight, baron or count might appear instructive and evocative, for many they are too much so, and force European ideals on an alien system. Take such admonitions too far, and discussion of Japanese history collapses into unreadable prose, thick with supposedly untranslatable concepts – *daimyō*, *sankin kōtai*, *katana*, *junshi*, *giri*. These concepts are necessary for appreciating the more impenetrable texts, but I have used them sparingly in this book. Hence, many will only show up once in the index, on the page where they are first mentioned, along with an English translation that I use thereafter: despite what some writers may suggest, very few of them really are untranslatable after all. I hope that this, at least, will help keep the narrative clear enough for the general reader, but still useful enough for the specialist, or the researcher who wishes to dig deeper in other sources.

A far greater problem in translating Japanese history for the general reader lies in the multiple readings afforded by the Japanese writing system. Japanese is written using a combination of Chinese characters and local phonetic scripts. Each character has a local, Japanese pronunciation and a classier Chinese reading, sometimes several. The meaning of a word is often more obvious as a glance than precisely how it should be pronounced – an issue that has contributed to the modern Japanese insistence on business cards. It is immediately clear to a Japanese reader that the book entitled *Gikeiki* can also be read as *The Chronicle of Yoshitsune*, that a book called *Shinchō Kōki* is obviously about Oda Nobunaga, or that a conflict called *Genpei* refers to a war between the houses of Minamoto and Taira. For someone unfamiliar with the characters and their multiple readings, this often makes it appear as if Japanese has two names for everything. I have done what I can to shovel such issues into the endnotes, where they will not interfere with the main narrative. In cases where a Japanese title is not uncommon in English sources, such as *Hagakure*, *Hakkenden* or *Chūshingura*, I give the term and its translation.

Many writers are tempted to discuss Japanese history as if it were hermetically sealed from the rest of the world. Although this is often how the Japanese liked to see themselves, Japan is an integral part of north-east Asia. Its dealings with the mainland in trade, piracy, cultural exchange and war were crucial influences in the development of a martial tradition that the Japanese themselves like to think of as unique. Hence, I make no apologies for my recurring focus on foreign contacts in this book – my own interests often lie on the border regions, where the Matsumae family carried civilization to the 'barbarians' of Ezo, where the Sō clan kept a constant vigil for hostile ships off Tsushima, and where the sailors of Satsuma pursued a secret suzerainty over the Ryūkyū Islands. We should remember that the ultimate authority of the samurai era, the Shōgun himself, was the 'Great General Who Suppresses the Barbarians', a military leader whose job was to defend Japanese culture from the predations and influences of unwelcome outsiders. By appreciating the impact of such foreign contacts, we can comprehend Japan's draconian reactions to them. Paramount among these, of course, is the 200-year lockdown during the Tokugawa Shōgunate, when the last of the great pre-modern foreign imports, Christianity, was ruthlessly suppressed.

It is often difficult in Japanese history to tell who is precisely in charge. For the millennium covered in this book, it was universally agreed that the ultimate authority rested with the emperors. And yet, even before the samurai period began in earnest, many emperors were puppets of their regents, such as the powerful members of the Soga and Fujiwara families. From 1192 to 1333, the emperors were obliged to delegate their authority to the Kamakura shōgunate, nine generations of supreme generals, whose authority was absolute, and largely hereditary. And yet, from 1203 to 1333, each Kamakura shōgun in turn delegated his authority to a *shikken* or shōgunal regent, a power behind the throne, each drawn from the family of the first Shōgun's powerful wife. With such multiple onion layers of authority, can we ever say who was on top?

Similar machinations can be found in the Muromachi period that followed, where shōguns from the newly paramount Ashikaga family soon found themselves en-meshed in rival claims to the imperial throne, and the meddlings of a 'retired' emperor, who was anything but retired. The Muromachi period was brought to a violent halt by the unification wars of the late sixteenth century, and the last line of shōguns, the Tokugawa family, became the de facto rulers of Japan throughout the period 1603–1867. The position of the Tokugawa shōgun, and that of his samurai retainers, was in turn mortally undermined by the return of foreigners en masse, particularly the 'Black Ships' of the United States of America, which forced Japan to re-open to foreign visitors in a triumph of gunboat diplomacy.

Having failed in his primary function, to 'suppress barbarians', the Shōgun did not last much longer. He was overthrown in the course of the Meiji Restoration, which began as competition between rival samurai elites, but ended with the Emperor regaining a nominal role as the head of state. The samurai were officially abolished soon after, and the last of their number entered the modern military or faded into the general population.

Although this is a factual account, fictions of the samurai play an important part in the way we understand them, and often in the way that they understood themselves. Some authorities, dazzled by cherry blossoms and tea ceremonies, have romanticized the samurai, preferring to see only the ornate accoutrements and poetic dalliances of their richest rulers and the owners of the largest estates. However, for most samurai, life was a tough regime of training and military service, hounded by vendettas and deprivation. Many of the conflicts of the samurai were aimed at gaining access to the luxuries and power of the privileged few – much of our modern misunderstanding of the samurai has its roots in the samurai's deliberate misunderstanding of themselves, the imposition of a code of honour and chivalrous protocol long after the wars were done. Japanese drama in the samurai era often hinged on the juxtaposition of Duty and Emotion (*giri* versus *ninjō*), contrasting one's personal desires with the draconian requirement to obey the orders of one's superiors.

The poster-boys and super-heroes of bygone ages exhibit different priorities at work. History is largely told by the winning side, but Japanese tradition retains a powerful affection for tales of the underdog and tragic failure – some of the most famous samurai in history were defeated by the same order that later lionized them. It is even worth arguing that many of the supposed virtues of the samurai were not fashioned in practice in the Middle Ages, but promulgated in protest in the early modern period, as the complaints and fulminations of a declining elite. Samurai heroes continue to come in and out of fashion: the last stand of Kusunoki had its day, but so did the wily machinations of Hideyoshi, the elegant, doomed nobility of Yoshitsune, and the unexpected Christian piety of Augustin Konishi. In this book, I have deliberately hit the high notes, but also taken the time to point out a few of the more obscure figures whose day will surely come again.

In the modern era, the samurai ethic came to be associated with conservatism and right-wing patriotism, often in opposition to modernist policies. Paradoxically, many of those figures that best evoked the samurai spirit at the close of nineteenth century were the same men who were crushed and broken by the new order. Even as they fought for the Emperor, they established a new world that would dismantle their domains, take away their swords, and effectively destroy the value of everything they had learned. The last of the shōgun's loyalists briefly huddled in a self-styled samurai republic in the north of Japan, before they were forcibly brought to heel. The fabled 'last samurai', Saigō Takamori, was one of the victors in the Meiji Restoration, who nevertheless found himself disenchanted with the direction of the new order and led a doomed rebellion of his own in 1877. Thereafter, what remained of the samurai spirit became part of the creed of the military faction that gained control of Japan in the 1920s and dragged the nation into the Second World War.

In the immediate aftermath, the Occupation authorities suppressed martial stories for fear they encouraged unwelcome fervour among the defeated Japanese. New heroes were co-opted from stories post-dating the samurai era – the brutal 'honour among thieves' of the *yakuza* gangsters, or the devious underclass espionage of the *ninja* assassins. But such a monumentally ubiquitous warrior class as the samurai could not be written out of history so easily. For a significant proportion of the Japanese population, the samurai *were* Japan. Not merely as warriors, but husbands, the aspirations of their children, the state validations of wealthy landowners, the clients of geisha, customers of inn-keepers and patrons of artists.

Soon after the departure of the American censor, samurai stories reasserted themselves in pot-boiler novels, comics and, as television came into its own, as Japan's default setting for costume drama. In the modern era, the samurai have become dramatic ciphers for Japan itself. The *jidaigeki* (period drama) remains a fundamental ingredient of modern Japanese media, presenting the samurai in a changing series of roles and conditions reflecting the way in which the Japanese see themselves.

In understanding the samurai, we also understand a crucial part of the soul of Japan. The ghosts of these old warriors can be seen everywhere in the modern world, in the power relationships between bosses and underlings, in the closed ranks of 'Japan Incorporated', in the rarefied levels of politeness and conflict avoidance to be found in the Japanese language. There is more, of course, to Japan than just the samurai. But the samurai have shaped so much of Japan, that it is impossible to see Japan without them.

1

STRONG FELLOWS
THE RISE OF THE WARRIOR CLASS

The Japanese archipelago stretches for a 1200-mile crescent in the Pacific Ocean, arching from south-west to north-east. Rarely more than 200 miles wide at any point, Japan's hinterland largely comprises soaring, forested peaks. Situated at the intersection of four tectonic plates, Japan is rich with volcanoes and hot springs, but also no stranger to earthquakes and tidal waves. Eighty per cent of Japan is covered with mountains – although the country's land mass rivals that of the state of California, barely 15 per cent of its 145,885 square miles is arable. During the samurai era, when swamps and forests were still being cleared away by farmers, it was even less.

In modern times, Japan comprises the islands of Kyūshū, Honshū, Shikoku and Hokkaidō, but the last of these is a relatively recent addition, and was untamed wilderness until very late in the samurai period. For much of the history of the samurai, it was the other three islands that constituted the homeland of the samurai and their subjects.

In Japan, one is rarely more than 100 miles from the sea. Between the three main islands sits a sheltered waterway, the 'Inland Sea' that formed the first great road of trade. Sailors making the perilous crossing from Korea would cling to the coastline of Kyūshū before entering the Inland Sea at the narrow Shimonoseki Strait. From that point in, sheltered from the worst of the storms that might have plagued them on the open sea, they could sail all along the inner coasts of Honshū and Shikoku. The centre of Japanese civilization in the pre-samurai era sat at the eastern end of this waterway, on the Kansai plain. Here, we find several of Japan's early capitals, including Asuka, Nara and Kyōto. Wherever the capital might be, it was assumed to be the centre of courtly culture, a refined place of poets and priests, elegant ladies and thoughtful scholars. It was palpably no place for a warrior, a recurring attitude in Japanese history in which the hedonistic, cultured court hires samurai to fight their battles, but prefers to keep them at arm's length in the capital itself.

East of the Kansai plain, mountains rise up again to wall off the rest of Japan. At the commencement of the samurai era, much of the land north-east of the barrier mountains was beyond the authority of the emperors. The tangle of forests and swamps was inhabited by the Emishi, a 'barbarian' people with a different language to the Japanese, who appear to have been descended from an earlier set of arrivals in Japan, possibly the prehistoric Jōmon culture whose ceramic artefacts can be found all over Japan.

Reading between the lines of ancient texts, the Japanese had long been advancing into Emishi territory. Chinese chronicles of the Tang dynasty describe northern Japan as a separate country of 'hairy people', two of which were presented to the Taizong Emperor as part of the retinue of a Japanese ambassador. There were, Taizong was told, two kinds of Emishi – the 'peaceful' ones who had accepted the arrival of the Japanese and assimilated into their culture, and the 'wild' ones who continued to cause trouble at the ever-advancing frontier. Little is known about the Emishi language, but their genes live on in a significant proportion of the modern Japanese. Fragments of their place-names can still be found in northern Japan, and elements of their technology and military style formed important components of what would eventually be known as the samurai.

Crucially, part of the new lands on the border marches turned out to be another area of flat ground, a plain easily twice the size of Kansai. *Kansai*, 'West of the Barrier [Mountains]' now had a new rival in *Kantō*, 'East of the Barrier'. Japanese history ever since has been characterized by tensions between the two plains. The Kantō region attracted ambitious frontiersmen and explorers, and, once cleared by generations of foresters, provided an incomparable source of horse-rearing pasture and land suitable for rice paddies. It should come as no surprise that the Kantō region was soon producing more rice, more horses and more men than the more established regions of the west. Before long, men of the Kantō region were playing ever more active roles in the politics back at court. Eventually, the Kantō region would come to dominate Japanese politics – while the capital remained in Kansai for 1,000 years, the true seat of power rested in Kantō. In the 1860s, this was finally recognized officially when the capital was moved from Kyōto to the city of Edo, which was only then renamed Tōkyō – 'Eastern Capital'.

Japanese history before the rise of the samurai is something of a blur. Archaeology tells us that there were separate waves of colonization from the Asian mainland, people who left middens of seashells on the virgin beaches and made the world's first documented ceramic pots. They developed rice agriculture and spread slowly along the land from the south-west.

Occasional references in Chinese chronicles talk of islands in the east, said to be the domain of the immortals. The first Emperor of China supposedly sent an expedition there in search of the elixir of eternal youth. The fleet of explorers never returned to China, although several local traditions in Japan will tell you where they landed, and where their descendants still live. Such prosaic legends of diaspora and dispersal are rather at odds with the legends of the Japanese themselves, which hold that Japan was the 'Land of the Gods', created from the droplets of seawater shaken from the tip of a jewel-encrusted divine spear.

Izanagi and Izanami, the god and goddess who give birth to the Japanese islands, also give birth to deformed, evil deities – said to be caused by the goddess' hubris in speaking first at their wedding. For the sake of appearances, they re-enact their wedding with the correct ceremonial in order to have better offspring – the first, but by no means the last, occurrence in Japanese chronicles of ceremonies and outward appearances being deemed crucial to the composition of luck and life.

Amaterasu, the Sun Goddess, is one of their many offspring, and regarded as the ancestor of the rulers of Japan, through her great-great-great-grandson, the first legendary emperor, Jimmu. It was Jimmu, so claim the earliest extant Japanese legends, who led his brothers eastwards from Kyūshū, all the better to rule all of Japan. The stories that follow contain multiple references to local chieftains bested by Jimmu and his family in combat – Japan might be the Land of the Gods, but it seems to have already been occupied when the ancestors of the emperors arrived. The first victories of 'Japanese' warriors were a world away from the armoured, sword-bearing samurai of tradition. A song purported to have survived from the time is a hymn to the power of clubs and stone maces.

> Though men in plenty
> Enter and stay
> We the glorious
> Sons of warriors
> Wielding our mallet-heads
> Wielding our stone-mallets
> Will smite them utterly.[1]

Chinese chronicles mention Japan as the land of Great Peace (*Dahe*, in Japanese: *Yamato*), or Origin of the Sun (*Riben*, in Japanese: *Nippon*) – the latter a reference to its geographical location, but fervently embraced by the Japanese themselves as a reference to Amaterasu. The Chinese also regarded the Japanese as savage barbarians, ruled over at one time by the shaman-queen Himiko, a veritable queen bee, attended upon by 1,000 women, and only a single male assistant – according to some sources, her brother. Dying unmarried, she was succeeded by a thirteen-year-old girl – is this a reference to a forgotten matriarchy in Japan, or the earliest indicator of underage puppet rulers functioning as mouthpieces for their 'assistants'?

Japan, however, seldom appeared in Chinese chronicles. It was only with the re-establishment of a stable empire in China in the late sixth century that the Chinese began to consider further embassies and contacts with the kingdoms on the periphery. Then, as ever, China was considered the centre of the world, and all other outlying regions as mere reflections of its glory.

The Tang dynasty was founded in 618, but Japan, presumed to still be a vassal state, did not send an embassy for another twelve years. The ambassadors returned full of praise for the distant Tang court, observing that the Taizong Emperor was a powerful military man, who had won his empire twice on the point of a sword – once as the prime mover of his father's grab for power from the preceding Sui dynasty, and again in a fratricidal skirmish that left him as the sole heir. Japanese ambassadors arrived only four years after this latter event, and were sure to have reported it back home.

In 645, Japan gained its own ruler in imitation of the proactive Taizong. The crown prince – the future Emperor Tenji – hatched a plot to kill one of his mother's hated imperial advisers. When the four co-conspirators proved to lack the will to carry it out, Tenji rushed his victim himself. With the bleeding minister wounded on the floor, the shocked Empress retired to consider the matter, whereupon the co-conspirators regained their courage and finished the minister off.

An unforeseen casualty in the purge was history itself. The father of the murdered minister died in what was supposedly a suicidal conflagration in his mansion, taking several treasures with him, including an irreplaceable chronicle of times gone by. All Japanese history before the seventh century is hence a matter of conjecture and innuendo, a massive 'Dark Age' without a point of textual anchorage, and with many issues, such as the precise relationship of Japan to Korea, infuriatingly unclear. Legendary tales of a Japanese empress who invaded Korea, may in fact be a garbled reference to precisely the opposite.

The Japanese interest in the Korean peninsula may have been more than simple neighbourliness – it seems more than likely that the ruling houses of Japan and southern

Korea were related, and that one was an offshoot of the other. But there is only a small portion of archaeological evidence to go on, limited still further by the attrition of time, and by the peculiar position of the Japanese emperors. Since Japanese tradition holds that Japan was created by the gods, and that the ruler of Japan is a direct descendant of the Sun Goddess, it is difficult to poke around Japanese antiquities with quite the same impunity as was afforded to archaeologists in Egypt, Italy or Greece. But there are, for example, extant multiple-pronged ceremonial swords, presented as gifts to Japanese rulers by Korean allies.

We should not be surprised that the Japanese had friends on the mainland. Such friendships were soon put to the test in 654 when the ruler of Tang China ordered a Japanese attack on the Korean nation of Baekje. If Japan were a loyal vassal state, as China had been led to believe, then it would have been a simple exercise.

From a distance, it might have seemed that Emperor Kōtoku was enthusiastically obeying. He initiated the Taika Reforms, a series of edicts that reorganized Japan in imitation of the Chinese system, redrawing boundaries and undermining the power of local strongmen, instead concentrating all authority in the hands of the Emperor, and creating new military districts. Men and supplies were moved from all over to Japan and concentrated in the southern island of Kyūshū, the logical launching point for any assault on Korea.

However, if we read between the lines, we might see that Kōtoku was anything but obedient. An imperial edict of 646 ordered the formation of new military units, specifying that each person should bring a sword, armour, bow and arrows, flag and drum. However, the term used for these men was *sakimori* – 'border guards'. Kōtoku was not planning an assault on his allies in Baekje; instead he was

preparing for the likely consequences when China found
out that he had ignored the order. The forces concentrating
in Kyūshū were not preparing to attack Korea: they were
preparing to defend Japan.[2]

Kōtoku may have hoped that China's expansion would
stop before it became his problem. It had, after all, been
many centuries since a single *imperium* had united the
mainland. The preceding Sui dynasty had lasted barely
forty years, in which time the upstart Japanese had
managed to rile the ruler of 'All Under Heaven' by
addressing him as an equal.[3] Perhaps Kōtoku hoped that
infighting, family feuds or revolution might soon reduce
the vigour of the Tang dynasty, and distract it from trouble
at its borders.

China would eventually overreach itself, but not before
uniting with the Korean kingdom of Silla to wipe out
Baekje, which ceased to exist in 660 when a combined
Chinese–Sillan force entered its capital. Along the same
lines of communication that had been used to carry
Buddhist missionaries and trade goods, a call for assistance
went out from the last defenders of Baekje. It travelled
across the narrow strait, past the island of Tsushima,
through the Shimonoseki Strait and into the Inland Sea.
Whatever offer was made in Baekje's name, it was clearly
tempting to the Japanese. The military response was so
huge that the Japanese capital was temporarily moved to
the southern island of Kyūshū in order to be close to the
shipyards.

The omens were bad. Empress Saimei, nominal ruler of
Japan, died during the preparations, but that did not stop
her martially minded son from continuing the project. A
fleet numbering hundreds of Japanese ships returned along
the Tsushima Strait, and to the mouth of the Baek River
that would take it to the site of the fallen Baekje capital.[4]

There, the Japanese ran into a smaller force of Chinese, which they fatally assumed would be easy to defeat. In the ensuing four days of military action, the Chinese scored four clear victories. 'In this action', wrote a Korean chronicler, 'they burned four hundred of the Japanese vessels – the flames and smoke rose to scorch the heavens, while the ocean's waters turned as red as cinnabar.'[5]

The Japanese fleet was bunched and crushed in the lower reaches of the Baek River, the ships forced too close together with little room for manoeuvre. Losses are estimated, even in conservative sources, at close to 10,000 men. It was, in the words of one historian 'the worse defeat for the Japanese in their pre-modern history'.[6]

The debacle literally formed the final page in the history of Baekje. The annals for that unfortunate kingdom peter out only a couple of years later, and subsequent kings of Baekje were merely honorary positions within the Chinese nobility. The survivors from the Baekje royal family either defected to the Chinese or sought asylum in Japan, where they endured as minor aristocrats. The news of the Chinese victory was sufficient to cause some outlying forts to surrender without even putting up a fight – emissaries arrived from the island of Cheju, and swore allegiance to the Tang dynasty before any trouble broke out. As the tattered remnants of the invasion force limped back home, Japan was gripped with the palpable fear of a Chinese–Korean counter-attack.

China was in the ascendant. The Tang dynasty, barely two generations old, oversaw a time of great prosperity. Empress Wu, favoured wife of Taizong's son, the crippled Emperor Gaozong, ruled in her husband's name, and was so sure of her success that she began planning for the rarest of rituals, only seen a handful of times in history, wherein the Chinese ruler announced to the gods that all was well under heaven. Japanese prisoners of war formed a reluctant part of the elaborate ceremonies, led along with captured Koreans, defeated barbarians from the inner Asian deserts and steppes, and vanquished Chinese rebels to the great mountain where Taizong was entombed. There, the multi-cultural entourage was presented to the late Emperor's spirit in symbolic offering. Surely, the Japanese were expecting to be executed, but the Chinese saw no need for human sacrifice. Instead, with the grim news that their souls would remain behind at the tomb, they were sent home.[7]

It was only now that Emperor Tenji, the instigator of the palace coup of 645 and brain behind the ill-fated Korean campaign, finally came to the throne in an official capacity – he had previously ruled from behind the thrones of other family members. He did so entirely convinced that it was only a matter of time before a Chinese counter-attack, and initiated a series of further reforms in order to prepare his country against invasion. Tenji moved his capital from Asuka to Ōmi, protected by mountains on three sides, and Lake Biwa on the other. The bearing of arms among Tenji's courtiers became commonplace, and it was no longer considered unusual to see a nobleman with a sword at his belt or with a bow and arrows. Border guards were set up with beacon-fires on outlying islands, particularly Tsushima and Iki facing Korea. Japanese soldiers and Korean refugees also constructed a long dike, fifteen metres high, around Hakata Bay – the largest natural harbour in Kyūshū, and sure to be the target of any large-scale landing. In a telling strategic move, several siege works were constructed at points along the Inland Sea approaching Tenji's new capital, as if Tenji were already expecting the outlying defences to crumble. The same period also saw the first national census, as Tenji's courtiers assessed the availability of manpower ahead of possible military conscription.

The reorganization of Japan's institutions was an ongoing, organic process spanning several decades. Provinces were reconstituted, and as conquests were made in the north-east border marches, new provinces were added. In imitation of the Chinese model, a ministry of priests was given precedence in government, with authority over rites and ceremonial. A ministry of bureaucrats was put in charge of more secular matters. Among the twelve ranks of civil servants, the lower six were referred to in state documents as 'servants' – *samurai*. At the time, the word did not specifically refer to a warrior, but the fact that it would eventually encompass military men is an indicator of the early low position of warriors within the imperial ranking system.

However, the expected Chinese attack never came. By the time of Tenji's death in 671, China faced a famine, a drought, and then a war with Tibet. If China had ever planned an invasion of Japan – and there is no evidence that China ever did – the Tang dynasty was preoccupied elsewhere, and was soon to begin its long, graceful decline. But if Chinese soldiers did not invade Japan in the late seventh century, they still made their presence felt. Although Tenji's son, Prince Ōtomo, was the late ruler's intended heir, Tenji's brother Prince Ōama, made a successful bid for the throne in a month-long civil conflict in the summer of 672.

Relying on the tactical advice of a prisoner of war from Tang China, Prince Ōama's attack lurched eastward to seize two crucial mountain passes that led to northern Japan. At first, the force comprised only a few men – Ōama rode with a small posse of horsemen and little supplies, counting instead on the goodwill and support of local strongmen. It was these local power brokers that then supplied Ōama with his army proper, amid promises of perks and power in the new order. Ōama's army then split into three, approaching the capital from both shores of Lake Biwa, while a third group ran for Naniwa to cut off Ōtomo's only decent escape route. What had once been a defensive strategy – the single route to the sea at Naniwa – was now a leading factor in the downfall of Prince Ōtomo, who had never expected that he would need to run away from his capital instead of protect it from putative invaders coming from the sea.

Even so, Ōama's victory was not assured. With a Korean military adviser of his own and the support of several powerful families, Prince Ōtomo scored an early victory when he duplicated his uncle's tactics, dumping any baggage or footsoldiers to send a swift squadron of horsemen cross-country to surprise his uncle's troops. When the two forces faced each other in a true battle, the *Chronicle of Japan* describes a distinctly continental confrontation. Soldiers appear to have been divided into units of archers, infantry and cavalry, while Ōtomo's forces are reported banging drums and gongs, which had simply been intended to scare their enemies, but may have also been a use of Chinese-style signalling to ensure coordinated responses from the men on the field.

Arms and armour also largely followed Chinese designs. There is little description of them in accounts of the time, but archaeological evidence from tombs and period figurines suggest that the soldiers who fought in Ōama's usurpation army carried straight swords, or spears or pole-arms with a distinctive, beak-like spike in imitation of similar Chinese weapons. The sole exception appears to have been in archery, where the Japanese had long been famous for using bows with an asymmetric design, held close to the bottom instead of at their mid-point. This seems to have been a decision made originally for technical reasons, as the earliest bows were made from an entire sapling, which would invariably have a springier branch end than root end. Hence, Japanese archers would clutch their bow low down the stave, with substantially more of the stave above the hand than below it. Likely to have been a more widespread style in ancient times, the asymmetric bow was already supplanted in China by compound versions made from several pieces of material, and hence with no need to conform to natural shapes or designs. However, the Japanese crucially kept their asymmetric bow design even when technology made it no longer necessary.[8]

Warriors on both sides wore armour made from strips of hardened hide or small iron plates, lashed tightly together with leather laces. Helmets were constructed from a more solid design, with additional hinged plates of hide or thin metal that shielded the jaw and the back of the neck. Mounted warriors, whose horse and saddle could bear a heavier weight for longer, tended to wear armour with a greater emphasis on metal plates, and with a flared skirt around the hips. In the case of both hide and metal construction, these armours were usually treated with lacquer to protect them against Japan's damp winters and humid summers.

When Ōama won, he did so thanks to superior numbers. His first ride east had not only secured him the mountain passes, but access to all the local chieftains beyond the pass to the north and east, who supplied him with sufficient cavalry to turn the tide in his favour. Conversely, Prince Ōtomo was only able to seek help to the south and west –domains that had heavily taxed to support the disastrous Korean campaign, lost many of their sons in the debacle at Baek River, and had faced further taxation and corvée labour in the years of preparation for a Chinese invasion that had never arrived. Understandably, such clans were unwilling to offer any further support to the latest incumbent.

His capital in flames, Prince Ōtomo committed suicide on a mountainside after fleeing the battle. His brief reign was scrubbed from Japanese history for many centuries, and Prince Ōama was enthroned as Emperor Temmu (r.673–86). Tellingly, his reign title translates as 'Heavenly Warrior'.

Temmu's reign has been widely regarded as a turning point in Japanese history. Not the least by Temmu himself, who may have been the first Japanese ruler to use the title of Emperor (*Tennō*) while living – his predecessors were only conferred with imperial status posthumously.[9] One of Temmu's sons was the chief editor of the *Chronicle of Japan* (*Nihongi*), an account of Japanese history clearly intended to replace and even supersede the accounts that had been burned during the purges of Temmu's brother. The *Chronicle of Japan* begins with the creation of the world by the gods and covers the 1,000 years that the Japanese believed had elapsed since Japan's first legendary ruler. But an impressive seven chapters from its total of thirty are devoted to the reigns of Temmu, his brother and his parents, spanning a little over forty years. These later chapters, culminating with the reign of Temmu's widow, were written within living memory of the events depicted, and may be reasonably assumed to be accurate, if biased. The preceding chapters lionized and mythologized Japan's rulers back in the misty past, refashioning the rulers of Japan as the divine descendants of the gods themselves.

Crucially, Temmu was a ruler who had been raised in a nation on a constant war footing. As a teenager, he had witnessed his brother seize power by arranging the brutal murder of a courtier; in his twenties, he had overseen the preparation of a massive invasion fleet; in his thirties, he had witnessed the countrywide preparations to ward of the threat from China. Having seized the throne from his own nephew, Temmu remained permanently on his guard. The *Chronicle of Japan* for the remainder of his reign is devoted largely to strategic affairs: life at Temmu's new court in Asuka was a constant round of tournaments, inspections and training. Late in his reign, he decreed:

> In government, military matters are the essential thing. All civil and military officials should therefore diligently practice the use of arms and riding on horseback. Be careful to provide an adequate supply of horses, weapons and articles of personal costume. Those who have horses shall be made mounted soldiers; those who have none shall be foot soldiers. Both shall receive training.[10]

But when Temmu talked of military affairs, he was talking of new institutions. Determined to kick away the ladder by which he had risen to power himself, he confiscated all heavy military gear from private hands. Crossbows, catapults and signalling devices (drums, flags and horns) were kept in district vaults. Meanwhile, court appointees were put in charge of sixty districts, where one of their duties was to maintain registers of the population. Although Temmu died before his system had been fully implemented, by the early eighth century an organization was in place that was designed to levy a conscript militia from local peasants. Heavy matériel was provided by the state from the district arsenals, but the conscripts were expected to bring their own sword and dagger, armour and a helmet made from wicker or straw, a bow and fifty arrows.

Much of the system was lifted, sometimes word for word, from Chinese military codes. On average, each household provided a single conscript. Fortune favoured the wealthy – those who could afford a horse were naturally able to promote themselves into the cavalry, while the sons of local potentates often spent their military service period on guard duty in the capital. For the poorer rank and file, guard duty was specifically *border* guard duty, stationed down in Kyūshū, or serving at one of the many signal-fires along the Inland Sea, linking the Kyūshū wardens with the capital.

There is some circumstantial evidence that most of the border guards were from east Japan. An anthology of contemporary poetry, intended as a snapshot of all aspects of life in early Japan, contains a conspicuous number of border guard laments, often referring to home villages in the east or an embarkation point at Naniwa – in other words, that their journey to the west was so long that it was necessary for them to board a ship in Kansai to cross the Inland Sea. For subjects in Kyūshū, Shikoku or west Honshū, simple maintenance of roads, watchtowers and signal fires was liable to take up much of the military service obligations. Geographically, east Japan was far from the likely point of contact with Chinese invaders, and so rather than providing fortifications and infrastructure, east Japan was best put to use providing men and horses. They also began to produce stories and narratives of a martial tradition, to which they regarded themselves as the rightful inheritors.

A legend of Japan's first ruler, Emperor Jimmu, tells of his war-band stopping at a place called Usa in the middle of one of their campaigns. The obscure village in northern Kyūshū seems to have been a position of some prominence, and was a place where Jimmu prayed for victory. A local 'princess' married one of his 'ministers'. When Jimmu's prayers were found to have been answered, the reputation of Usa went up in the world. Later known as a prominent shrine, Usa came to signify all that was divinely steered in the actions of the Japanese state. Close contacts with Korea, probably giving it early access to new Buddhist mysteries, also helped Usa keep up with the times, and it was periodically reported as the place where ministers prayed for a sick emperor's recovery or a beleaguered emperor's victory.

The local god was an agriculture deity or patron saint of fishermen, until the time of the legendary fifteenth Emperor, Ōjin, his birth apparently signified by the divine appearance of eight banners. It was with the name 'Eight Banners' (*Hachiman*), that the Usa shrine came to be most associated, eventually passing the name on to the local deity. Hachiman came to be known as the God of War, and it was to him that some of the early Japanese courts prayed for victory. In time, he came to be regarded as the patron deity of many samurai clans. Hachiman, or rather, his effigy, officially visited the sacred city of Nara in the eighth century, and his shrine maidens, chewing laurel leaves and deep in religious trances, functioned as prophetesses. At times when even the oracles of the Sun Goddess were silent, Hachiman had something to say. For certain warriors in the provinces, Hachiman came to be associated with their victories. He was adopted as the patron deity by several factions of warriors that would become influential in Japanese politics.[11]

As the threat from China faded, new uses were found for the soldiers. The period 774–812, known as the 'Thirty-Eight Years War', saw a series of military expeditions against the Emishi of northern Honshū.

Precisely who the Emishi were is a matter of some debate. They have a multiplicity of names, and the names themselves a multiplicity of explanations. Some sources conflate them with the Ainu, a group of bear-worshipping, conspicuously hirsute natives who may have entered prehistoric Japan by way of a land bridge from Siberia. Emishi itself was once written with the characters for 'hairy men', then with the characters for 'shrimp barbarians' – this may have been an attempt to match pre-existing tribes with fanciful descriptions from Chinese chronicles, but is more likely to have been descriptive – perhaps of their diet, hairstyles, or of a particular kind of whisker favoured by the warrior males. There may even have been a military origin in the two weapons that made the Emishi most formidable – in Japanese, a *yumishi* is a bowman; in the lost language of the barbarians, an *emushi* may have been a sword.[12]

Court reports of early Japan note that the Emishi tattooed their skin and wore their hair in a form of topknot. Although widely described as hunter-gatherers, they also appear to have adopted agriculture in places. Contacts were not always violent, although the Emishi appear to have had no written culture, and accepted gifts of armour, flags and drums from Japanese emperors with a degree of bafflement. It seems that in some cases the Emishi did not realize that they were surrendering. Some military 'conquests' ended without a single casualty, with victorious Japanese generals reporting an Emishi surrender, but actually meaning that a colony had been established and nobody had yet decided to attack it. In other cases, some Emishi seem to have welcomed the arrival of new faces and new luxuries from the south. Far from presenting a barbarous danger, one might even argue that some Emishi only began to present a threat when they began to appreciate what 'civilization' was, with early miscegenation and cultural contacts giving way to later arguments over law, tax and obligations.[13]

Government-sponsored colonization programmes sent groups of people to the north, settling in areas around newly constructed forts such as Akita and Taga (modern Sendai). These 'forts', however, were nothing like the anti-invasion fortifications built in the south. No stone-work was used in their construction – instead they usually comprised a wooden palisade on an earthwork surrounded by a ditch. The roofs were thatched – suggesting that colonists did not expect prolonged trouble from the supplanted local Emishi, or that the Emishi style of combat did not extend to siege or arson attacks on government property. In many cases, the 'colonists' *were* Emishi, of the 'peaceful' variety, while the government troops merely watched for any trouble from their unassimilated 'wild' cousins.

The Emishi, it seems, did not stay peaceful for long when their new masters imposed unwelcome tax burdens. Annoyed at the locals' lack of willingness to adhere to the new order, the court dispatched first one punitive expedition, then another, in a series of ill-fated pacification exercises that eventually stretched into the Thirty-Eight Years War.

The punitive expeditions followed the designs that the Japanese had adopted from Chinese military codes. The bulk of each force comprised infantrymen, armed with spears or straight, stabbing swords. Archers were also in evidence. The wealthiest members of the expedition brought their own horses. Many of the unmounted troops carried shields of a design far removed from that familiar to Europeans. A Japanese 'shield' was more like a long wooden plank with a hinged pole to hold it up. It was not readily portable because it was never intended to be carried in battle; instead it functioned as a temporary wall, behind which archers or infantry could duck during the initial exchange of arrows in a battle. Such shields rather implied that there was a set of gentlemanly rules to any battle, and that both sides would have to agree to play along. The Emishi entirely ignored this implied order, and instead remained highly mobile, mainly on horseback. They retained the element of surprise, and excelled at striking and running.

Although lumped together as one mass of barbarians, the Emishi also seem to have had an organizational structure of their own that the Japanese did not understand. Rare Japanese victories in skirmishes, sufficient to 'pacify' any given locality, were simply ignored by Emishi in the next valley. Campaigning was halted in 778, only for a new group of Emishi to steal across the frontier and burn settlers' villages in another part of the north. From the safety of the court on the Kansai plain, the government ordered ever larger expeditions to quell the northern disturbances.

Strangely, the war in the north was not permitted to trouble the rest of Japan. In the western regions, the situation was so peaceful that the government actually began dismantling the old conscript system. Conscript soldiers had a reputation for being unreliable and poorly trained, and their use was abolished over most of Japan. Soldiers were expected to be recruited 'in emergencies', but with no invaders arriving from the Chinese mainland, the likelihood of an emergency was considered to be remote, with the exception of the new northern provinces of Mutsu and Dewa, still thick with unpacified Emishi.

This policy may have streamlined costs and organization, but it also created a new vacancy that was readily filled by professional soldiery. While southern and western Japan did away with much of its military organization, the north and east remained a constant proving ground for martial men. For now, these warriors were the underlings of the court – lowborn men out to win fortunes, or the sons of minor nobility determined to carve out a domain for themselves on the borderland. They remained the respectful servants of the court nobility, acting in the name of a distant capital that many of them never even visited.

This very distance from court interference may have contributed towards the forging of the samurai. There was no place on the frontier for feeble, theoretically minded generals – these were soon weeded out. Instead, the warriors on the frontier began to adopt new ideas learned from their enemies. This included the use of the Emishi themselves; we might even argue that the Thirty-Eight Years War lasted an entire generation because it took that long for assimilated Emishi to grow up and fight for the Japanese cause against their own cousins.

Not every Emishi convert stayed faithful. The renewed attacks in 780 were actually caused by internal tensions among the Japanese colonists. One had insulted the ancestry of Azamaro, a warrior in the service of the Japanese. Affronted, Azamaro killed the Japanese leader and returned to his roots, leading a force of Emishi against the Japanese colonists he had once helped. The Japanese counter-attack stalled for literally months while its leaders at the burned ruins of Fort Taga fussed over supplies and logistics:

> They swarm like bees and gather like ants . . . but when we attack, they flee into the mountains and forests. When we let them go, they assault our fortifications . . . Each of their leaders is as good as 1,000 men.[14]

The worst Japanese defeat came at the Koromo River in 788, when a force of 2,000 men broke away from the main body of the army and forded the river in an attack on the base of the Emishi leader Aterui. The Japanese were victorious in the initial assault, in which they outnumbered Aterui's men six to one. The Japanese pursued the Emishi, forgetful that they were straying far from the main body of the army. The 300 Emishi were reinforced by another 800, and then a further 400 arrived and cut off their escape route. A survivor's report of the incident betrays the ongoing bafflement among government troops about what constituted true battle:

> Those who died in battle for the state were 25. While 245 were struck by arrows, those who drowned in the river were 1,036. Those who returned without belongings were 1,257.[15]

Only a handful of men had engaged the Emishi in what the court would have reasonably expected to call 'combat'. Much of the rest of the Japanese appear to have fled in chaos from the scene, trying and largely failing to swim for safety. Though a court reader might be able to massage the figures in some reports – after all, only twenty-five men had died in hand-to-hand fighting – the full statistics imply that 1,000 men drowned in ignominious retreat, while the remainder dragged themselves onto dry land on the far riverbank, a hail of Emishi arrows streaming down around them. Their drums, gongs and other barbarian-scaring paraphernalia lay broken and forgotten on the enemy shoreline.

Back at the capital, Emperor Kammu had no trouble in reading between the lines. The generals had prevaricated in the safety of their forts, and whined incessantly about supplies, until only a direct order had set them on their way. They had then lost thousands of men but barely inflicted a few dozen casualties on the Emishi.

Finally, the Emperor sent a general who could do the job. Sakanoue no Tamuramaro, the descendant of exiled Korean aristocrats, described in dramatic, demonic terms as having a 'yellow face and red hair'. Legendarily, Tamuramaro scored his victory through trickery, erecting giant paper lanterns on hilltops in order to draw the curious Emishi out of cover. This, however, seems to be a later spin on events, designed to explain similar activities undertaken in local festivals in north Japan. In fact, Tamuramaro defeated the Emishi by turning their tactics against them.

The Emishi's ultimate weapon was the mounted archer – a man using a long bow, which was held asymmetrically with the hand close to the lower end. This left the bow itself towering above the wielder, but allowed a man to fire from horseback without tripping over himself. The samurai soon adopted this tactic themselves; however this style of bow use still encumbered the samurai, forcing the average mounted archer into a relatively small field of fire to his left-hand side. It remained difficult to swing one's bow hand over to the right while on horseback, an encumbrance that often forced samurai to face their opponents obliquely, riding around them in an anti-clockwise direction. Such considerations placed stronger emphasis on speed and manoeuvrability – samurai archers were vulnerable on their right side to other samurai archers, and would need to constantly jockey and reposition to keep their enemies in their field of fire.

The Emishi also used long, curved blades, designed so that a rider might slash downwards at infantry, or clash with mounted opponents. Similar blades have been found in the graves of northern Japanese colonists, and appear to have been adopted by most veterans of the Emishi wars. In the years that followed, as veterans returned to their home provinces with stories and skills from the north, the curved blades spread throughout Japan and entirely supplanted their straight predecessors.[16]

It was also during the wars against the Emishi that the

government discontinued the construction of iron-armour plates, and instead mandated that armour would be henceforth made solely out of hardened leather, as this was less liable to rust, easier and quicker to manufacture, and more durable. The iron plates stayed in use, but faded from sight due to standard wear and tear.

Instead, the design of warriors' armour began to reflect the increased role of mounted archery. The top of the helmet remained the toughest point of the armour suit, and its neck guard flared out even further.[17] This afforded the maximum protection and deflection from arrows fired from *directly above* the wearer's head. While this might seem strange at first, it suggests that when charging at their enemies, Japanese soldiers would do so with their heads low and eyes down, presenting the arrow-deflecting curves of their helmet head-on to the foe.

With the need to keep both hands free for using a bow, no shield was possible. Instead Japanese warriors began to favour large, shield-like attachments that formed square pads attached to their shoulders. Made of overlapping hide plates like the rest of the warrior's armour, these square shoulder guards formed strong defences when a rider's hands were down at his horse's reins, but would lift up and out of the way if he grasped his bow and prepared to fire an arrow. In adding square, box-like structures to the warrior's silhouette, the addition of these shoulder guards created another piece in the slow accretion of what we now think of as the style of the samurai.

In 794, as the wars in the north reached their final phase, Emperor Kammu moved its location once again. After several previous locations, including Asuka, Ōmi, and most recently in Nara, the court was relocated to a city that would become known as *Heian-kyō* ('Peaceful and Tranquil Capital'). Remaining, with only the briefest of interludes, the capital of Japan for the next 1,000 years, the city would come to be known simply as *Miyako* ('The Capital'), or by the name that it has today: *Kyōto* ('Capital City'). Kammu, whose mother was a descendant of a Korean king, seemed intent on recreating the world that the exiled nobility from the Asian mainland had left behind. The new capital was designed in deliberate nostalgia for a lost world. Its layout, with an inner imperial citadel in the north and square city blocks in a checkerboard pattern, was deliberately conceived in imitation of Chang-an, the capital of distant Tang China. But whereas the capital may have been conceived in imitation of the Chinese model, Japan's military system was going its own way.

One casualty of Japanese warfare over the next few years was the *ōyumi* or crossbow. Seemingly imported from China, the crossbow existed in several variant forms, and was in use as both an infantry weapon and as an artillery piece. In this latter form, installed on mountings on castle walls like the Roman *ballista*, crossbows appear to have been formidable weapons, highly prized by generals. The presence of an *ōyumi* at a Tsushima watchtower seems to have been such a grand prospect that the weapon's name was eventually assigned to the town where it was based. However, the *ōyumi* is also something of a mystery. When they were commonplace, nobody thought to draw them or describe their construction – *ōyumi* were simply used in battles and regularly reported to devastate enemy lines. If they came into Japanese hands during the Korean wars, their intricate manufacture and maintenance was only sustainable for a few generations. As the Korean and Chinese military advisers faded into the local population, the number of competent operators or mechanics dropped off. By the ninth century, *ōyumi* were still reported in district armouries, but rarely mentioned on the battlefield.

Instead, district commanders griped about the cost of maintenance, or filed plaintive reports with the court, requesting instructors be sent to teach their men how to use the legendary weapons. The weapons show up in Tsushima, close to the mainland, and also in border forts in the wilder frontier of the north-east – yet even there they appear to have swiftly degraded, their triggers jamming or sights left uncalibrated. Whatever an *ōyumi* was, its delicate mechanism, expensive springs and bowstrings became harder to replace. By 914, a general described the few remaining crossbows as 'empty nostalgia', gathering dust in local armouries, entirely beyond the comprehension of local troops. A few large-scale versions persevered in northern forts, but no extant examples survive for modern investigators to assess.[18]

It probably did not help the crossbow's fortune that it seemed primarily designed for defence rather than attack, in an age when relatively few battles on Japanese soil were fought under siege conditions. As decades passed with no sign of the much-awaited invaders, the crossbows fell into disrepair. Nor should we discount the influence of a form of martial snobbery among the Japanese. The acceptable face of martial valour, throughout the history of the samurai, required great achievements in swordsmanship and archery – both skills that required long years of training. The crossbow, like the arquebus many centuries later, may have been seen as an unwelcome equalizer, operable by any conscript, but sufficient to turn such a man into the nemesis of any samurai standing in his line of sight. There is an intriguing class-based dilemma about the fate of the crossbow – it required a skilled artisan to manufacture, and the wealth of an aristocrat to maintain, but was liable to be crewed by lowly border guards. Despite its high-tech allure, it seems to have been shunned by the samurai, who saw no glamour or glory in its use.

Crucially, it was during the wars in the north that the court gave up on its Chinese-influenced system of conscription. Instead, it largely replaced the discredited part-time peasant footsoldiers with mounted archers, to be drawn from the wealthier members of the population who could bring their own horse. Known variously as *kondei* ('Strong Fellows'), *kenshi* ('Strong Warriors'), or *senshi* ('Select Warriors'), this new militia was intended to guard local granaries and district offices, and to serve at guard posts throughout the capital and the rest of Japanese islands. Some 10,000 of the early Strong Fellows were Emishi – referred to as prisoners of war in the sources, but more likely to be the scions of wealthier 'peaceful' Emishi, scattered throughout Japan on military service, but also as hostages against further rebellions from their northern relatives. The posting of such Emishi warriors throughout Japan certainly helped teach the northern 'barbarians' about Japanese culture; it also introduced the tactics and technology of the northern wars all over Japan, where an entire young generation learned the new fashions for winning wars – swift horsemen and curved swords.

With no foreign wars to fight, the function of the Strong Fellows was largely civil – guard duty and police actions. The requirement to bring one's own horse ensured that in many areas only the sons of local strongmen had the necessary requirements. It became a self-fulfilling prophecy – a military career was only available to those who could demonstrate experience and equipment that were only available to military families. Where Strong Fellows were not drawn from local elites, they were usually found to have their origins in the Kantō region, where former colonists had taken advantage of the reforms on land clearance to snatch large parcels of arable land for them-selves. The conquest of the north may have pacified the border areas, but it had also radically shifted the balance of power. Whether the court realized it or not, the Kansai region was no longer the centre of wealth and power. Piece by piece, the balance of control in Japan was shifting eastwards, to the Kantō plain.

2

THE FIRST SAMURAI
THE TAIRA AND THE MINAMOTO

Marriage customs in the capital city usually kept the parties in their family homes. In what was either a quaint custom or a chilling relic of forgotten rapes, it was considered dashing for a nobleman to steal into his lover's home at night, his face concealed. Concubines remained at the homes of their fathers, where they would also raise the children of their trysts. Regardless of the pretence of secrecy, the children thus fathered were all considered legitimate, and granted princely status.

The Tale of Genji, sometimes considered the world's first novel, has left us an impression of life for the courtiers of the capital. With the enforcement of peace farmed out to the rural warrior families, the nobility could indulge themselves in endless rounds of court ceremonial, genteel arts, and religious worship. *The Tale of Genji*, purportedly the work of the court lady Murasaki Shikibu, is a world of poetry and banquets, and of predatory 'romances' as princely youths force themselves on protesting court ladies. It is also a world of constant intrigue as the courtiers jostle over positions in the elaborate hierarchy. As had been their practice for centuries, the fathers of the Fujiwara clan ensured that their daughters became the chief wives of the emperors, so that the Fujiwara remained the most powerful and influential clan at court. If our sole source for this period were *The Tale of Genji*, we might be forgiven for thinking that martial matters were a thing of the past. True enough, there are moments in the narrative where the courtiers attend an archery contest, or threaten each other with swords, but military matters are largely absent. Civilization, in the eyes of the courtiers, was only to be found at the capital. Those samurai that kept order in the outlying regions were regarded as uncultured, mannerless country bumpkins.

The warriors in the capital, however, liked to claim that there was something different about them. Local language began to distinguish between *tōgoku no musha* ('Warriors of the Eastern Lands'), and *miyako no musha* ('Warriors of the Capital'). This latter group, it was implied, were better educated and more refined than the louts they commanded in the provinces. Rather than refer to them as warriors at all, the courtiers damned them with faint praise by referring to them as *samurai* ('servants').

By the time of the grandchildren of the fiftieth Emperor, Kammu, the imperial family was already too unwieldy. With the Fujiwara often serving as regents in their name, the emperors found other uses for their time. The fifty-second Emperor, Saga (r.809–23), was no exception, fathering at least fifty children. Determined to reduce the burden on his treasury, he informed some thirty-two of them that they were no longer members of the imperial family, but founders of a new offshoot clan. Entire branches were lopped off and deprived of their imperial status, instead granted new surnames and established as new houses. Some princes were informed that they were now the *Taira* ('Peace'); others that they were now the *Minamoto* ('Source').[1]

The downgrading of entire arms of the imperial house was initially a success. It packed off large numbers of younger sons to the provinces and reduced the drain on the imperial resources. However, it also created a tempting middle ground between the capital and the provinces – a group of disenfranchised nobles, many with wealth, but all with a tradable name. Just as the Fujiwara clan had insinuated themselves into the world of the court, wealthy provincials soon attached themselves to the newly formed clans. Sons of the Taira and Minamoto were promising matches for the daughters of provincial strongmen, adding a noble cachet to outer clans. The daughters were similarly highly thought of, and many husbands took on the surname of their wives in recognition. Even those Taira and Minamoto fallen on hard times still had their name to trade; numerous noble-born debtors adopted their provincial creditors as their heirs as a form of payment in kind, ensuring that the Taira and Minamoto names were soon firmly ingrained in provincial landholdings. The names of many clans were wiped out in this period, not through military conquest, but through their willing adoption of a distaff imperial pedigree through marriage or adoption.

The tenth century's greatest upheaval was brought about as a result of part of this manoeuvring over birth. Its instigator was Taira Masakado (d.940), a warlord in the Kantō region who seemed used to the rough justice and militarized conflict resolution of the area, but who

eventually allowed the brusque nature of provincial disputes to spill over into open warfare with emissaries of the
imperial court.

Masakado's father had been a general in charge of
maintaining peace in the north, the second successor to the
role previously held by the great Sakanoue Tamuramaro.
He was thus a man with considerable wealth in the north,
and an even larger sense of entitlement. He seemed unable
to reconcile the free rein of a war of conquest with the
reserve required as an official in peacetime; nor did he
inherit his father's rank. While others were in charge of
suppressing the north, Masakado was caught in between
two classes – he was too nouveau to be a court aristocrat,
but not quite wealthy or powerful enough to be a high-
ranking clansman. Like many of the Taira clansmen, he was
caught on the cusp – only five generations previously, his
branch of the Taira had been princes. Now they were stuck
in the provinces, with the prospect of ever-diminishing
class rank.

The origins of the conflict at first seem bizarrely trivial.
At first, it was little more than a dispute over a woman –
specifically, over his impending marriage to his cousin, the
daughter of Taira Yoshikane. Between the lines, we can see
the class-related machinations of surnames and residence;
in fact, Masakado's marriage to the woman was already
approved, the dispute was really over whether his bride
should come to his residence or he should go to hers. It
would appear that Taira Yoshikane would have grudgingly
accepted Masakado as a son-in-law, with whatever financial
or material wealth he might bring, so long as Masakado
acknowledged Yoshikane as a superior by undertaking an
uxorilocal marriage – i.e. joining the family of Yoshikane,
instead of demanding that the bride 'leave' her family to
join Masakado's. The Taira, of course, were well used to

this sort of politicking and took it particularly seriously. Although a courtier might have found such posturing laughable, Yoshikane considered himself a cut above Masakado because Yoshikane's branch of the Taira family was much closer to the court. Yoshikane's father had been a prince, and Yoshikane may have preferred a princely son-in-law, in order to steer his descendants back into the nobility.

Ironically, of course, there was not even an issue over the name, as both bride and groom were of the Taira clan. However, it seems that there was considerable loss of face for Yoshikane if his daughter slummed it with a lower-ranking samurai, and the argument soon escalated.

Other local clans soon got involved – Masakado's first battle was against forces led by Yoshikane's brother-in-law, a Minamoto. It was, however, not enough for Masakado to simply win; he vengefully torched over 500 houses (i.e. several villages) of enemy supporters. The chronicle of his uprising makes it clear that this act was a calculated atrocity:

> Masakado went about burning the homes . . . from the great compounds of the wealthy to the tiny houses of those who abetted them. Any who ran out to escape the flames were surprised with arrows and forced back into the fires . . . How sad it was! Men and women became fuel for the fires, and rare treasures were divided among strangers . . . That day, the voice of the flames contended with the thunder as it echoed; that hour, the colour of the smoke battled with the clouds as it covered the sky.[2]

In a later conflict, directly with Yoshikane, Masakado faced him with '100 mounted warriors' – in other words, 100 cavalry but also the 1,000 or so footsoldiers likely to have accompanied them as squires and henchmen. Footsoldiers remained an important component in this period, and Masakado's access to troops waxed and waned conspicuously in relation to the farming season and impoverishment through famine. Although the top-ranking combatants, most prominently discussed in extant chronicles, were horse-riding samurai, much of the combat during Masakado's insurrection bore a close resemblance to the 'Chinese' style of armies on foot that had been employed in earlier wars.

Masakado won, but balked at killing Yoshikane. It was, after all, surely now self-evident that Masakado was the stronger warrior and better man. Actually killing Yoshikane would have invited censure. However, Masakado was already in trouble back in the capital. A complaint had been lodged concerning his arson attack on the villages, taking his action from boisterous and inconsequential squabbling in the provinces to a crime that required courtly attention. He escaped the consequences thanks to his highest-ranking ally back at the court, the incumbent Fujiwara Regent, and was pardoned completely in 937 with the granting of a national amnesty.

Presumably, the court had hoped that cooler heads would prevail. But Yoshikane was still smarting after his defeat, and soon marched out against Masakado again. This time, Yoshikane pointedly played politics, facing Masakado with a statue of the founder of the Taira clan borne at the head of his army. It might not have impressed Masakado, but it was enough of a psychological statement for many of his men – even if he had been forced to flee from their most recent battle, Yoshikane was still Masakado's nominal superior, and if Masakado opposed him, he sinned against his clan.

Masakado's forces withdrew, while Yoshikane mercilessly burned Masakado's nearby forts and supply dumps.

Masakado's luck continued to falter – he was laid low with beriberi and lost several stragglers to the pursuing enemy. One of them was his wife, the source of all the conflict, who fell back into her father's custody when Yoshikane's samurai caught up with her boat. In an unexpected romantic touch, her brothers later allowed her to sneak back to her husband against her father's wishes – just one of the many dramatic touches that has ensured that the story of Masakado has survived the centuries.

Yoshikane tried another tactic, offering samurai status to one of Masakado's footsoldiers if the man reported on the weaknesses in Masakado's camp. Whatever intelligence Yoshikane may have gained, it was not sufficient to defeat his enemy. A second strategy saw Yoshikane sending an ally to the court to report Masakado's behaviour. Masakado must have known that the ruling would not go in his favour, as he sent a military force to prevent the message getting through, but failed. By 938, Masakado had been summoned to the court to account for his actions; he did not go, but instead sent a letter outlining his grievances against Yoshikane.

The skirmishes continued, although Yoshikane had died of natural causes by 939. If this really were nothing but a family dispute, then that should have been the end of it, but the progress of the war had already created new enmities. In particular, Masakado had it in for his cousin Taira Sadamori, who had once promised him support but defected to Yoshikane. It was, to Masakado's great annoyance, Sadamori who had rushed back to the capital to tell tales, and Sadamori who appeared (rightly), to be on track to be appointed to the post once held by Masakado's father, that of the general in charge of keeping order on the frontier.

Meanwhile, and more crucially, Masakado began acting as if he were the overlord of the Kantō. He intervened in a local dispute unrelated to his ongoing war, and handed down a judgement in favour of one of the local lords. The loser in the dispute, naturally, refused to recognize Masakado's authority, and ran to the capital to complain that Masakado was plotting against the court. There were further exchanges of letters from the government, demanding to know what Masakado was up to in the provinces, followed by further protestations of innocence. The final straw came when, amid what appears to be a time of food shortages all around, Masakado was ordered to police the behaviour of a local Fujiwara nobleman who had been accused of withholding taxes, withholding famine relief and burning neighbours' grain houses. Instead, Masakado sided with the underdog, refusing to cooperate with sources friendly to Sadamori, and instead turned on them. By doing so, he ceased to be in a position to offer any excuses for his behaviour – he was allied with a rebel and fighting forces loyal to the government.

Masakado did not work alone. He seems to have been part of a coterie of disaffected Kantō men who believed that they were better suited to power than others closer to the court. Supposedly on the advice of a shaman or fortune-teller who described him as 'the new Emperor', Masakado began to style himself as the rightful ruler of the Kantō region, not in the Emperor's name, but in the Emperor's place. In making such a claim, Masakado was the first to truly acknowledge that Kantō was bigger, wealthier and more powerful than the Kansai region to which it was supposedly subordinate. What had once been a mere province was now asserted as a nation in its own right, with the power to dismiss the authority of the emperor in Kyōto.

Tardily, the court arranged for an army to be sent after Masakado. The hated Sadamori was among the commanders sent after him, and as the groups pursued each other around the region, a group of Masakado's soldiers captured Sadamori's wife. On hearing this, Masakado immediately realized her value as a hostage, and ordered that she 'not be shamed'. This command, however, arrived too late, since she and her companion had already been raped. In a bizarre footnote to Masakado's rebellion, he attempted to mollify the victims by sending them gifts of fine clothes and interrogating them in the subtlest manner possible, with an apologetic poem, asking where the 'flower separated from the branch now dwells'.

Sadamori's wife deftly deflected this query as to her husband's whereabouts by writing her own response, that the 'scent of flowers told her she was not alone' – either a polite acknowledgement of Masakado's implied apology, or an icy comment that she would be avenged. The other victim was blunter, comparing her dishonour to 'flowers scattered on the wind', and stating that her barren heart would bear no fruit for her captors.[3]

The winter campaign now turned to spring, threatening both sides with the loss of many of their troops as planting season began. Masakado was forced to demobilize most of his army, whereas Sadamori's government-appointed army was able to retain more of its number through the promises of imperial rewards. By the time the two 'armies' faced each other for their final battle, Masakado's great host had been reduced to only a handful of his most faithful and fanatical followers. Masakado originally had the upper hand, fighting with the wind behind his arrows, although in the chaotic pursuit of his fleeing foes, he suddenly found their positions reversed. No account of Masakado's last battle is all that clear on his demise, but the evidence suggests that he was struck by a random arrow in the confusion, and that the celebrant Sadamori sent a lowly warrior over to 'twist off his head' later on.

Already in death, Masakado had acquired a legendary status. He was seven feet tall (supposedly); he had two pupils in his left eye (possibly). His mother, it was suddenly alleged, had been a serpent, who had licked him all over soon after his birth, imparting an iron-hard invulnerability to his whole body, with the fatal exception of one weak spot – variously his forehead, the top of his head, his right eye or his temple, depending on the account. This single flaw, it was said, had been learned by one of his concubines, who had told one of his enemies: the same archer who brought him down. When his head was brought to the capital for inspection, it supposedly came alive and demanded to know the location of the rest of his body. Other stories claim that it actually flew away in search of the body. Shrines dotted around Japan claim to hold different relics of Masakado's dismembered corpse, although the head's final resting-place, Kubizuka ('Head Hill') in what is now Tōkyō, would long be regarded as a site protected by a powerful curse. As a rebel who stood up to the imperial regime, he has enjoyed mixed fortunes in the centuries since his demise, but has come to be regarded, often to the embarrassment of later emperors, as the patron saint of the Kantō area.[4]

The tale of Masakado offers a grotesque window into the superstitions and savageries of combat in the tenth century, not merely in his own behaviour, but in that of his opponents. In one of its sidebars, we hear of Sadamori's quest for a male foetus – the crucial ingredient in a magical cure for a bad wound that he has sustained. He first orders his pregnant daughter-in-law to give up what she is carrying, and is only thwarted by a doctor who tells him that his unborn grandchild would not be suitable. Instead, he slices up a pregnant kitchen maid, although her foetus is female, and hence useless. It is only with yet another death among his retinue that he finally obtains the foetus required. The horrific story may be an invention, although its details are true to folk remedies of the period, in which powdered foetus was indeed used as a cure for battle wounds.[5] More poetically, perhaps, it alludes to a new state of affairs among the samurai clansmen, in which they are literally feeding on their own.

In the rebellion of Masakado, we see a small but important shift in the nature of samurai combat. Previous wars had always been rationalized as border conflicts against foreign hostiles, and there would be more to follow on the frontier in the following century. But Masakado could not be written off as an ignorant, brutish barbarian, unfamiliar with Japanese ways. He was a Taira, and his bid for power in the Kantō region was not externally directed, snatching lands from a foe conspicuously branded as somehow different. Instead, it was internal, fighting against a foe that was demonstrably not only of Masakado's type, but even of his clan lineage and family. Hence, Masakado's rebellion was the first acknowledged incident in which the new warrior class turned on itself. The participants in Masakado's rebellion were not in opposition because of their loyalty to higher, courtly powers in a political struggle. Although both sides periodically paid lip service to propriety and rules of engagement, they fought in a conflict that was samurai on samurai.[6]

The best-known account of Masakado's uprising, the *Shōmonki*, is also the first of the *gunkimono* – martial tales loosely equivalent to the Viking sagas, told and retold as public entertainments by minstrels who would talk through the events and launch into songs and poems at the right moment. Such performances offer a new and rich strain of materials on the samurai, although they also come with their own problems.[7]

It is, for example, in the story of Masakado that we first hear of a warrior charging into battle after *announcing his name*. This is not merely a designation to tell one Japanese person apart from another – every person had one of those, even if they were so prosaic and blunt as First Son (Tarō), Second (Jirō), Third (Saburō), Fourth (Shirō) or Fifth (Gorō). An actual surname in Japan was a statement of presence on the tax register; it announced to all present that one was a member of a landed family, and hence had a military obligation to perform and a homeland to defend. Such announcements in the *gunkimono* do not seem to be mere dramatic licence or acknowledgements of relatives present in the audience. Instead, they seem to reflect a growing custom that would resonate throughout the samurai age, as warriors insisted on announcing their names and lineages before entering battle.

This was also not merely a matter of martial pride. Such grandstanding was intended to make it clear to all observers – friend and foe – who were taking part in a battle. The conferral of military honours, spoils and acclaim rested on precise counts of opponents defeated. Samurai were expected to collect the heads of their enemies as grisly trophies of success. The verb for beheading, in this context, retains a visceral sense of the battlefield – it is not the stark, slashing *kiru* of a ritual execution, but the unpleasant, gritty *kubinejikiru*, literally, 'head twisting off and cutting', wrenching the head from the neck with the aid of a dagger or butcher's knife. Where such collection was not immediately possible, it was helpful if witnesses to a combat were able to say for sure who had taken part in it. In some cases, the implication is clear that the head is not being collected from a corpse, but from a still struggling opponent, pinned down and butchered like an animal.

Hence, we see in the announcing of names the early stirrings of a general battlefield vanity among the samurai.

Even as armour enclosed its wearer and rendered him indistinguishable from his allies, the armour's decoration was rendered more elaborate in order to tell him apart. Lacing patterns began to incorporate sigils and crests, samurai began to favour brightly coloured battle-flags, and helmets began to gain distinctive headpieces. Even as the samurai assembled into clans and houses and fought as part of great armies, each individual did all in his power to single himself out among the crowd. This served another purpose – for any observers, it would also be immediately clear who was retreating. In making themselves easy to identify, the samurai pushed themselves into a martial attitude that would brook no surrender.

The need for identity, and for ever more intricate armour led to another change in materials from days of old. Whereas armour lacings had previously been made of leather, this material was no longer deemed appropriate. It was only available in relatively short lengths, and, perhaps more tellingly, in a limited number of colours. As samurai began to rely on ease of identification to others, they began to favour silk armour lacings that could be dyed with more vivid colours.[8]

One of the reasons for the delayed court response to Masakado's insurrection was that his was not the only one. An unrelated second 'revolt', this time in the west, also kept the court occupied, although without quite the legendary status of Masakado's epic insurrection. Fujiwara Sumitomo (c.893–941) was an administrator in Iyo province, a coastal region on the Inland Sea. As his name implied, he was already part of the great courtly Fujiwara clan, although presumably a low-ranking official with similar grievances about being posted so far from the pleasures of courtly life. In 939, a rival Fujiwara governor accused Sumitomo of plotting an insurrection, and prepared to head to the capital to warn the court that Sumitomo had set up a signal system of watchfires designed ahead of a rebellion. The accusation appears to have been well-founded, since Sumitomo managed to overtake his rival en route, cut off his ears and nose, stole his wife and killed his children.

This rather surprising behaviour for a Fujiwara suggests a very different background. Sumitomo was the great-nephew of a prominent Fujiwara regent, but his branch of the family had fallen on hard times. Like Masakado, he was stuck out in the provinces with little hope of getting closer to the capital. Sumitomo, however, was not in league with farmers-turned-soldiers, but with fisherman-turned-pirates. Far from being a mere government appointee, Sumitomo had until recently been the 'chief of the pirates', commander of a fleet of up to 1,000 ships that had preyed on shipping in the Inland Sea. A government amnesty in 936, in which up to thirty separate bands of pirates were allotted land in exchange for giving up their ways, seems to have been written up in courtly records as a victory whereas it was probably more of a collection of protection money. The 'pirates', liable to have been legitimate residents turning to crime amid the famines and deprivations already reported in the 930s, only remained quiet for a while, before rising up again, with Sumitomo at their head.

Although it is Masakado's rebellion that gained all the attention from historians, it was Sumitomo's that was taken far more seriously by the court at the time. Masakado was based in the Kantō region, still regarded as a distant vassal, whereas the Inland Sea was still the heart of the Japanese self-image. Western Japan was home to many prominent nobles, and many fiefs operated by residents of the capital or their family. Notably, Sumitomo was also one of the courtiers' own, and treated in a different way to the provincial Masakado. Instead of sending an army to deal with him, the court sent a proclamation, offering him a junior court rank if he stopped his predatory ways. This only worked for a few months; if the government had hoped to set a thief to catch a thief, leaving Sumitomo in charge of policing the activities of lesser pirates, the attempt failed. Instead, a force was sent to the region to deal with Sumitomo with extreme prejudice, successfully enticing one of Sumitomo's most trusted lieutenants to defect, and using the information he offered to hunt down and destroy Sumitomo's fleet in 941. Justice caught up with Sumitomo two weeks later, when he was apprehended and beheaded.[9]

Masakado and Sumitomo were mere symptoms, and dealing with them did not remove the underlying causes of their rebellion. There was, however, a century of relative peace after the suppression of their insurrections. Resources had been assigned to local elites, and the prospect of resisting the court grimly demonstrated to be a suicidal act. The turn of the eleventh century saw the pinnacle of courtly life, best summarized today in the genteel cultural pursuits of the aforementioned *The Tale of Genji*, a story of intrigues and romances circulated among court ladies of the time by its putative author Murasaki Shikibu.

The Tale of Genji is interesting to the samurai historian for its *lack* of relevance. Lady Murasaki's Kyōto is a world away from the seacoast where pirates burned their enemies alive, or the brutal tallies of samurai in the provinces twisting off their opponents' heads in order to compare their battle prowess. But Murasaki's characters, while in a more privileged position than the samurai, are still beholden to the same concerns. Genji himself, the 'shining prince' of the story, is arguably a prime candidate for the kind of rustification that so troubled the samurai of the era. The son of a concubine of a former emperor, he is downgraded to commoner status and given a Minamoto surname, barely clinging to a court position. We might readily imagine a second- or third-generation descendant of Murasaki's protagonist falling on times so hard that life in the capital is no longer a possibility. At that point, perhaps a new life and new opportunities awaited on the frontier, perhaps by marrying into one of the powerful provincial clans. Class – what we might call the difference between old and new money – is a permanent obsession for Murasaki's characters. Behind the opulence of the brocades and fine furnishings, the sophistication of the exchanges of poetry, the gossip and dalliances and intrigues of furtive romances, there is the ever-present shadow of a savage world beyond the capital, where these peaceful pursuits are not possible. Of course, even in the capital one was not entirely protected from murder, natural disasters, disease, famine or drought, but life there was appreciably better than anywhere else in the archipelago. The population of Japan in the year AD 1000 was perhaps five million people, of which only 1 per cent lived within the civilized precincts of the capital. The court itself, a further subcategory, sustained a refined, cultured lifestyle for a mere 5,000 souls, while the rest of Japan struggled in medieval squalor. No wonder the samurai were so keen to be part of life in Kyōto.[10]

Famines and epidemics in the eleventh and twelfth centuries led to a contraction in the population of Japan. New lands were less cleared at the end of this period than they were re-opened. But whether newly cleared or farmed for a long period of time, the acquisition of land was a sure way to luxury. Provincial lords took up residence in the capital, leaving the administration of their distant domains to underlings. Land was cleared by men in search of tax breaks, 'gifted' to local temples in order to obtain tax exemption, and then administrated in the temple's name by the man who had cleared it. Occasionally, in those cases where 'cleared' land was merely a claim staked on an abandoned piece of farmland or pasture, there would be conflicts over ownership when the original owners returned.

It was not until the 1050s that such squabbles over re-settlement were supplanted by a true war once more. This time, the focus shifted back to the northern frontier, where a new generation of samurai fought over the right to rule the area. Much like their counterparts in the distant capital, the samurai had evolved a sense of upper and lower hierarchy, between which aspirants would rise through the making of good matches and the exercise of ominous power. During this period, the samurai still saw themselves as 'Japanese', while the descendants of the Emishi were still an underclass of 'non-Japanese'.

The 'peaceful' Emishi of the north turned out not to be so peaceful after all. Many of them remained resolutely uninterested in the pursuit of farming, so they remained mobile and difficult to tax. In times of shortage, this also turned roving hunters into roving brigands in the eyes of local authorities. Six counties in the north fell under the leadership of one clan, the Abe, who progressively gained greater power. Areas of farmland were fenced off behind stockades, and guarded by Abe troops, until the Abe clan rose to prominence as the de facto rulers of the region. When they decided to disobey what they regarded as an unreasonable request to pay tax and perform corvée labour, the official governor, a member of the Fujiwara family, was obliged to send an expedition to bring them to heel. When the punitive force was defeated by the locals, the dispute escalated into an uprising.

The court's reaction was confused. A new governor was appointed in the form of Minamoto Yoriyoshi, a samurai with a fierce reputation who was sure to give as good as he got. But before Yoriyoshi could even take up office in his new posting and raise an army, the court announced an amnesty for the northern rebels.

The Abe seized on the opportunity, and swiftly swore allegiance to the new arrival. Instead of another war, the north was plunged into five years of blissful tranquillity. The Abe paid all the required tributes, usually in horses and gold from local mines; their leader even adopted a personal name in imitation of Minamoto Yoriyoshi's.

What happened next remains a mystery. As the end of Yoriyoshi's five-year term approached in 1056, a group of his soldiers were massacred at the Akuto River, a tributary of the Koromo that ran through the six counties. Contemporary reports claimed that there had been a clash between a Minamoto retainer and Sadatō, eldest son of the Abe clan leader. A request from Sadatō to marry the Minamoto official's daughter had been rebuffed, and in such a way as to imply that Sadatō was an unworthy husband. If the Abe clan had been hoping to co-opt themselves into the Minamoto, they were sorely mistaken. Five years of good behaviour apparently counted for nothing, and Minamoto Yoriyoshi went on the offensive.[11]

The resulting conflict plunged the north back into old enmities and alliances. Sadatō's father was killed in the early battles, but the son swiftly took over the father's power base, and had little trouble raising troops and resources from the immediate area. Meanwhile, Yoriyoshi found that despite his initial victory he was starved of manpower. Blaming local commanders for his early setbacks, he executed one on doubtful charges, causing further loss of morale and goodwill among the native population. Many local allies swiftly left the territory in order to escape conscription, forcing Yoriyoshi to lean on the long supply routes back into the Kantō area. The absence of men in the region contributed to already failing food supplies.

However, the timing of the conflict seems almost too convenient. Yoriyoshi was widely suspected of orchestrating the skirmish on the riverbank in order to provoke the locals into war and allow subsequent looting with government sanction. His initial advances were pushed back to the fort at Taga, and his requests for additional men met with cool indifference from a court that was largely persuaded he was the architect of his own misfortune. Desperate to score a victory quickly, Yoriyoshi marched in winter snows – an anecdote from the time relates that he embraced his fellow warriors to warm their bodies.

Surviving accounts of Yoriyoshi's campaign first appear to be little removed from descriptions of Masakado's revolt. Armies are still a mix of mounted samurai and infantry with spears and swords. Notably, however, there is no mention of shields – the cumbersome planks appear to have been forgotten or discarded for campaigns on the frontier.

The rebels were also of a different stripe. Whereas earlier conflicts with Emishi emphasized hit-and-run attacks by horsemen, people led by Sadatō seemed much more attached to their land. When facing superior forces, Sadatō's men turned earlier fortifications against them, retreating to the confines of old forts, and forcing their pursuers to conduct a siege. Such measures were particularly galling to Yoriyoshi, who lacked the manpower and supplies to simply wait out his enemy. The rebels would fire arrows or drop rocks or boiling water from the palisades. When a fort seemed ready to fall, Sadatō's rebels would simply open the gates and make a mounted charge for safety. In some cases, this would be suicidal, but in many others, it seems to have been enough to smash a hole through the ranks of the besieging samurai.

In later tales of the war, the unforgettable star of the conflict was Yoriyoshi's eldest son Yoshiie (1039–1106).

Only a teenager at the start of the conflict, he survived to tell and retell his exploits in the capital, with an emphasis that he was no mere warrior:

> He shot arrows from horseback like a god; undeterred by gleaming blades, he lurched through the rebel's encirclements to emerge on their left and right. With his great arrowheads he transfixed one enemy chieftain after another, never shooting at random but always inflicting a mortal wound. He galloped like the wind and fought with a skill that was more than human. The barbarians fled rather than face him, calling him the first-born son of Hachiman, the god of war.[12]

Hachiman was already gaining prominence as the patron deity of the Minamoto. Addressing Yoshiie in affectionate jest as 'Hachiman Tarō' was a compliment to him and to his father, since it equated Yoriyoshi with the god himself.

In one early conflict on the banks of the Koromo River, Yoshiie pursued Sadatō and a group of men to a fort. Inevitably, Sadatō's men rushed out in a breakout, and Yoshiie found himself in lone pursuit of the wounded enemy leader.

Their encounter in the forest speaks volumes about the aspirations of the new warrior class. Yoshiie, so he claimed, yelled angrily that Sadatō had turned his back on his enemy, and that he should turn to receive a message. When Sadatō did, Yoshiie hit him not with an arrow, but with a line from a poem: 'The threads in your robe have come undone.' It was a deliberate, complex pun, which could also be interpreted as 'Koromo castle has been destroyed.'

Sadatō replied immediately with a line from the same poem: 'Over the years, the threads become tangled, and it causes me sorrow.'[13]

Yoshiie let his bow drop, and Sadatō lived to fight another day.

In this highly improbable but much repeated story, we see new priorities coming to the fore. Both Yoshiie and his enemy aspire to courtly graces, and each sees a worthy and noble opponent. In what is more likely to have been a desperate spin on Yoshiie's failure to kill or capture his enemy, the story of the poetry duel seems almost tailor-made to resonate with an audience in the distant court.

Despite such pretence of gentility, the war in the north ended in a brutal massacre. The last stand of the Abe occurred in the fort of Kuriyagawa, in the northern reaches of the Koromo River – a location that implies they had been pushed to the very edge of their territory by the samurai advance. The fort was set on fire, and the Abe mounted a final charge, this time with no hope of escape. When Sadatō's teenage son was found among the captured soldiers, Yoriyoshi at first prepared to free him in recognition of his brave performance on the battlefield. However, his associate Kiyowara talked him out of it, warning of the consequences of a vengeful enemy's son permitted to grow to adulthood. Suitably persuaded, Yoriyoshi ordered the thirteen-year-old boy to be executed.

Coughing, choking women of the Abe clan fled from the burning stockade, only to fall into the hands of the besiegers. A wife of one of the Abe leaders cried out to her husband that she was sure to follow him in death, and threw herself off a cliff, clutching her three-year-old infant to her.[14]

With the execution of young boys and the suicide of women to avoid rape, it is perhaps understandable why the Minamoto might hope to push a more courtly version of themselves upon their return to the capital. Perhaps we can see a different conflict at work here: the attempts of the

Minamoto to ingratiate themselves with the nobility once the war was over. For Yoriyoshi's part, he returned from the war and submitted a pointed report. Instead of limiting his report to accounts of battles won and a statement of obeisance to the Emperor, Yoriyoshi bullishly noted that the war had cost him a great deal of personal expense, particularly as the taxes he had expected to amass as governor had been uncollectable in a war zone. Moreover, while he thanked the Emperor for his new promotion, he forcefully and rather rudely suggested that a dozen of his followers had been overlooked for commendations. Until such time as the Emperor complied with his wishes, Yoriyoshi would not take up his new post as the governor of distant Iyo province in Shikoku. Accordingly, his presence at the capital served as a constant reminder that the Emperor owed him a favour.

Yoriyoshi's comments came across as typical samurai belligerence, although they may have hidden more immediate concerns. Despite the boasts of Yoshiie's superhuman prowess in battle, the tide of battle was only turned when Yoriyoshi had enlisted the support of a rival local elite in fighting against the Abe. Yoriyoshi had enlisted the help of Kiyohara Takenori, a local potentate whose assistance had turned the tide of the war when all else failed. In return for his service, Kiyohara had expected to be rewarded with a sizable part of the spoils of war, including some sort of official recognition that he was the warlord of the north. Even as he reported a victory for the samurai, Yoriyoshi may have been secretly worrying that his new allies would themselves rise up in revolt unless he could somehow incorporate them officially within the imperial system.[15]

His son Yoshiie got a similarly rude awakening in the capital. Although he seems to have been the darling of some courtiers, who could not get enough of his war stories, one member of his audience commented that he lacked a true education. Although appointed as a governor of the north, Yoshiie refused to take up his new post, perhaps in the realization that regardless of what the court might think, the true ruler of the north was Kiyohara Takenori. Veiling his refusal to depart with the Confucian excuse that he did not want to be too far from his aging father, he lurked in the capital as a reminder of the kind of man required to enforce the Emperor's peace in the outlying regions.

Twenty years later, Yoshiie returned to the north as an older, wiser man, or so he would often claim. In fact, he appears to have been dragged back into a rematch among the northern players. Tensions within the family of Kiyohara Takenori were to blame. His son, Sanehira, was assumed to be his heir, but Sanehira's mother had an ominous past. She was the widow of a Fujiwara clansman who had sided with the Emishi, and hence had distant ties to the court nobility. To make matters worse, she was the sister of the former Abe leader Sadatō, and had arrived in her second marriage with a son from her first.

Sanehira, meanwhile, had no sons of his own, and hoped to maintain his family line by adopting a son and marrying that son to a woman of the Minamoto. In the eyes of many of the veterans, he had adopted airs and graces unbefitting the inexperienced son of a local headman. The final straw supposedly came at the wedding of Sanehira's new heir, when a former associate of his father arrived bearing a tray of gold, but was ignored while Sanehira played a game of go. Throwing the tray into the garden in disgust, the supplicant stomped out – once again, we may wonder if this picturesque bit of drama has been overlaid on true events after the fact. Whatever the cause of the quarrel, the insulted official had soon joined forces with Sanehira's resentful younger brother, and, more importantly, the elder half-brother who might reasonably be seen by many parties as the rightful heir to much of the north. There is also a certain karmic irony that Kiyohara, who had so famously urged Yoriyoshi to murder any potential troublemakers before they matured, should find his own sons and stepson feuding over his domain.

Minamoto Yoshiie was dispatched to the north in the role of governor, but essentially as a mediator in the conflict. Somehow, he allowed himself to be drawn into the conflict as a combatant, purportedly when he was inspecting one of Sanehira's forts, which was then attacked by the rebels. Sanehira's wife then supposedly announced that it would be unseemly for her, as a woman, to lead the defence of the fort in her husband's absence, encouraging Yoshiie to reluctantly take over.

Amid such monstrous family feuding – we should bear in mind that Sanehira's wife was also the mother of one of the rebels Yoshiie had just been persuaded to attack – Yoshiie put paid to the rebels with great speed. But with Sanehira inconveniently dead of an illness shortly afterwards, the supposed instigator of the war was gone. His brother and half-brother duly reported to Yoshiie at Taga Castle and offered their surrender.

Yoshiie's attempt at mediation was doomed. He ordered that the region be split between the surviving half-brothers. Depending on one's allegiance, this either deprived Kiyohara's last surviving son of half the territory that was rightfully his, or dangerously restored a scion of the Abe family to half the land that his family had lost a generation previously. Before long, the Kiyohara heir led an army against his Abe stepbrother, killing his wife and children. The Abe heir complained to Yoshiie, and Yoshiie led Minamoto forces in a mission of vengeance.

Amid all this confusion, it was not lost on many participants that the Minamoto had effectively switched sides. They were now prosecuting a war *against* the rightful heir of their former ally Kiyohara. When Yoshiie eventually ran his enemy into retreat, killed him and restored order in the region, he handed control of the territory to the grandson of the original Abe leader that his own father had spent half his life fighting.

The situation was so sensitive that Yoshiie refused to be reminded of it. When an enemy retainer berated him for his lack of loyalty, Yoshiie had the man's tongue cut out. In order to instil a fanatical competition among his own men, Yoshiie instituted a system that rewarded valour with honoured seating for the best fighters at the end of each day. This incentive was perhaps less successful than its corollary – Yoshiie also ordered that the *worst* fighters be made to sit in a designated area for cowards, creating an escalating anxiety to outdo each other among his men.

Yoshiie returned to the capital sure that he had made the best of a bad situation. The most dramatic story of his campaign seems to be another tale tailor-made for a courtly audience, in which Yoshiie the shrewd commander notices that a flock of geese landing in a nearby rice field suddenly fluttered back into the air. Rightly guessing that the geese had happened upon something in the field that should not be there, Yoshiie gave the order to attack, and flushed out thirty enemies waiting in ambush. The story bore repeating, it seems, not merely to add to the fame of Yoshiie, but also as an acknowledgement to friends among the courtiers – the aphorism 'When soldiers lay in ambush, wild geese scatter' had been something Yoshiie had picked up from a scholarly mentor during his days in the capital.

If Yoshiie were hoping to persuade the court that he was on their side, he was sorely mistaken. He returned to the capital full of tales of daring, and humbly submitted a request to the court to execute the enemy ringleaders. In granting assent, the court would effectively acknowledge the just nature of Yoshiie's mission. However, the request met with courtly obfuscation. Yoshiie's motives in entering the fray had been called into question, as had the rationale behind his inadvisable decision to split the territory between the two rivals. Nor was the court ready to order the massacre of the survivors of a family that had apparently been diligent taxpayers for twenty years.

When he learned of the court's unwillingness to acknowledge his actions, Yoshiie took matters into his own hands. He threw the collected heads of the Kiyohara rebels into a roadside ditch, and parcelled out rewards to his men from his own treasury.

Such behaviour, like that of his father, was sure to annoy the court. Yoshiie was relieved of his governor's post in the north and pointedly not given another position. In the eyes of the court, this turned him into nothing more than a commoner. But the censure of the court held little sway with the samurai themselves. If Yoshiie was disliked at the court but independently wealthy, what need would he have to seek the court's approval?

Court sniping at Yoshiie continued for several years. On one occasion, other landowners were forbidden from signing over their holdings to him by a government concerned over his still-growing wealth. On another, his brother and rival, Yoritsuna, was appointed governor of the north, in a move that could have provoked hostility between them. Regardless, Yoshiie's celebrity was unassailable, and late in life, Yoshiie shaved his head and became a Buddhist monk, ostensibly in atonement for the many deaths he had caused. However, his discovery of religion hid another change in the balance of power in the capital.

Shirakawa, the seventy-second Emperor, had abdicated from the throne in 1086 and gone into seclusion himself. As a 'retired' emperor, he was freed from many of the distractions of court ceremonial, but still entitled to an entourage and the chance to manipulate his successor from behind the scenes – the throne now being occupied by his four-year-old son. While Yoshiie and his fellow warriors remained ostracized from the court itself, he enjoyed the support of his men and the confidence of the Retired Emperor. In particular, they enjoyed the honours that were heaped upon them by the Retired Emperor in thanks for their generous donations to his temple-building programme. Shirakawa's policy of ruling from the cloisters was to make him, and many later retired emperors rely increasingly on a power base that was not drawn from the old noble houses like the Fujiwara, but from the new clans such as the Minamoto and the Taira.

3

THE LATTER DAYS OF THE LAW
THE HŌGEN AND HEIJI INSURRECTIONS

According to Buddhist tradition, there would be three ages following the death of Gautama Buddha around 500 BC. The Former Days of the Law would see Buddhism gaining ground and finding followers in a millennium of gradual growth, and local belief in Japan dated the end of this period to AD 552, the time of the arrival of Buddhism on Japanese shores. A middle period of a mere 500 years would characterize the apex of Buddhism before even the law of Gautama Buddha would enter a period of decline and fall. It was widely believed among Japanese Buddhists that these Latter Days of the Law commenced around 1052, and that the growing unrest and instability in Japan was a sign of these end times.

It can be helpful to frame the rise of the samurai in the late eleventh century within this particular interpretation of the end of history. A belief that a golden age was past and society was falling into the hands of evildoers was common, as was the sense, albeit nothing to do with Buddhist tradition, that the mandate of heaven might have been revoked. Whereas the rulers of Japan in the age of Emperor Temmu considered themselves appointed by heaven and ruling through a form of divine right, the eleventh century saw the samurai rebelling against this established order. The concept of the 'Latter Days of the Law' (*mappō*) made it easier to argue that unwelcome laws issued from false authorities, and that true sincerity lay in disobedience to an unpopular order.

The imperial family made no bones about using samurai supporters as pawns in their own struggles. A quarrel between Yoshiie and his brother Yoshitsuna was largely engineered by imperial backers behind the scenes. Yoshiie's later years were haunted by the growing realization that his own son Yoshichika, was at odds with a rival faction in the capital. Yoshiie ordered his son, then a governor in Kyūshū, to return to the capital and present himself, but Yoshichika refused. Yoshiie died in 1106, in his late sixties in his monastery retreat, fretting that someone would inevitably be sent to deal with Yoshichika by force. Within a year of his death, the meteoric rise of the Minamoto under his command would come crashing down.

The samurai selected to bring Yoshichika to heel was a fellow supporter of the Retired Emperor Shirakawa, named Taira Masamori. Masamori had donated land in a nearby prefecture to Shirakawa's Buddhist order, and been promoted in thanks swiftly up the civil ladder until he was a provincial governor. In 1107, Masamori was sent to Kyūshū to deal with the apparently rebellious Yoshichika, reporting success in barely a month, and returning with Yoshichika's head to a rapturous welcome.

Soon afterwards, the new leader of the Minamoto clan, Yoshichika's brother, was killed by an unknown assassin. The leadership of the clan passed into the hands of a fourteen-year-old boy, Tameyoshi, who was immediately ordered to pursue one of his own clansmen, who was accused of the murder of his predecessor. After returning to Kyōto with the clansman's head, Tameyoshi was given a contemptuous reward for his services, and made a police chief instead of a provincial governor.

Tameyoshi's lowly reward reflects the waning position of the Minamoto clan in Kyōto, although this fall in fortunes was not reflected out in the countryside. In the Kantō region, the Minamoto remained a powerful authority, and Tameyoshi's many sons continued as scions of a wealthy dynasty with many associated vassal clans. Although the Kantō region was the heartland for the Minamoto, their associate allies were scattered across Japan. One of Tameyoshi's sons, repeating a family pattern, was reprimanded for causing trouble in Kyūshū. The son failed to appear when summoned to Kyōto to answer for himself, leading to the punitive dismissal of Tameyoshi from the capital. He was replaced as the clan's official leader and representative with another son, Yoshitomo, who arrived in the capital embarrassed by the activities of his half-brother, and determined to avenge his father's disgrace. That, at least, is the version of the tale as understood by the Minamoto. We might easily present a similar account of events from the point of view of the court aristocracy that would paint Tameyoshi as a bad seed from a bad family, whose life in the capital was characterized by a number of unseemly incidents. The scandal over his son was merely the final straw – Tameyoshi was also reprimanded for starting fights on six occasions, and for harbouring criminals on three. It is perhaps more understandable in this light that the mainstream courtiers regarded the Minamoto as thugs with ideas above their station, and no great surprise that the Minamoto and Taira were often found to be at odds with one another, while the courtiers looked on.

While many courtiers may have looked upon the Minamoto and Taira as belligerent nuisances, it was only a matter of time before the sense of entitlement of the samurai found a new outlet. If the old order kept the samurai in their place, then the samurai were sure to succumb to the allure of a *new* order. In the middle of the twelfth century, a long period of rule behind the throne by a retired emperor came to an end, pitching a pretender against the throne and erupting into armed conflict in the capital. The rebellion, known as the Hōgen Insurrection after the period it took place, featured samurai on both sides, brought the violence of the borderlands to the capital itself, and was the first small step on the path to a full-blown samurai government.[1]

Despite abdicating in 1123, Retired Emperor Toba had steered the Empire from behind the scenes, first through his son Sutoku, and after Sutoku was persuaded to abdicate in turn, through Sutoku's brother the Emperor Konoe. The teenage Konoe's death without an heir in 1155, and that of Retired Emperor Toba in 1156, led to sudden unrest over a long-burning dispute within the imperial family. Soon after Konoe's death his elder brother Go-Shirakawa was enthroned in his place, to the surprise of many in the capital. Go-Shirakawa, a man in his late twenties, had never been seriously considered as emperor material, and was better known for his love of music. The new enthronement was in fact a move by Konoe's mother and her allies within the powerful Fujiwara family, who hoped to present their enemies with a fait accompli. However, a rival court faction favoured an even older brother, the Retired Emperor

Sutoku, who had abdicated on Toba's orders in 1142 and regretted the move ever since. Sutoku was a decade older than Go-Shirakawa, and considered himself to be a far better candidate. Moreover, if the court would not accept a Retired Emperor coming out of retirement, Sutoku had a son of his own whom he hoped to place on the throne while he ruled as Regent.

Toba's death only came after a long illness, giving the factions plenty of time to make their plans. On the day of the funeral, Yoshitomo led forces from the Minamoto clan on Go-Shirakawa's orders across Kyōto to arrest Fujiwara Yorinaga, on suspicion of intrigues against the throne. They did not find Yorinaga, but occupied his house and confiscated his badge of office.

Although named as the seventy-seventh Emperor, Go-Shirakawa was still the underdog, and it is telling that his faction should lean on the support of the out-of-favour Minamoto clan. Unfortunately, so did Fujiwara Yorinaga, calling Tameyoshi out of exile, leading to a tragic standoff between Tameyoshi and several of his sons, against his own eldest son Yoshitomo and the majority of the Minamoto clan.

Our best account of this battle, the *Hōgen Monogatari*, differs from earlier war tales. Whereas former samurai sagas invariably took place on the distant frontier, the civil war conflict arising from the 1156 succession dispute involved a battle in the capital itself, with the court actively employing its samurai vassals in an internal struggle that broke out into open warfare on the streets of Kyōto. The *Hōgen Monogatari* is also noticeably more dramatic and confused; it clearly accreted over many decades of telling and retelling, and its narrative often flies off on tangents to recount the inconsequential deeds of participants whose descendants were presumably close to hand at forgotten performances. It is, as the Japanese speaker may have already noticed, not a *–ki* (chronicle), but a *monogatari* (story).[2]

At his mansion, Fujiwara Yorinaga consulted with his Minamoto vassals about the best way to deal with the intrigues. He was advised to arrange a night assault on the enemy compound, setting fires on three sides to drag the foe out into combat. It would be, he was told, a tough battle, but the element of surprise would stand them in good stead. Not unlike a game of chess, there was only one person in play of any strategic value. The rebels would not even need to kill all their enemies in order to complete their mission; they would only need to capture Emperor Go-Shirakawa. If the mansion was aflame and the compound was under attack, then Go-Shirakawa's men would be sure to bundle him into a palanquin and run for safety. At that time, the Minamoto archers could simply shoot the palanquin bearers, stranding Go-Shirakawa in the open and delivering him to his foes.

However, Yorinaga was a scholar and a politician, and refused to listen to advice from trained warriors, instead demanding that a great struggle required a great battle. He demanded an old-fashioned standoff between armies, and ordered his men to prepare for one. Interestingly, Yorinaga's assessment of the rules of engagement demanded an order of battle – he appears to have expected the dispute to eventually be resolved by agreeing a mutually acceptable time and place, an exchange of arrows, some name-calling and announcement of lineages, a few episodes of single combat, and then a grand mêlée. This, at least, was how Yorinaga, a lifelong courtier appointed to office in his teens, would have imagined all battles should be resolved. After all, although anything might go when fighting the barbarians of the old frontier, when it came to conflict between gentlemen, that was how matters were settled in all the great songs and poems. In this, Yorinaga appears to have mistaken the dramatic licence of countless bards for an accurate guide to the rules of engagement.

Across town, his enemies had a similar conversation with a very different outcome. The monk and former minister Fujiwara Michinori sought the advice of Minamoto Yoshitomo, who similarly counselled him to arrange a night assault. Unlike Yorinaga, Michinori readily agreed with his military specialist. Michinori, it seems, had no qualms about ending the dispute with a swift, surgical strike at the heart of his enemy's forces.

Before dawn on the morning of 11 July 1156, three samurai groups converged on the late Retired Emperor Toba's compound. There were, perhaps, only 600 horsemen in the attacking forces, outnumbered three to one by the defenders. Two of the attacking groups were Minamoto; the third comprised men from the Taira clan. Although three of the compound's gates were attacked simultaneously, we only have a surviving account from the west side.[3]

There, a lone Minamoto defender, Tametomo, gained legendary proportions among later Japanese storytellers. Despite being only one of many defenders, it is Tametomo whose defence of the west gate would be embellished and augmented over the centuries, until it sometimes seems as if he was holding off the Taira single-handed. Most famously, a single arrow from Tametomo passes clean through one attacker and lodged in the armour of another, convincing Kiyomori, the leader of the attackers, that it might be wise to break off. His son, Shigemori, however, does not see the danger that Tametomo presents. Taira Shigemori was a teenager who had never been in battle before, and had arrived decked out in a clearly identifiable style:

> Beneath his armour, red brocade he wore
> Lacing like the leaves of arrowhead
> A bright-rimmed helmet, marked with silver stars
> Flared for arrow-warding, brightest red[4]

Shigemori had marked out Tametomo for himself, and recited his lineage, announcing his courtly rank, his father's name and rank, his grandfather's name and rank, his highest-ranking ancestor, and, inevitably, the fact that his twelfth-generation ancestor had been the Emperor Kammu. He then announced that he was nineteen years old (i.e. eighteen by our count) and that he had never fought in battle before. Before his father Kiyomori could stop him, Shigemori called out to Minamoto Tametomo, a veteran of dozens of battles, and demanded that he show himself.

Shigemori had picked an opponent far out of his own league. Tametomo was a legendarily powerful warrior. Kiyomori ordered his own men in to protect and somehow escort his son out of harm's way. The Taira attackers fell back under a relentless onslaught from Tametomo's men – the boastful Shigemori was successfully spirited away, but Tametomo and his fellow defenders pushed them back. At that moment, reinforcements arrived for the attackers, in the form of horsemen led by Minamoto Yoshitomo.

In an uneasy standoff, Yoshitomo waited a mere fifty paces away from Tametomo, his enemy and brother. Yoshitomo announced that he been sent on the orders of the Emperor Go-Shirakawa, immediately establishing that he was an agent of the ruling authority. Tametomo was having none of it, announcing that he had been sent to oppose him, on the orders of Retired Emperor Sutoku.

It is easy to see why the author of the *Hōgen Monogatari* should choose to zero in on these two men among the hundreds of combatants. They were two samurai brothers, each opposing the other, serving two imperial brothers, similarly locked in dispute. Yoshitomo, the elder, tried to pull rank, telling his sibling that he was sure to lose all divine support – not only disobeying his brother, but readying his bow to loose an arrow at his own flesh and blood. Tametomo had a ready response, noting that he was remaining loyal to their father, while Yoshitomo was opposing him – a thorny question of filial piety that any Confucian scholar could spend happy months unravelling. Who was the more loyal? Who was the better gentleman?

Tametomo answered with a symbolic gesture. He shot at his brother with a humming-bulb arrow, a noise-making device intended more for signalling than combat. The arrow glanced off Yoshitomo's armour, and Yoshitomo led his samurai in a renewed assault.

The battle continued as the sun rose, and seemed to favour the defenders, with Tametomo's side down by two deaths and two wounded, while Yoshitomo was down by fifty-three dead and two hundred wounded. There is no extant account of what was happening at the north and south gates, which were also under attack, but it was presumably a similar state of affairs. Perhaps realizing that things were not going in his favour, Yoshitomo sought and received permission from his Fujiwara masters to set fire to the west side of the mansion. In a dry summer month, and on a building largely made of wood and paper, the flames quickly caught and the defenders abandoned their stronghold. The Retired Emperor Sutoku fled on horseback, surrounded by his samurai supporters, with the valiant Tametomo bringing up the rear. The entire party was able to flee by the east gate, which the attackers had neglected. Presumably, this is because the attackers knew that there was little chance of escape to the east. Sutoku and his protectors soon found themselves in the foothills of the mountains encircling Kyōto, and split up. After two days in the open, Sutoku and two henchmen sneaked into a temple in north Kyōto, run by another brother. This sibling, however, favoured Go-Shirakawa, and handed the errant pretender over to the authorities. Within the week, the pretender's lead warrior Tameyoshi also appeared back in Kyōto, presenting himself at the house of his victorious son Yoshitomo; he was clad in the robes of a priest, and claimed to have renounced violence. If this was an attempt to remove himself from retribution, it failed.

The disturbance at the mansion, which was burned to the ground during the fighting, was regarded by at least one commentator as the beginning of the 'age of the warrior'. But it was the aftermath, rather than the battle itself, that truly established the intrigues of the samurai era. Although the Emperor Go-Shirakawa's faction had been preserved and a usurper thwarted, neither of the samurai clan leaders received a reward that they regarded as just. Minamoto Yoshitomo was made a fifth-rank, junior-grade courtier, and master of the stables for all his hard work, which might have sufficed were he not made to endure the sight of Taira Kiyomori receiving a higher rank and a provincial governorship, despite having played little part in the skirmish beyond the rescue of his own son.

Members of the Fujiwara, Minamoto and Taira clans had fought on both sides, but the punishments caused the disparate factions to begin uniting along lines of clan affiliation, instead of personal allegiance. Among the Fujiwara, Yorinaga had bled to death from an arrow wound during the battle, and so was beyond punishment. Other errant members of the Fujiwara clan, as well as the pretender Sutoku, were sent into exile – arguably a fate worse than death for the courtiers, who would be forced to slum it in the countryside, far from their beloved capital.

Exile from Kyōto was the traditional courtly punishment for misbehaviour, but after dealing in such a manner with his own relatives, the victorious Fujiwara Michinori applied an unexpectedly rough justice to the samurai participants. When it came to the rebel ringleaders, Michinori insisted on battlefield punishments unseen in the countryside for centuries. The Taira were obliged to execute several of their own, as were the Minamoto.

Despite fighting bravely for the authorities, Minamoto Yoshitomo was put in an impossible position, ordered to execute his own father, Tameyoshi. Understandably, he refused, and another Minamoto clansman took on the gory task. Pointedly, the lieutenant did this so that a Minamoto would not die at the hands of a Taira, and killed himself in contrition shortly afterwards. Already, there was a simmering resentment growing between the Minamoto and the Taira, particularly when the executions of the Minamoto extended not just to Tameyoshi but to nine of his brothers, including a seven-year-old boy.

Only Tametomo, the brave defender of the compound, survived the putsch by successfully remaining on the run for a month. By the time he was captured, there appears to have been an element of guilt among the courtiers about the handling of the victory, and Tametomo was sent instead into exile.[5]

Among the deaths of the Minamoto involved in Sutoku's failed bid for the throne, we see the first reference in any Japanese text to a peculiar custom that appears to have evolved among the samurai of the Kantō plain. One of the samurai among the would-be usurpers is surprised by enemy reinforcements, and commits suicide. Although the act is simply related in many extant texts of the *Hōgen Monogatari*, at least one relates that he and his men 'do not have time to draw their swords or cut their bellies'.[6]

Belly cutting, or *seppuku* (commonly known as *hara kiri*) seems to have already become established among eastern samurai as a means of escaping from impossible circumstances. Since ancient times, a belief had persisted among the Japanese that the soul resided in the abdomen; among the samurai of the Kantō region, this conviction appears to have transformed into an increasingly ritualized form of suicide. Although samurai in war tales continued to simply 'fall on their swords' when facing impossible odds, the odd customs of *seppuku* seem to take the coup-counting and points-scoring of samurai battles into the afterlife. By killing himself in the most painful way imaginable, a samurai was able to avoid capture by his enemies and any accusation of cowardice. The agonies of *seppuku* would soon come to gain a new role off the battlefield, as a means of sincere protest or heartfelt contrition.

At the most basic level, *seppuku* afforded a samurai some semblance of a warrior's death, dying by the sword. As the years passed, it gained additional accoutrements – a white kimono, the perceived need for a parting 'death-poem', and the presence of a lieutenant, usually one's best friend or most trusted servant, who could be expected to hack off the samurai's head either when he completed the fourth and final cut of the belly-opening, or at any previous juncture when the suicide showed a moment of hesitation. Arguably, the awful self-wounding of *seppuku* may have even been a form of protection for the lieutenant – no samurai could willingly strike off the head of his own lord, unless doing so was the only possible release from an inevitable and agonizing death. Hence, *seppuku* was a means of imposing a new obligation on one's loyal servants, allowing them to offer execution as a blessed release, insulating themselves from any accusations of foul play.

If *seppuku* seems strangely savage, we might also bear in

mind the alternatives that awaited samurai who allowed
themselves to be taken alive – such as crucifixion or being
burned alive – and the fact that *seppuku* was usually a
private affair, and not a public execution surrounded by
gawping commoners. All these factors may have pushed
the samurai into favouring *seppuku*, and what was once
a bizarre affectation among a small group of samurai soon
became a trend and then a custom as the samurai era
proceeded.

Only two years after Minamoto Yoshitomo had sacri-
ficed half his family in support of Go-Shirakawa, the
Emperor abdicated in favour of his own teenage son, thereby allowing Retired Emperor Go-Shirakawa and Fujiwara
Michinori to set themselves up as Regents. That, at least,
was the plan, but Michinori's behaviour soon annoyed
some of his own clansmen, leading one disgruntled Fujiwara to seek an ally in a new insurrection. He found a
willing accomplice in Minamoto Yoshitomo, who offered a
new strategy.

It was, argued Yoshitomo, not possible to simply re-run
the events of the Hōgen Insurrection. He would have to
oppose his former accomplice, Taira Kiyomori, who had
many loyal samurai in the capital. Seizing control of certain
strategic buildings in the capital might be possible, but the
Minamoto would also need to rely on a much larger force
of Minamoto warriors to be brought in from the distant
Kantō heartland. Regardless of the risk, Yoshitomo agreed.

'I will act,' he is supposed to have said, 'even if it costs
my life.'[7]

In December 1159, Yoshitomo made his move. With
Taira Kiyomori and his immediate family out of the capital
on a month-long pilgrimage, Yoshitomo's men seized the
Regent's residence, captured the Retired Emperor Go-
Shirakawa, and put both him and his son Emperor Nijō

under house arrest. Dealings with the imperial family were bloodless and calm, but such care was not matched by other units of Yoshitomo's rebels. Across town at Fujiwara Michinori's residence, Yoshitomo's men killed the guards and set fire to the building. Determined to execute Michinori, and sure he would be in disguise, they killed every man fleeing the burning building. Michinori, however, was nowhere to be found. In his absence, Yoshitomo's faction took advantage of their imperial captors by persuading them to grant them prominent positions in the government. Michinori was eventually found a week later literally underground, buried alive with a hollow bamboo tube as an air supply. His retainers spun this as an idiosyncratic form of suicide, although it is more likely that it was a cunning hiding place, given a careful spin by servants who did not wish to admit to concealing a fugitive.

Michinori's body was exhumed, and his head exhibited on a spike. The coup appeared to have passed without a hitch, although there was still no indication of how Taira Kiyomori would react. From his Kyōto residence, the Rokuhara, loyal Taira samurai sent a message to the travelling pilgrim. Hearing that his allies in the capital had been murdered or displaced, Kiyomori first considered running for the Taira heartland in Kyūshū to seek reinforcements. This was certainly what the Minamoto had been expecting him to do. Perhaps realizing that such a delay would allow time for a whole army of Minamoto samurai to rush down from the Kantō region and occupy Kyōto, Kiyomori instead went straight back to the capital. En route, he picked up a guard of several hundred samurai from districts loyal to the Taira.

Slipping back into the capital at roughly the same time as Michinori's head was being exposed, Kiyomori returned to his Rokuhara mansion and sent a polite note to the

Minamoto faction, implying that he accepted their coup as a fait accompli. In fact, he merely hoped to lull the Minamoto into a false sense of security. A week after Kiyomori's return, a fire at the imperial palace allowed some of his agents to slip inside with an ox-drawn carriage. There, they picked up one of the Emperor Nijō's concubines, along with Nijō himself, disguised as a woman. Nijō, of course, was only thirteen years old, and a combination of youth, heavy make-up and voluminous kimono easily hid his true identity, particularly when the guards would have been reluctant to peer too closely at a member of the imperial family. We may assume that the concubine was present in order to ensure that the guards would also hear a female voice as the carriage stopped at the checkpoint.

Even as Nijō successfully slipped past the checkpoint, his father the Retired Emperor Go-Shirakawa escaped by an even more daring ruse. Humbly dressed as a low-ranking member of the imperial retinue, Go-Shirakawa climbed on a horse and rode nonchalantly out of another gate, before galloping to the safety of a nearby temple.

The first that the Minamoto clansmen heard of this subterfuge was when heralds announced that Emperor Nijō was at the Rokuhara. Government officials were ordered to assemble at the Rokuhara, which was termed the 'new palace' – the implication being that the country was in an unspecified state of emergency, and that the actual imperial palace had somehow been compromised. An irate Yoshitomo remonstrated with his Fujiwara accomplice, who was found drunk with some of his concubines a mere stone's throw away from the place where his charges had slipped from his grasp. The two vital bodies in the coup attempt were now in the hands of the enemy, and Yoshitomo's only hope was to seize them back before the puppet emperor decreed that it was Yoshitomo's turn to find his head on a spike. But Taira forces were already en route towards the imperial palace, led by Kiyomori's son Shigemori, who had once so unwisely challenged Yoshitomo's father to a duel. Shigemori led some 3,000 mounted warriors, bearing thirty red banners – here we see the first stirrings of medieval Japan's enduring juxtaposition, the red of the Taira versus the white of the Minamoto.

At one of the gates of the imperial palace, Shigemori keenly began introducing himself once more, calling out the Fujiwara within for a fight. The Fujiwara, however, refused to respond to such bluster, gingerly edging back from trouble. Instead, Yoshitomo ordered Minamoto men to attack. A Minamoto champion yelled out his lineage in the same fashion as Shigemori, and then charged into battle at the head of over a dozen horsemen – later minstrels might have implied that the skirmish was a form of single combat, but there were many participants on each side. The battling horsemen wheeled and galloped around the palace grounds, giving later storytellers ample time to admire the scenery of orange trees and cherry trees. Neither side was prepared to fight with fire – they were after all, on palace grounds. Nor was there any reason for the Minamoto to cling onto the palace, since neither the Emperor nor Retired Emperor was there.

The fight eventually left the imperial palace behind and drifted westward several blocks, until it reached the riverbank near Kiyomori's mansion, the Rokuhara. The reason given for this depends on which side one believes. Taira accounts suggest that this was Kiyomori's plan all along, and that his son had carefully lured the Minamoto across town in a series of feigned retreats. The Minamoto samurai rather thought that they had *chased* the Taira across town, and now had them trapped with their backs to the wall. Other stories of the day suggest that either the combatants had mutually agreed to take their fight away from the Emperor's palace, or that a group of wily Taira had occupied the palace while the Minamoto were chasing after Shigemori's men. Both sides seem to have thought that they had the upper hand – the Taira because they could now regroup and repair at will by simply dropping into the Rokuhara; the Minamoto because Yoshitomo was expecting reinforcements from another clan branch. However, although the reinforcements arrived, they simply watched the continuing mêlée, as the Minamoto combatants slowly exhausted themselves. Eventually, it became clear that the Minamoto were outnumbered and without support, and Yoshitomo's dwindling group was forced to flee.

Our main source for the Heiji Insurrection (once again, named after the era in which it took place) is the *Heiji Monogatari*, another tale that emphasizes narrative over historical fact. However, the *Heiji Monogatari* also shows the allegiances of the Taira and Minamoto leaving behind their multi-nuclear, incomprehensibly complex allegiances, and coalescing into the simple, uncompromising red-versus-white of clan-versus-clan.

There is still a sense that the Taira and Minamoto clans are upstarts in the genteel capital, disingenuously proclaiming their loyalty to an imperial order that both are seeking to subvert. There is also a sense that these descendants of frontier warriors are very wealthy, but unlike the poetic, art-appreciating courtiers of the capital, mark their difference by cherishing sumptuous weapons and armour. When Taira Shigemori rides out into battle, we are treated not only to a recitation of the colour and style of his armour (this time with a butterfly mounting on his helmet, and a dragon's head design), but also the announcement that he is bearing Kogarasu ('Little Crow') the antique heirloom sword of the Taira clan, forged more than three centuries earlier, and said to have been one of, if not the, first curved swords to be created by samurai swordsmiths.

The Heiji Insurrection was a low point in the fortunes of the Minamoto clan, and was followed by a new set of reprisals and executions as Kiyomori sought to purge the ringleaders. Splitting into three, the departing Minamoto were soon lost in a massive blizzard, in which Yoshitomo's son Yoritomo was cut off from the rest of the group (in some versions, openly abandoned by his father). Yoshitomo eventually found brief sanctuary with allies in a nearby province, but these proved to be fair-weather friends, and he was murdered in his bath. Others of Yoshitomo's family and followers were rounded up and many were executed in the capital, but there were several key survivors.

One was Yoshitomo's thirteen-year-old son Yoritomo, whose mother was, thanks to the bizarre intricacies of court life, also technically Kiyomori's stepmother. Thanks to her special pleading on her son's behalf, Kiyomori relented and sent the boy into exile at the edges of the Kantō region. Another was Tokiwa, Yoshitomo's newest concubine, who had fled Kyōto in the snowstorm when news drifted back of the Minamoto's defeat. She was hobbled by her three young sons, two of whom she led by the hand through the snow, while the youngest, Yoshitsune, was bundled in her robes. Unsurprisingly, Tokiwa did not get far, but when brought before Kiyomori she was offered an unexpected deal. Kiyomori offered to spare her three sons, on the condition that the boys would go into a monastery, and Tokiwa into Kiyomori's harem. Needless to say, despite the protests of Kiyomori's stepmother that the surviving Minamoto boys would be sure not to bear a grudge, their survival ensured that reprisals would follow a generation later – in particular, the half-brothers Yoritomo and

Yoshitsune would return to avenge their clan against the Taira. In the meantime, however, Taira Kiyomori relished his kingmaking role.

Kiyomori wasted no time in insinuating himself into the capital, and in 1160 became the first samurai to be awarded a senior courtly rank. As his Taira allies enjoyed similar promotions and honours, he managed to manoeuvre his sister-in-law into bed with Go-Shirakawa, ensuring that the son born of that union was on a fast track for the throne, crowned as Emperor Takakura in 1168. Among many accolades heaped upon Kiyomori in the years after the insurrection, Kiyomori had become the Prime Minister in 1167. In 1171, Kiyomori secured the greatest coup of all by marrying his daughter Tokuko to the reigning eightieth Emperor Takakura. As Kiyomori's plans became more obvious, even the Retired Emperor Go-Shirakawa began to make attempts to rein him in. In 1177, Kiyomori broke up a conspiracy of Fujiwara nobles to remove him from power – although Go-Shirakawa was not directly implicated, he was rumoured to have been behind the failed plot. Tokuko duly provided the Emperor Takakura with an heir in 1178, presenting Kiyomori with the irresistible opportunity to arrange the incumbent ruler's abdication, and put the infant on the throne. At last, the ruler of Japan would be a boy of Taira stock, and since he was too young to make decisions for himself, his grandfather Taira Kiyomori would volunteer as Regent.

The decision did not go unopposed, but with no Minamoto in town to resist the Taira, Kiyomori's regime change was bloodless. Kiyomori arrived in Kyōto with several thousand Taira samurai, whose presence easily enforced a series of sackings in the government that removed any opponents to his reign. Some forty government officials were ordered out of office and replaced with

Taira sympathizers. Retired Emperor Go-Shirakawa, now no longer of any use to Kiyomori, was confined to his mansion and powerless to resist.

Taira Kiyomori is the grand villain of many extant medieval war tales. Reading between the lines, amid many libellous accusations of cowardice and incompetence, we see the shadow of an artful schemer, but also of a man who continued to suffer the ever-present samurai affliction of class envy. In the *Tale of the Heike* (*Heike Monogatari*), the grand epic of the rise and fall of the Taira, Kiyomori's over-achievement and intrigues are his answer to a lifetime excluded from the Kyōto in-crowd. His own son, Shigemori, headstrong but well educated, remonstrates with him about his failure to grasp the finer points of etiquette. As part of his many power plays, Kiyomori takes holy orders as a Buddhist monk, but still feels able to don armour and pick up a sword when the time comes to arrest Go-Shirakawa. Shigemori is scandalized at this, in a scene that depicts the idealistic, naïve son whose education and high moral standards have been largely paid for by the scheming intrigues of the wily father of whom he disapproves. For Kiyomori, the ends justify the means on every occasion.

Two years later, in 1180, Kiyomori's infant grandson was enthroned as the eighty-first Emperor Antoku, rendering his hold on the court complete. History, however, was due to repeat itself, as Kiyomori's malleable young ward was enthroned to the great annoyance of Prince Mochihito, a twenty-nine-year-old son of Go-Shirakawa who considered himself to be a far better candidate. The Prince sent a message to the distant strongholds of the Minamoto, ordering them to kill Kiyomori, his followers, 'and other rebels'.[8] Of course, the decision was not Prince Mochihito's alone – he was encouraged in his act by Yorimasa, a

septuagenarian Minamoto clansman, and the same Minamoto who had failed to support Yoshitomo in the battle on
the riverbank. Mochihito's decision was partly based on
resentment, partly on the influence of Yorimasa, and partly
on subtle influences such as the claims of a physiognomist
that he had the face of a future emperor. Such superstitions
would never have swayed Kiyomori, but were enough to
push Mochihito into action:

> If the warriors of the Minamoto clan ... do not extend Us
> help, they will be regarded in the class of Kiyomori and the
> others, and will deserve capital punishment. But if the
> Minamoto clan ... offer Us their distinguished service, they
> will definitely be rewarded for their contributions when
> Prince Mochihito accedes to the throne.[9]

In the proclamation of Prince Mochihito, we see an
ominous foreshadowing of many future conflicts. It was
delivered, albeit at first in secret, as a communiqué not from
an emperor, but from an emperor-to-be. It outlines the
crimes of Kiyomori and Shigemori, and pointedly plays a
religious card by claiming that they have corrupted Buddhist teachings. It hedges its religious bets by also suggesting that 'the gods' will look favourably on samurai support
for Prince Mochihito, and promises rewards for his
supporters upon victory. Within the span of the turbulent
twelfth century, the definition of a samurai's 'loyalty' has
shifted dangerously into a new area. Once the pawns of
power-players in the imperial capital, they are now seen to
be active agents in the intrigues. 'Loyalty' is no longer a
question of service, however reluctantly, to an incumbent
ruler. In the proclamation of Prince Mochihito, we see the
stirrings of a lethal concept: that a samurai might be 'loyal'
to the idea of what an emperor might command, even if that

emperor is not yet on the throne. It is only a short step from this to a reversal in which the emperors become the pawns of the samurai, and that the exercise of samurai loyalty is in the support of one's own choice as imperial ruler, rather than obedience to whoever is actually on the throne.

Reading between the lines of many accounts, there were other problems in Japan. The week after Prince Mochihito's secret missive saw the capital assailed by a powerful whirlwind, taken in hindsight as a grim portent. The more objective historian might prefer to read something else into the descriptions of adverse weather – 1180 was a year in which bad rains had left many expecting poor harvests, suggesting that at least some of the unrest may have been over food rather than samurai honour.[10]

Kiyomori heard of the seditious proclamation within a fortnight, through reports of Minamoto forces on the move in the countryside, although he had not seen a copy of the precise text. He soon took steps to lock down the capital. The Retired Emperor Go-Shirakawa, sure to be meddling somewhere soon if not already, was transferred to a more secure house arrest location, and 300 Taira warriors arrived at Prince Mochihito's own mansion with the intention of dragging him away to exile in distant Tosa. Adopting a ruse that had been known to work before, the Prince let down his long hair, put on women's robes and shielded his face beneath a large woman's hat. It was a rainy night, with the moon peeking through intermittent clouds. A group of samurai accompanied the disguised Mochihito as if they were his bodyguards, holding a large umbrella above him as he scurried down the street to safety. Prince Mochihito was so keen to reach sanctuary that he does not appear to have given much thought to his demeanour. When faced with a large ditch in the road, he bounded across it in an athletic leap, leading passers-by to shake their heads at the lack of ladylike airs among modern women.[11]

Unaware of such suspicious activity close by, the Taira samurai barged into Prince Mochihito's mansion, brandishing Kiyomori's official order and demanding that the guards hand their boss over. Refusing to believe that Prince Mochihito was away on a pilgrimage, they forced their way into the main building, starting a fight with the loyal Minamoto guards, many of whom were unarmoured, unprepared, and only wielding ceremonial weapons not designed for true combat. One in particular, Nobutsura, inflicted conspicuous casualties on the Taira attackers, with nothing but a battered and bent sword made only for show. Well acquainted with the corridors and rooms of the mansion, Nobutsura led his assailants on a wild goose chase that bought Prince Mochihito plenty of time to get to safety. It was only when the end of his sword broke off that he conceded defeat, and only then that he realized his dagger had been lost, and he had no chance of committing *seppuku*.

Securely tied, the unrepentant Nobutsura was dragged before Kiyomori, who watched in silence from behind a screen while lieutenants questioned him. The point of order, as far as the Taira were concerned, was that Nobutsura had fought off men who had plainly identified themselves as the bearers of a command in the name of the Emperor. Nobutsura scoffed in reply that any idiot could claim to be a representative of the Emperor, and that it was his policy as a guardsman to demand proof, rather than letting any brigand or pirate into his zone of responsibility. The implication now was that rather than providing that proof, the Taira samurai had simply drawn their swords, immediately turning Nobutsura from a would-be rebel back into a loyal guardsman who had merely been doing his job. Here, too, we see ominous signs of a shift in emphasis among the samurai – it was now possible to directly disobey an imperial command, as long as one can come up with a rational doubt.

Although they had originally had every intention of executing Nobutsura, the Taira samurai began to regard him with grudging respect. His resumé, only available after the heat of battle, noted that he had received a citation for valour some years earlier while serving as a guardsman to the Retired Emperor. Nobutsura boasted that if he had been equipped with more than a toy sword, he would have killed far more of the Taira. There was plainly no point in torturing him, as, even if he knew of Prince Mochihito's destination, the pretender was long gone. Nor did it seem prudent to execute someone whose sense of duty appeared unimpeachable. Consequently, Nobutsura was sent into exile, and lived to fight another day.

Meanwhile, Prince Mochihito failed to find sanctuary at the first temple he approached, and eventually holed up in the Miidera at the foot of Mount Hiei on the outskirts of Kyōto. After a week of fruitless negotiations, Kiyomori ordered his samurai to drag the Prince out of Miidera by force. The monks of the temple complex, no stranger to swords themselves, would be sure to resist, but Kiyomori seemed prepared to commit sacrilege.

One of Kiyomori's men was Minamoto Yorimasa, who had preserved his position precariously in the capital ever since the day he refused to come to the aid of Yoshitomo on the riverbank. Now an old man, troubled by a generation spent in the service of his clan's enemy, Yorimasa finally decided to take a stand. On the eve of the attack on Miidera, he set fire to his own house (an irreversible act comparable to burning one's boats or bridges) and ran to Miidera, ready to join the defenders.

The attack was postponed while Kiyomori and his men worked their charm on other monks in the vicinity, hoping to reduce the number of supporters of the Miidera coterie. Realizing that his time in the capital was limited, Prince Mochihito resolved to run to the west, hoping against hope that faithful Minamoto warriors would already be advancing towards him on the road from the Kantō plain. With Yorimasa and Yorimasa's fifty henchmen and several hundred other supporters and dependants, Prince Mochihito fled the capital in a panicked departure that reputedly had him falling several times from his horse.

The fugitive pretender made it as far as Uji, the upper streams of the river that flowed from Lake Biwa towards the sea. At the time, the river was fast flowing with water from the spring rains, and the Uji bridge was the only crossing for some miles around. Accordingly, the Minamoto ripped up the planks of the bridge as they crossed – an act of discrete vandalism, leaving the bridge itself intact, but still ensuring that any pursuers would take a day to restore it. It was not a moment too soon, as a massive force of Taira numbering several thousand troops was soon at the riverbank and firing arrows across the stream.

The modern River Uji bears no resemblance to the churning rapids of Japanese legend, and so we cannot know what possessed Yorimasa not to simply run. Presumably, the river was not quite as impassable as the Minamoto had hoped, and Yorimasa already suspected that his pursuers would attempt to ford the fast waters. The Minamoto fired volley after volley of arrows across the river at the Taira on the opposite bank, but their ammunition was limited. When the arrows ran out, the Taira were sure to attempt a crossing, in numbers overwhelming enough to put warriors on the Minamoto side.

It was a fateful decision for Minamoto Yorimasa. A generation after he had let his clan down on the banks of another river, he resolved to do the right thing by the pretender. He packed Prince Mochihito off in the company of a small group of guardsmen, and informed the rest of the Minamoto present that they would be holding the Uji crossing against the Taira samurai. Accounts of the numbers involved vary – some court diaries suggest that the Taira may have outnumbered the Minamoto by perhaps three to one, a few hundred horsemen against a few dozen. Less reliable accounts put the Minamoto defenders at a mere 50 men, while the Taira attackers numbered some 28,000![12]

Among the Taira was a samurai with experience of river crossing – a man who had been involved in one of the many forgotten inter-clan skirmishes that appear to have characterized life in the Kantō plain. While the other Taira continued to cover them with arrows, he led a squad of 'horse-rafts' – rows of mounted warriors plunging into the fast waters, with foot soldiers clinging onto the saddles:

> If someone is drifting away, let him grab onto your outstretched bow. Hold your line while you cross . . . stay firm in the saddle and stand in your stirrups. Pull your mount's head up if it goes under, but not so far over that it goes back in the water. Stay light on your mount, try to let the water carry [the weight]. Don't use your bow in the water, not even if you are under fire. Keep your neck guard down at all times, but not so far that your helmet-top is presented to the enemy. Cross in a straight line; do not let yourself be carried downstream. Do not try to ride upstream. Come on! Into the water![13]

The vanguard having proved that the river was not impassable, it was now a matter of honour for the other Taira to follow suit, and the rest of the samurai were ordered into the water. Even as the forces clashed on the riverbank, there were screams as less able riders and mounts were sent spinning downstream to their deaths – sometime later, their bloated, armour-clad bodies were found bumping against a weir among the fish. However, sheer force of numbers allowed many Taira to cross.

The Minamoto were hopelessly outnumbered. Yorimasa's sons died in the fighting, alongside many other Minamoto and their warrior monk allies. As Yorimasa attempted to lead a tactical withdrawal, he was struck in the knee by an arrow, and unable to go any further. He ordered one of his lieutenants to kill him, but the man refused. After a heated exchange, in which he refused to break the rules of propriety by killing his lord, the lieutenant offered a compromise: 'I will have the honour of decapitating you if you first commit *seppuku*.'

Yorimasa hastily tore open his stomach, thereby providing his lieutenant with the necessary rationale to end his suffering. His death poem survives, and had been written sometime earlier, alluding to his regret that he had waited until his seventies to take a stand on behalf of his clan:

Like a dead tree that has never put forth flowers
My life has passed in loneliness
To this melancholy end.[14]

The Battle of the Uji River also spelled the end of Prince Mochihito's rebellion. The Prince himself did not long evade his pursuers, and died from an arrow wound soon after the battle. His demise, however, was known only to his immediate followers, who kept it quiet while the proclamations continued to circle among the Minamoto samurai. As the news spread of Yorimasa's last stand on the Uji River, the rumour persisted that Yorimasa had been successful, and that even now Prince Mochihito was heading east to join with his loyal Minamoto followers.

Among the Taira, ignorance about the death of Prince Mochihito prompted Kiyomori to take drastic measures. In a gesture that shows the magnitude of his concern he moved the infant Emperor Antoku and the two surviving Retired Emperors to Fukuhara on the coast of the Inland Sea, effectively moving the capital of the country for six months. It was only after the Taira and their lieges slunk back into Kyōto towards the close of the year that Kiyomori took military action. With news drifting in of thousands of Minamoto on the march in several different parts of the east, Kiyomori sent three of his own sons at the head of armies to deal with their problem. Their first targets, oddly, were not Minamoto strongholds, but two strongholds of warrior monks, 'which have become enemies of the court, in the one case by harbouring the Prince, and in the other by going to meet him'.[15]

The temples were razed to the ground with immense loss of life. Kiyomori's holocaust against the Buddhists bought him nothing but further trouble, and perhaps even an attack of conscience. Within weeks, the aged dictator had succumbed to a powerful fever, legendarily said to have raised his body temperature so high that his bathwaters would boil. On one occasion, the feverish Kiyomori was convinced that he saw a pile of skulls in his mansion garden; on another, he was awoken by a giant's face staring down at him. The Taira, specifically Kiyomori, were plagued by strange omens and hallucinations, including ghostly laughter and phantom noises, such as that of a tree falling in a palace ground where no trees stood. Taira archers were posted in shifts, shooting a constant barrage of humming-bulb arrows into the air – the screaming arrows were thought to scare off evil spirits, but cannot have done much for Taira morale.[16]

All the while, reports drifted in of thousands of Minamoto mobilizing in the east. Paramount among them, by the end if not at the start, was Minamoto Yoritomo, the son of Yoshitomo exiled after the Heiji Insurrection and spared through his mother's intercession. He had spent his adult life on the remote Izu peninsula, and was now on the move. His first encounter with Taira forces, on the road from the Kantō to the west, was a disaster for the Minamoto. Camped in a bad position, facing a massive Taira army and surprised by a rearguard assault in the middle of a fierce summer rainstorm, Yoritomo was forced to flee, and took refuge in a cave where, according to legend, he was discovered by a Taira samurai, but allowed to escape. He somehow made it across the short strait to the Izu peninsula, and began to regroup his scattered forces. By luck or by design, Yoritomo's route required him to make a complete anti-clockwise circuit of what is now Tōkyō Bay, a journey that took him right through the heartland of the Kantō plain – he was sure to have rounded up the largest possible number of willing warriors. The first sign of Yoritomo's return was relatively minor – a raid on a Taira mansion in Mishima that was little more than brigandage, but before long he was at the head of a true army, and heading west. By the time he reached the natural fortress of Kamakura, his father's old headquarters, he had been accepted as the commander of a vast group, not only of Minamoto warriors, but of his in-laws the Hōjō clan, his cousins among the Miura, and many other powerful Kantō clans.

Soon after reaching Kamakura, Yoritomo heard that a huge Taira force was heading out to meet him. The Taira army, however, lacked the fanaticism or will of the Minamoto – many of the 'Taira' soldiers were little better than conscripts, who swiftly deserted when they saw the size of the Minamoto force. While Kiyomori and his Taira clansmen enjoyed an immediate hold over the court, the

Taira power base had always been to the west, along the coast of the Inland Sea. We might call Kiyomori a big fish in a little pond, whose sway over the capital brought him to a pre-eminent position only for as long as his authority was not challenged in the provinces by brute force and sheer numbers. The east had always favoured the Minamoto, and Yoritomo's army notably combined several other clans that had once been antagonistic towards one another, but were now united under a Minamoto leader. By the time Yoritomo faced his Taira adversaries at the Fuji River, the 'Minamoto' forces, both real Minamoto clansmen and allies carrying Minamoto banners, outnumbered the Taira ten to one.

The battle, however, was fated not to take place. A group of Minamoto samurai planned a night assault on the Taira, but disturbed a huge flock of sleeping birds in the marsh. The birds took flight in a flurry of squawks and splashes, inadvertently suggesting to the Taira that the *entire* Minamoto force was poised to attack from the wetlands. Consequently, the Taira fled before the Minamoto assault could even commence. That, at least, is how the *Tale of the Heike* describes it. It is far more likely that the Taira commander, a son of Kiyomori, was smart enough to see that he stood no chance at all against a force ten times the size of his, and ordered a withdrawal. It is unlikely that thousands of Taira warriors would be so easily spooked by a flock of birds, but the image feeds into the popular folklore that the Taira forces were dominated by ineffectual courtiers. The allure of a Taira panic was irresistible to storytellers among the Minamoto, and certainly did not look good back in Kyōto. The news was devastating to Kiyomori. Still bedridden with fever, the old Prime Minister had failed to put sufficient samurai muscle in the field to hold off the Minamoto advance. Drawing ever closer to the capital, Yoritomo was now heard to be doling out fiefs to his best troops – acting as if he were already a figure within the legitimate government, instead of a warlord on the march.

Burning from his fever and expecting the worst, Kiyomori finally died early in 1181. His infamous last words poetically combined his long-running contempt for religious matters with his legendary desire to win against his Minamoto enemies:

> My sole regret is that I have yet to see the severed head of Yoritomo, the exile in the land of Izu. After my death, build no temples or pagodas to my memory. Chant no sutras for my soul. Bring me the head of Yoritomo and set it before my tomb. That need be your sole devotion.[17]

Within the span of a year, both sides in the nascent conflict had lost their figurehead. Kiyomori had been the main target of Prince Mochihito's proclamation, but now both Prime Minister and Prince Pretender were gone. Prince Mochihito's bid for power, the supposed catalyst for the unrest, was now demonstrably at an end, but Yoritomo's forces continued to pursue their Taira enemies. Kiyomori's manipulations in the capital had briefly made him the power behind the throne, but his legacy was the terrifying prospect of imminent war between the two clans whose opposition he had nurtured.

4

THE PROUD DO NOT ENDURE
THE GENPEI WAR

The Hōgen and Heiji Insurrections were the prelude to one of the most devastating and far-reaching wars to be fought on Japanese soil. In the street scuffles of Kyōto in the 1150s, we see the origins of vendettas and enmities that would explode a generation later. The unsuccessful revolt of Prince Mochihito in 1180 was merely the opening act, a skirmish over court protocol that escalated into total war.

Shortly before Kiyomori's death, Yoritomo had offered him a deal:

> Just like old times, the Minamoto and Taira [should] stand side by side, and . . . serve you. The Kantō would be under the control of the Minamoto, and the Western Sea would follow the desire of the Taira. Both could be rulers . . .[1]

It is interesting to speculate what might have happened if Kiyomori had accepted, as he had the power to do so. Yoritomo would have been rebranded as a member of the establishment, and presumably left to police his own actions in the east. The Taira, meanwhile, would have held on to their ancestral lands along the coast of the Inland Sea. But Kiyomori would not accept it, and the vehemence of his dying words attests to his refusal to write off the Kantō plain merely to appease Yoritomo. In not accepting the compromise, and by dying so that his last command could never be recanted, Kiyomori plunged Japan into a cataclysmic civil war.

Ostensibly, the Taira fought to uphold the old order, in the name of the infant Emperor Antoku, grandson of Kiyomori. The Minamoto were fighting the ghost of Kiyomori, refusing to acknowledge his bid for power behind the scenes. Despite the involvement of dozens of clans of varying sizes, the only colours that were important were red and white – regardless of a samurai's family affiliation, in the coming conflict he was either a supporter of the Taira or Minamoto. Using component characters from the clans' names, the conflict is usually referred to as the Genpei War. Its effects would continue to resound for centuries.[2]

The literature of the Genpei War is immense. Among its many chronicles and adventurous narratives are the *Tale of the Heike* (*Heike Monogatari*), a narrative of the decline and fall of the Taira, and the *Chronicle of Yoshitsune* (*Gikeiki*), a long account lionizing one of the most famous and tragic generals of the Minamoto. There are also diaries of aristocrats and innumerable plays, legends and local folktales. The Genpei War also forms the opening sequence of the *Mirror of the East* (*Azuma Kagami*), an account of the government formed by the ultimate victors, heavily favouring the new powers that would deftly snatch true authority from their hands.

The first lines of the *Tale of the Heike* sum up the tragedy that is to come:

The Gion bell tolls, sounding the knell that all things must pass. Like the colours of the summer camellia, prosperity is ever followed by decline. The proud do not endure; they are like a dream on a spring night. Even the mighty meet with destruction, until they are as dust before the wind.[3]

Although Yoritomo was the most famous of the Minamoto, he was by no means the sole leader. The Taira believed that they would only secure their position by defeating Yoritomo, but would not be able to even reach him until they had fought their way through other, independent uprisings by other Minamoto clansmen. Minamoto Yukiie, the man who had delivered the proclamation to the rebels in the first place, ran into an army led by the sons of Kiyomori across the Sunomata River, near what is now Gifu city. The roles of the Battle of Uji were reversed – this time it was the Minamoto who were obliged to ford a river, and the Taira who waited calmly on the opposite back, picking off the bedraggled attackers as they emerged from the water. The Battle of Sunomata was a total victory for the Taira. Several leading Minamoto were killed, and Yukiie barely escaped with his life. The victory should have allowed the Taira to surge eastward to deal with Yoritomo as well, but with provisions in short supply, the Taira dawdled.

Meanwhile, Yoritomo wasted no time in searching for new allies. He wrote a secret letter to the Retired Emperor Go-Shirakawa, seeking his approval. With Prince Mochihito gone, Yoritomo would hope to rely on Go-Shirakawa's support, rebranding his rebellion as a loyal action against a usurper. Go-Shirakawa, however, did not offer Yoritomo the support he was hoping for.

Better support came from Kiso Yoshinaka (1154–84), a cousin of Yoritomo whose adventurous life was the subject of many samurai legends. Yoshinaka had been born as a Minamoto, but had lost his father in 1155 in the midst of a samurai conflict. Raised by adoptive parents in the Kiso region of Japan, Yoshinaka took their surname as his own, but was ready and waiting for Prince Mochihito's proclamation, and an enthusiastic supporter of the rebellion. However, it did not follow that he was also a supporter of Yoritomo. Inheriting many of the Minamoto samurai fleeing the Battle of Sunomata, Yoshinaka maintained a dangerous military presence to the north of Lake Biwa, the edges of his domain a mere forty miles from the capital. But his relationship with his cousin Yoritomo was wary at best, and instead of joining forces against the Taira, the two were only prevented from fighting each other by intense negotiations. At Yoshinaka's urging, Yoritomo guardedly agreed that they should set aside their differences and unite against the Taira. Yoshinaka's eldest son was sent to Yoritomo, purportedly as the bridegroom to Yoritomo's daughter. However, since the boy was eleven and the girl merely six, we might reasonably see this for what it was – the offer of a hostage as a guarantee of future cooperation.

For now, Yoshinaka bore the brunt of the Taira counter-offensive. A Taira army marched out the capital to deal with Yoshinaka in 1183, running into his forces first at Hiuchi Castle, a stockade set among rocky mountain crags, encircled by a deep moat. The moat, however, was not a natural feature, but a lake around the castle formed by the construction of a nearby dam. When the Taira eventually worked this out – according to legend, by reading a letter shot out to the besiegers by a would-be defector within the castle – they demolished the dam and ruined Hiuchi Castle's best defence, causing the Minamoto to flee to their next position.

That, at least, is how the Taira were encouraged to view their progress. Yoshinaka was far more pragmatic, and cannot have seriously expected Hiuchi to be the uncrossable line against the enemy advance. Instead, Yoshinaka happily permitted the Taira to continue their march across his territory, stretching out their supply lines and allowing his own scouts repeated opportunities to assess the Taira's morale and general direction.

The Taira ran into Minamoto forces again near Ataka, in another short skirmish that soon saw the Minamoto running. But Yoshinaka had no need to engage the Taira directly. He was, instead, biding his time for the chance to inflict a decisive defeat; in the aftermath of Ataka, he was now entirely convinced that the Taira army would be heading onwards by a single mountain pass, at Kurikara. Yoshinaka's forces were split into two groups, while a third, phantom force was implied through the judicious placement of white banners so that their crests could be discerned poking above the top of a nearby ridge.

At the beginning of June 1183, the Taira and Minamoto armies met at Kurikara Pass. The sight of the phantom flags on the next hillside had kept the Taira bottled in their place, but Yoshinaka distracted them by making a conspicuous display of samurai protocols. Despite the presence of thousands of men on both sides, the initial combat was a model of battlefield etiquette. Fifteen Minamoto samurai rode out to fire humming-bulb arrows at the Taira. The Taira sent fifteen of their own to respond in kind, in a duel that was less of a battle than a sport. After a while, the screaming arrows were replaced with pointed ones, for a contest that was somewhat more serious. The fifteen men were raised on each side to thirty, then fifty. By the time the combat had escalated to a hundred men on each side, the day was already getting late, and the Minamoto offered no response to the next set of challenges from the Taira, retreating instead to their tents. The day had been, for want of a better word, a thoroughly 'civilized' samurai encounter, which should have been clue enough to the Taira that the notoriously uncultured Yoshinaka was up to something.

As the sun set, Yoshinaka made his move. A group of Minamoto samurai had made a laborious trip around the mountain to approach the Taira from behind. They launched into an attack from the rear, while in the front and on one side, Yoshinaka launched an attack of his own. In a move that immortalized him in samurai history, Yoshinaka's secret weapon was a herd of angry cattle, charging towards the Minamoto lines, each with a flaming torch tied between its horns.

Faced with an unstoppable stampede, panicked by the sudden Minamoto ambush, the Taira fled into the night in the only direction from which they had not been attacked, plunging in the darkness over the edge of the steep ravine, and tumbling to their deaths in the Kurikara valley below. Even those who realized that they were approaching a cliff edge were unable to stop themselves from being shoved over by the onrush of thousands of others:

'Come no further! Turn back! Turn back!' yelled the warriors, but the retreat, once commenced, was difficult to quell, and the foremost warriors plummeted into the Kurikara valley. [The others] could not see the men [falling] ahead of them, and assumed that there was a path down into the valley. Sons fell after fathers, brother fell after brother. Lords fell with their retainers. Men fell on horses, horses fell on men, such that the valley filled with the crush of seventy thousand samurai of the Taira. The rocks ran with blood like springwater, piling hills of corpses. To this day, they say the gorge is scarred with arrow-holes and sword-cuts.[4]

Ironically, a second Taira force had actually defeated the luckless Minamoto Yukiie not far away, but Yoshinaka was able to catch up with his colleagues and deliver a second knockout blow at the Battle of Shinohara. Having dealt a crushing defeat to the army sent to chastise him, Yoshinaka now did the unthinkable and marched on Kyōto.

The news of his approach sent the townsfolk into a panic, and courtiers answered their concerns impotently with prayers for deliverance and for the Taira to somehow regain the upper hand. Merely because the Taira had many of the prominent court positions, it did not immediately follow that they enjoyed the population's entire and unfettered support, and several fence-sitting lords threw in their lot with Yoshinaka as he approached.

In late July, with Yoshinaka's 50,000 men almost upon the capital, the late Kiyomori's children decided to run for it. It was a decision of some finality: the Taira torched many of their homes behind them, in recognition that the capital was lost. Kiyomori's son Munemori, now the Regent, rushed to the residence of the Retired Emperor Go-Shirakawa, to inform him that the time had come to flee. However, Go-Shirakawa was unwilling to serve another round as a Taira pawn, and had already fled. Instead, Munemori arranged for the departure of his sister Tokuko and her son, the six-year-old Emperor Antoku, who clambered into a palanquin along with the hurriedly snatched imperial regalia, the mirror, sword and jewel. Kiyomori's old mansion, the Rokuhara, was torched as the Taira left town, creating a pall of black smoke that drifted ominously across the river towards the capital as its self-proclaimed rulers fled.

The next day, the Retired Emperor Go-Shirakawa came out of hiding, and swiftly re-established himself in the capital. He named the Rengeō-in, a temple that had been built in his honour by Kiyomori, as the new imperial palace, proclaimed that the Taira were his sworn enemies, and settled down to await the arrival of the capital's new masters. He did not have to dwell at the Rengeō-in for long before a carnival of white banners could be seen on the mountain road. Thousands of Minamoto, all brandishing their standards, limped the last few miles into the capital, exhausted after a long campaign and punishing march. It was a shock for both sides. For the Minamoto, who had been expecting the opulent city of legend, Kyōto was quiet and hungry, the smell of the smouldering Taira palaces still carried on the wind, and the remaining occupants were gaunt and half-starved. For the townsfolk, some of whom hoped to welcome the Minamoto as rescuers from years of Taira intrigues, the new arrivals were disappointingly common.

The letters and dispatches of Yoritomo had always been impeccably drafted, properly following the rules of protocol, always firm in their assurance that Yoritomo was the son of a noble house. But Yoritomo was still somewhere to the east. Instead, the people of Kyōto had to contend with his cousin Yoshinaka, the victor of the bloodbath at Kurikara valley, who, through no fault of his own, had been raised by gruff countryfolk in a distant province.

The presentation in the *Tale of the Heike* of Yoshinaka's arrival at the capital is visibly played for laughs, with an ever-escalating series of faux pas. It is one of the liveliest passages in the entire tale, and offers not only light relief after the melancholy departure of the Taira, but a chilling presentiment of how far the old order has fallen. A local courtier requests an audience with Yoshinaka and is announced as the Lord of Nekoma, Yoshinaka does not reply in kind, but instead sniggers that Nekoma sounded a bit like *neko*, meaning 'cat'. The fuming nobleman is ushered into Yoshinaka's presence only to have a bowl of food thrust into his hands in what Yoshinaka clearly regards as homespun hospitality. This only makes matters worse, as Lord Nekoma looks on aghast at the filthy crockery. Yoshinaka protests that it is the best bowl in the house, as he has snatched it from the altar himself, thereby revealing that he has scandalously plundered a nearby shrine. When Lord Nekoma storms off after another round of off-colour cat gags, Yoshinaka sets off to the court. He is barely prevented from heading off wearing nothing but his *hitatare*, the undergarment for armour, as if presenting oneself at a black-tie affair in a T-shirt and dungarees. Instead, he throws on a garish ensemble of robes, entirely mismatched, as if the previous 200 years of genteel court culture had been for nothing. Cluelessly, he addresses his ox-cart driver as 'cow boy', and the driver (a former Taira employee) has the last laugh by setting off at a jaunty pace, causing Yoshinaka to pitch over in his carriage. Yoshinaka, who has plainly never ridden in a carriage before, has to be shown that there is a handhold inside to prevent him losing his balance. He takes childish glee in this discovery, but pig-headedly insists on exiting from the rear of the carriage (according to protocol, only to be used as the entrance), despite the tutting of nearby courtiers.

'There were', claims the despairing *Tale of the Heike*, 'many other ridiculous incidents like this, although people were too afraid to speak of them.'[5] Most crucially, Yoshinaka and Yukiie were summoned to the presence of Go-Shirakawa and given the task of hunting down the Taira. Only a week earlier, the Taira had been the family and Regents of the Emperor – now they were regarded as his captors, and rebranded as rebels. Pointedly, Yoshinaka and Yukiie were given their roles as *members* of the Minamoto clan. Behind the scenes, Go-Shirakawa also sent missives to Yoritomo, asking him to come to Kyōto – it was still not clear who was the acknowledged leader of the Minamoto, but Go-Shirakawa appears to have hoped that it would turn out to be Yoritomo, and not Yoshinaka, who was already being characterized as the 'wild monkey of Kiso'.[6]

While Yoshinaka the conquering hero bumbles around Kyōto like an ignorant buffoon – validating and strengthening court prejudices towards all samurai from the provinces – the *Tale of the Heike*'s depiction of the Taira in retreat is awash with symbols of misfortune and isolation. The Taira retreated not only from the capital, from the Kansai plain itself. They lingered for a single night at Fukuhara, Kiyomori's old estates on the coast near modern Kōbe, before taking to their ships. Although they still had the infant Emperor and the symbols of his power, they were already witnessing catastrophic losses of support. Munemori addressed several hundred wavering vassals, admitting that much of the Taira's good luck appeared to have run out, and exhorting them to stay loyal as the clan retreated to bases on the Inland Sea:

> Rejected by the gods and forsaken by the lord [Go-Shirakawa], we have departed the capital on a wandering journey. Unsure of our destination, we think of the ties of karma, the connections from a previous life that unite even those who merely share the shade of the same tree. What other life joins us together, if we drink from the same stream? Thy pledges to our house were not made yesterday; thy service is hereditary, like unto our grandfathers . . . In service to our Emperor, who bears the Three Artifacts, who will not travel to distant countryside, to the edges of the mountains?[7]

One by one, the followers announced their allegiance to the Taira, their mournful boasts only accentuating the desperate nature of the situation. In the *Tale of the Heike*, Munemori only mentions distant mountains and rural retreats, but his followers reply as if they are already expecting to have to leave Japan itself. For them, quitting the capital is as drastic a decision as running for distant Korea or Manchuria, legendary countries that none of them have even seen, or even 'the edges of the clouds and sea'.

The *Tale of the Heike* claims, with only a mild degree of poetic licence:

> Only yesterday they were ten times ten thousand warriors, pointing their bridles at the foot of the eastern mountains. Today, they were but seven thousand men, casting off their moorings and heading to the western sea. The sea was sunk in clouds, as the curtain of night drew across the day. Evening mist wreathed lonely isles, and on the sea, the reflection of the moon.[8]

The excitement over Kyōto's 'liberation' at the hands of the Minamoto was short-lived. Far from bringing order to the capital, Yoshinaka's arrival plunged it into chaos. His men, often hungry, went on foraging exped-itions that turned into urban looting, and a climate of fear and uneasy violence descended on the city. Nor was there any love lost between Yoshinaka and the Retired Emperor Go-Shirakawa. Both agreed that they should put a new sovereign on the throne, but disagreed over the selection. Citing his loyalty to the proclamation of the late Prince Mochihito, Yoshinaka insisted that the throne should now fall to Prince Mochihito's son. Go-Shirakawa's faction disagreed, proposing instead the four-year-old younger brother of the incumbent Emperor Antoku. While argu-ments persisted, Go-Shirakawa fretted over conditions to the east, in the Kantō region and beyond. His proclamations, calling for the collection of tax and the restoration of order, cited Yoritomo as his enforcer.

Yoshinaka may have been notoriously brusque, but he was not stupid. Even he could see that his cousin enjoyed greater favour with the Retired Emperor. Instead of carrying out his orders to hound the Taira to the west, he returned to the capital, and demanded that Go-Shirakawa should clarify who was the leader of the Minamoto. Go-Shirakawa refused to do so, although his communiqués to Yoritomo in the east had demonstrated escalating levels of concern about the presence and attitude of Yoshinaka. In a heated exchange with Go-Shirakawa, Yoshinaka was given a blunt ultimatum – he was to spare Kyōto conflict within its own streets by leaving town, either to pursue the Taira or to fight his own clansmen among the approaching Minamoto.

Yoshinaka took a third option that nobody had suspected. Out of desperation, he initiated a coup within the capital, in imitation of the old Hōgen and Heiji disturbances. With 1,000 loyal horsemen, he seized Go-Shirakawa's residence, captured the Retired Emperor and Antoku's infant brother, and murdered any who stood in his way. In the aftermath of his sudden putsch, the heads of some 100 palace guards were displayed on stakes along the riverbank, along with several hundred officials who had got in Yoshinaka's way. Several dozen officials were dismissed from office to be replaced by Yoshinaka sympathizers. At the dawn of 1184, Yoshinaka's conscience was salved when he arranged to have himself awarded with a new title. In imitation of commanders of days gone by who had been conferred with special commissions to suppress the barbarians of the east, he was proclaimed *Seii Tai Shōgun* ('Great General Who Suppresses the Barbarians'). In a telling change, there not really being any barbarians available, this was subtly rebranded *Seitō Tai Shōgun* ('Great General Who Suppresses the East'). The East was now the enemy, and the East was Yoritomo.[9]

It is at this point of the story that the most famous of Genpei War figures re-enters the narrative: Minamoto Yoshitsune, last seen as a babe in arms, clutched to his mother's breast as she fled during a snowstorm after the Heiji Insurrection. Yoshitsune had been sent into a monastery after the execution of his father, but had somehow escaped to the north, and was raised among Minamoto sympathizers. Some historical records, which there is no need to doubt, suggest that he presented himself at the camp of Yoritomo, his half-brother, as early as 1180, shortly after the Taira were spooked by a flock of birds at the Fuji River. Supposedly, the half-brothers met in a tearful encounter – 're-united', albeit that they had never met before. Although little is said about Yoshitsune in the intervening years, he suddenly appears again in the army that Yoritomo sends to deal with Yoshinaka in 1183, sometimes credited as its leader, sometimes credited as a high-ranking clansman under the authority of his cousin Noriyori.

Legends and folktales of the Genpei War are riddled with stories about Yoshitsune, not all of them unbelievable. We hear not only of his victories, but his great reversals of fortune and even embarrassing occasions when he makes mistakes – it is these incidents of human failing that bring a sheen to his stories, not of legend, but of reportage. However, not every Yoshitsune story has the ring of truth. Japanese legend suggests that he was trained not by warriors but by a band of crow-demons, the *tengu*, in the mountain forest near his temple. Hence, there are allusions in some accounts to tricks and spells Yoshitsune has picked up from the *tengu*, such as the ability to stamp his feet and disappear.

We need not dispute that the historical Yoshitsune was a noble warrior among the Minamoto. Unlike the uncouth Yoshinaka, his temple upbringing had given him a cultural sheen, while still bringing him military training. We need not even question one story about his wanderings in the north, where he is alleged to have seduced the daughter of a local lord merely to gain access to the man's rare copy of Sun Tzu's *Art of War*, a Chinese strategy manual in which the young Yoshitsune took great academic delight. We might wonder how such a prominent figure, connected so memorably to the purge that ended the Heiji Insurrection, might have found it so apparently easy to simply leave the capital and head north to be with allies of his clan. Such a question certainly bothered some of his enemies, one of whom accused him of once being a catamite or porter for a mere merchant.

However Yoshitsune got out of Kyōto, he was able to reach the north in time for the ceremonies of manhood – i.e. his late teens – among Minamoto sympathizers, before journeying south again to join the forces of Yoritomo. By the time he arrived, he did so in the company of several loyal followers. Some of these associates were minor nobility at the head of groups of soldiers, but one in particular stands out in samurai history, although he was not technically a samurai.

If Yoshitsune is the Robin Hood of Japanese folklore – a noble warrior who falls on hard times, ultimately persecuted by a hateful regime – then Benkei is his combination of Little John and Friar Tuck, a great hulk of a man with famously bloodshot eyes and superhuman strength. Benkei was one of the *sōhei* warrior monks, an independent class of fighters whose martial prowess seems to have stood them in good stead during the upheavals at the capitals. According to legend, Benkei had stationed himself at the Gojō bridge in Kyōto, supposedly as the result of a religious vow, and had been dutifully relieving passers-by of their swords, with the intention of retiring to a monastery on the collection of his thousandth sword. With 999 swords already achieved, he was looking forward to completing his collection, when the thousandth victim turned out to be Yoshitsune. According to Japanese folklore, Yoshitsune bested Benkei on the bridge, leading the awestruck Benkei to pledge lifelong allegiance to the plucky youth.

This, at least, is the most enduring version of the legend, found in countless works of fiction and drama, immortalized in a strangely cartoonish statue at the site of the modern Gojō bridge, in a clockwork diorama in the grounds of Nagoya Castle, puppet shows (in which Yoshitsune's superhuman leaps gain extra height) and in hundreds of comics and prints. And yet, even the oldest versions of the tale cannot agree on some of its most basic points. Does Yoshitsune hold off Benkei with a sword, or does he use a fan as shown in many versions? If he uses a fan, is it a 'war-fan' (i.e. a type of mace) or is it *actually* a fan? Surely he has a sword, since Benkei has demanded that he hands it over?

Such minor issues are swamped in the earliest extant accounts, which cannot even agree on who is bullying whom. In the folktale and Nō play *Benkei on the Bridge (Hashi Benkei)*, it is the fourteen-year-old Yoshitsune who goes on a killing spree on the bridge, determined to slay 1,000 enemy souls in memory of his departed father. It is Benkei who is the thousandth opponent, but still Benkei who is defeated and swears allegiance. There are enough versions of this tale clustered at the older end of the extant manuscripts for us to suspect that they are truer to the image of Yoshitsune during his own lifetime, and that the roles of the protagonists were only reversed in later centuries in order to uphold the image of Yoshitsune as a fine, upstanding young man, and not a vengeful mugger.[10]

Regardless, Yoshitsune dominates the latter half of the *Tale of the Heike*, a position reflecting his later fame and tragic fate. Even in its early stages, he is set up as a hero who cannot win – he fights for fame and recognition within the army that is supposedly doing the bidding of Yoritomo, but eventually finds too much fame and too much recognition, incurring Yoritomo's envy and, ultimately, revenge.

Once Yoshinaka has sent the Taira on the run, it is Yoshitsune who arrives on the scene, first to deal with Yoshinaka – taking the fight to the Taira is left until the Minamoto have dealt with their own factions. The two contending Minamoto forces met, with an element of poetic justice, at the same Uji River where a Taira arrow had ended the imperial bid of Prince Mochihito. Yoshinaka had already dismantled the famous bridge. The river presented just as difficult an obstacle as it had to the combatants in 1180, but many of the Minamoto would have known it would be possible to ford it. In fact, while Yoshinaka's men drew up on the western bank ready to defend the road to the capital, the problem among their enemies was not *if* the river could be forded, but who would ford it *first*.

One samurai stood in his stirrups and bellowed his name and lineage across the river. Just as he was ready to charge, a second samurai politely warned him that his saddle was not securely fastened. As the first challenger dismounted to check, the second laughed and galloped into the river, determined to be the first across. Angry at the trick, the duped horsemen yelled after the charging warrior that he should look out for the nets in the water – the existence of which he may have simply made up in order to distract his ally.[11]

In another telling incident, one of the lead horses fell with a Minamoto arrow in its head. Its rider, Shigetada, pressed onward on foot through the waters, using his bow as a staff and straining against the current. As he neared the far bank, he sensed someone behind him, and turned to see another mountless samurai, his godson, clinging onto his armour. The older samurai grabbed hold of the struggling boy and bodily threw him ashore, but instead of thanking him, the young warrior bragged to all around that he was the first Taira to the other side.[12]

This is an early example of another samurai affectation, the desire to be *sakigake* – out in front, first in line, the first warrior to clash swords with the enemy. It was not enough merely to be present, a true samurai had to conspicuously demonstrate his lack of fear, and his eagerness to engage the enemy, even if, as in this case, the claim was somewhat laughable – the young warrior had only got there because he had been clinging to another man's armour for dear life.

Any chuckles over the boastful boy soon evaporated as the Minamoto samurai charged up the bank. Shigetada, thwarted in the effort to be first across, was nevertheless the first to draw blood. The *Tale of the Heike* has him asking the name of an enemy, and on hearing the answer that he faces a kinsman of Yoshinaka, he rides up, grapples with him, and 'twists off his head' with the menacing words: 'You shall be today's first offering to the god of war.' Before long, battle is joined, and the Taira forces failed to hold out.

The victory at the Second Battle of the River Uji was widely remembered as being Yoshitsune's, although he was merely a lieutenant within an army that was officially led by a senior clansman, Minamoto Noriyori. Hindsight, particularly in the more fictionalized accounts of the Genpei War, has tended to retroactively assign the command to Yoshitsune, as if doctoring his resumé to reflect his later fame. In fact, Yoshitsune and Noriyori seem to have quarrelled over their precise relationship in the command structure, with Yoshitsune sometimes claiming to be a leader, and at other times deliberately deferring to Noriyori, usually in order to allow himself the chance to barge his way to the front line in battle.[13]

Regardless of who had been in charge, the news soon reached Yoshinaka that one of his three forces had been defeated. Yoshinaka had made initial efforts to take a stand, and had even put out feelers to the ousted Taira, but it seems that the news of the fall of the defences at the River Uji was sufficient to cause him to give up. He abandoned his plans to make a second stand at the mansion of Go-Shirakawa, and instead set out on the run, on horseback, with forty of his most trusted samurai. Even as Yoshitsune was welcomed by a beaming Retired Emperor Go-Shirakawa, Yoshinaka was galloping away from the capital, and clearly expecting that his days were numbered.

It is during the retreat of Yoshinaka, as he says his goodbyes to his dwindling numbers of henchmen in a series of breakouts and battles, that the *Tale of the Heike* off-handedly drops in one of its most debated scenes. With Yoshinaka's retinue now dropped to a mere seven riders, the fugitive general dismisses the samurai Tomoe Gozen – a woman:

> With her white skin, long hair, and attractive face, Tomoe was the most beautiful. She was also a strong archer and a spirited soldier, on horseback or on foot, fit to confront a demon or a god, she was worth a thousand warriors. She

was superb at breaking in wild horses, she was fearless in rough descents. Whenever battle was drawn, Yoshinaka sent her as his first captain in heavy armour, with a great sword and a powerful bow. She won greater glory for her name than the other warriors. And now that all had fallen or fled, she was among the final seven riders.[14]

Suddenly, out of nowhere, the *Tale of the Heike* introduces a samurai woman – not in the broad sense of a wife or mother, but as an active combatant. Tomoe's precise position is unclear – she is first mentioned as one of two 'attendants' but is clearly described in martial terms as a front-line captain. Despite this, Yoshinaka shoos her away, telling her to die wherever she pleases, but not at his side:

> I shall die in battle. Or if I am wounded, I shall take my own life, but it shall not be said that Lord Kiso [i.e. Yoshinaka] came to his final end in the company of a woman.

The *Tale of the Heike* has Tomoe wilfully resisting his order, until, finally getting the message, she lets her horse dawdle to a halt on a forest path.

'I wish for a worthy foe,' she muses, 'that I may show my lord one last fight.'

As if on cue, thirty enemy horsemen hove into view, and Tomoe rides into their midst, surprising one by dragging him across her saddle and 'twisting off his head' – it is implied that she rides out of the forest and snatches one unawares. With that, she turns and gallops for freedom, casting aside her armour and weapons as she goes, disappearing from the record as swiftly as she arrives.

Needless to say, Tomoe's page in the *Tale of the Heike* is one of the most-read and most-studied. Is she included as yet another disapproving indicator of the rough ways of the provinces, that Yoshinaka would have such an Amazon among his forces? But she is not alone – the text also mentions a second female 'attendant', Yamabuki, whom Yoshinaka has had to abandon, ill, in the capital. A variant text, the *Genpei Jōsuiki*, mentions yet another woman warrior active in the same period, and yet Tomoe is still regarded as something of a rarity.

Were there many other warrior women among the samurai, whose tales went untold, presumably because of the same chauvinism that led Yoshinaka to regard Tomoe's presence as somehow shameful? Women among the samurai were certainly expected to know how to fight, although they do not appear to have been expected to take part in campaigns. Going off to war, it seems, was a man's job, although his wife was expected to know how to defend the home. A woman's weapon of choice, from the era of the Genpei War onwards, was a *naginata* – a sword blade mounted at the end of a long pole. Once a weapon used by warrior monks, the *naginata* appears to have gained a wider prominence by the twelfth century, valued in particular for its usefulness in unseating a horseman. A *naginata* was the great equalizer, allowing a footsoldier to hold off a mounted samurai by effectively extending his (or her) arm. A *naginata* came to become a prominent inclusion in the dowry of a samurai wife, and *naginata-jutsu*, the martial art concerned with its use, remains a primarily female sport in modern Japan.

However, Tomoe is not recorded wielding a *naginata*, unless perhaps that is what the *Tale of the Heike* means when it points out that she has a 'great' sword. She does have a bow, but in her sole recorded encounter we see her grappling on horseback and, considering the logistics of 'twisting off', using little more than a long knife. Perhaps Tomoe's presence in the tale serves another purpose.

Perhaps deliberately, we see her present not long before Yoshinaka meets his end. When she is left alone on the forest path, she thinks aloud, and the writer puts words in her mouth that could have only come from Tomoe herself. In other words, either she is an entirely fictional creation, or the tale is implying that we have Tomoe's story because *Tomoe herself has told it*. In a tale that undoubtedly has many moments of speculation and outright fiction, the sudden cameo of Tomoe adds a note of reportage. Pointedly, Tomoe escapes – she does so against overwhelming odds, but not in a superhuman way. There is no kung-fu showdown here, no special effects martial epic or massive, theatrical defeat of dozens of foes. Her getaway is brutal, quick and entirely believable.

A variant text of the same story has Yoshinaka dismissing Tomoe so that she can return to his native land to tell his story. She survives the Genpei War and eventually marries the Minamoto official Wada Yoshimori (1147–1213). Although the historical Wada family were wiped out in an uprising in 1213, Tomoe herself evaded the violent ends of her husband and son, and is said to have survived, living as a nun into her nineties. Three sites in modern Japan claim to be the location of her grave, and in Kisomachi, the hometown of Yoshinaka in today's Nagano prefecture, her statue stands guard beside his, a *naginata* in her hand.[15]

Setting aside the sudden appearance and disappearance of Tomoe, the end of Yoshinaka comes soon afterwards. In the *Tale of the Heike*, it is presented as a squabble between him and his last remaining henchman, a man who is determined to preserve his honour. It is no longer a question of whether Yoshinaka will die, but merely how. When another fifty warriors ride out of the woods, Yoshinaka's henchman Kanehira realizes it is all over and urges him to commit suicide. His rationale is rooted in the grisly points system of collected heads – if Yoshinaka takes his own life, then no enemy samurai will be able to claim the merit for slaying him.

Grudgingly agreeing, Yoshinaka rides off while Kanehira makes a last stand, firing off all his arrows and charging into the newly arrived horsemen. Yoshinaka rides on through scenes of desolate February cold. His horse either drops through ice or misjudges the depth of a nearby paddy field. Either way, it sinks and drowns in the mire, and when Yoshinaka looks back to check on his pursuers, he is struck in the face by an enemy arrow.

Back at the main fight, Kanehira hears what he has been afraid of all along – a henchman shouting out his lineage and identifying himself as the killer of Yoshinaka. Hearing that it is all over, Kanehira yells to his enemies that he no longer has a mission to protect his lord, demands that they witness how the bravest of the samurai meet death, and then leaps off his horse with his sword in his mouth, killing himself instantly.[16]

There is a certain irony that the *Tale of the Heike*, a saga whose very name implies that its subject is the fortunes of the Taira clan, should devote page after page of its main narrative not merely to the Minamoto enemies of the Taira, but to the long-running squabble among them over who should be in charge. But in dealing with the tragic fate of Yoshinaka, the story puts his killers in Kyōto, where they receive the undying gratitude and favour of the Retired Emperor Go-Shirakawa. In particular, Yoshitsune gets a lot of the credit, much to the annoyance of his half-brother Yoritomo, who still claims to be the leader of the Minamoto forces, despite not having yet left his power base in the east. It is Yoshitsune who brings the head of Yoshinaka into Kyōto; it is Yoshitsune who is ordered to take the battle to the Taira. Notably, it is also Yoshitsune who is left out of military dispatches and honours proclaimed by Yoritomo in late spring 1184. Never one to avoid stirring trouble, Retired Emperor Go-Shirakawa cheered up the forgotten Yoshitsune by awarding him two court positions – a sinecure in the Imperial Guards and a position in the Bureau of Metropolitan Police. Whether calculated to annoy Yoritomo or not, it surely did so.[17]

Pointedly, it is now Yoshitsune who leads the Minamoto to their next victory. His sometime superior, Noriyori, is clearly in a subordinate position by this point. Yoshitsune stabs straight for the heart of the Taira by marching on Fukuhara. Although only recently and dramatically abandoned by the Taira, Fukuhara had been reoccupied while the Minamoto were settling their differences elsewhere, and seemed intended as the headquarters of a Taira counter-assault.

However, the main Taira forces were not at the ruined Fukuhara itself, but at Ichinotani (literally, 'valley one'), a narrow scrap of beach with the sea to the south and steep cliffs rising up close by to the north. The Taira were unquestionably masters of the sea, and the Minamoto had no navy worth speaking of. With the cliffs presumed impassable, there were effectively only two approaches to the base, from the east and west along the beach. An off-hand conversation in the *Tale of the Heike* hints at the human cost of samurai warfare. The Minamoto debate how to cross dangerous terrain in pitch-black night, only for Yoshitsune to brightly suggest that they 'light big torches in the usual way'. This is soon revealed to be a euphemism for setting fire to the homes and fields of nearby commoners, whose possessions are burned in a vast conflagration merely to light the way of their Minamoto liberators.[18]

Supposedly, the Taira are surprised by a night assault, and several of their commanders give up on the outer approaches to Ichinotani, instead taking to their ships and sailing for safety across the Inland Sea to Yashima on the island of Shikoku. Others, however, hold the line at Ichinotani, occupying it not only with footsoldiers, but with cavalry detachments and some of the last, dwindling examples of that ancient siege crossbow, the legendary *oyūmi*.

Yoshitsune sent the main body of his force to attack from the west, taking a smaller body of samurai along the perilous eastern route. It is here that the *Tale of the Heike* turns upon the unique knowledge of the Kantō plainsmen. The combatants might be fighting over a coastal fortress, but the tactics that won the day would prove to be equestrian. In an age before military intelligence or mapping, in an area where none of them had been before, the Minamoto men argued over the best way to approach Ichinotani over the treacherous terrain that protected it to the east. On the canny advice of his cavalrymen, Yoshitsune puts a golden saddle on the oldest local horse he can find. This juxtaposition of finery and age is no poetic conceit, but a deliberate attempt to put something reflective and clearly visible on top of an animal that is most likely to instinctively know its way across the rough terrain. The old horse was then driven ahead of the Minamoto forces, and duly found the ideal path.

The ability to take a horse across rough terrain was highly prized among the Minamoto. We have seen it before, listed among the attributes of the beautiful samurai girl Tomoe, and it crops up again at this point in the *Tale of the Heike*, when the Minamoto begin to wonder just how 'impassable' the cliffs above Ichinotani really are.

In search of local knowledge, the towering warrior monk Benkei brings an old huntsman to Yoshitsune. The man is questioned about the terrain of the cliffs, and at first confirms their suspicions, that the 300-foot gorge and subsequent 150-foot drop to the beach form an impassable barrier. But it is Yoshitsune who asks the old hunter if deer can be found on the cliffs. When the old man answers in the affirmative, Yoshitsune replies with a rare quality in samurai – wit: 'Sounds like a regular pasture. If the deer can go there, then the horses can go there, too. Right, you shall be our guide.'[19]

When the old man pleads that he is too infirm to show the riders the way, they conscript his son, binding up his hair, and giving him a samurai name (Yoshihisa). It is a mere aside in the *Tale of the Heike* account, dwarfed by later dramatic events at the Battle of Ichinotani, but it is a telling moment of battlefield promotion. In later centuries, when social classes in Japan were fixed and immobile, the samurai countenanced no such actions. But here, amid the expediencies of the Genpei War, we see a boy transformed from a huntsman's son into a member of Yoshitsune's inner circle. It is notable that Yoshitsune's band of followers contains such a mixture of classes and professions, foreshadowing the multi-racial bands of brothers of our own war movies.[20]

The *Tale of the Heike* highlights horsemanship and lateral thinking in the Battle of Ichinotani. At first, the camp is quiet in the night, with only the crackle of watchfires, and the mournful sound of someone among the Taira playing a flute. Into the middle of this calm, Yoshitsune leads seventy horsemen in a foolhardy descent down the cliff, in a surprise attack that throws the Taira into chaos. However, there is also wisdom among the Taira – just before Yoshitsune charges into their camp, the *Tale of the Heike* pauses to admire the intelligence of a Taira watchman, who frowns in suspicion at the sudden sight of foxes and rabbits fleeing down the steep cliff. He muses that for the small animals to be making such a risky descent, they must be fleeing something even larger – a realization that strikes him mere moments before the Minamoto ambush.

Only a tiny fraction of the Taira samurai would have suspected that the Minamoto were such a small force, all but parachuting into their midst. For the bulk of the Taira camp at Ichinotani, the sound of conflict in the centre of the camp was a sure sign that their outer defences had fallen. Hence, understandably, they commenced an unruly retreat, sprinting for their ships, hoping to run for open water to join their comrades at Yashima.

It is here, as the Taira flee for their lives, that the *Tale of the Heike* interjects one of the most famous stories of the conflict, fated to form the basis of many kabuki, Nō and puppet plays in the centuries that followed. As the Minamoto flood into the Taira camp, the samurai Kumagai Naozane sees a figure in high-ranking armour sloshing out into the sea. Instinctively, he calls out to him, taunting him that it is bad form for a commander to turn his back on his foe. The samurai stops, turns and fights, but is no match for the experienced Kumagai. Kumagai knocks of his helmet, and raises his sword to deliver the deathblow, only to look into the eyes of a terrified teenage boy, the sight of whom reminds him of his own son. Kumagai hesitates and askes for the boy's name. The boy refuses to give it, and simply says that his head will be recognizable enough when presented to Kumagai's superiors. Wavering, Kumagai hears the approach of his own allies. Tearfully, he beheads the boy, who is later revealed as the nobleman Taira Atsumori. It is only when rifling through his possessions in search of something to wrap the head in that Kumagai finds a small bag containing a flute. He realizes that he has just killed the musician whose music he heard the night before, and muses that none of the uncultured Minamoto have a flute with them. The thought reinforces his own regret and adds, once again, to the sense that court life has rendered the Taira unsuitable for the samurai life. But this is not presented as a snide attack on effete courtiers – rather, it is the Minamoto who are losing out. Traumatized by what he has become, Kumagai eventually drifts away from the samurai life, and ends his days as a Buddhist monk.[21]

Conspicuously, in the aftermath of Ichinotani, it was Yoshitsune who was rewarded with an honorary court position in recognition of his achievements. His supposed superior, Yoritomo, received no such honour – further signs of a widening rift between the two brothers. Nevertheless, it was Yoshitsune who continued to bring the fight to the Taira, a year later, when he headed out at the head of a naval force towards the Taira's base at Yashima. In doing so, he was leaving behind the land, where the Minamoto were widely known to have the upper hand, for marine combat, at which the Taira had so far been the undisputed masters.

Yashima is a towering, imposing crag on the Shikoku shoreline. We can assume, as did the Minamoto, that the Taira's first action on arrival would be to post watchmen on the heights, who would be able to see almost all the way to Ichinotani. This time, there would be no surprise attack: the forces were sure to approach each other with ample foreknowledge of who was where.

One of Yoshitsune's own men, the adviser Kajiwara Kagetoki, appointed by Yoritomo and hence speaking with the weight of the distant 'leader', suggests that the Minamoto boats have 'reverse oars' in order to allow them to flee. The cryptic comment, presumably referring to the possibility of fixing a rudder at either bow or stern, is met with scorn from Yoshitsune. Kajiwara, clearly taking umbrage at such treatment, comments that Yoshitsune only knows how to attack, like a 'wild boar', and that he will be remiss in his duties as a leader if he does not also consider the possibility of withdrawing to fight another day.[22]

Although an apparently minor incident, the argument between Yoshitsune and Kajiwara is a critical moment. Losing face by almost coming to blows with his leader, Kajiwara files a deeply negative report with Yoritomo of Yoshitsune's behaviour. Whereas Yoritomo might have previously regarded Yoshitsune's rise as the result of luck or even meddling by the court, he was now presented with the suggestion that Yoshitsune was disrespectful and foolhardy.

In truth, it does not seem unreasonable to claim that Yoshitsune was subsisting largely on luck. He sets out for Yashima in the middle of a storm, amid great protest from his underlings. The *Tale of the Heike* discreetly has him 'allowing' all but five boats to stay behind, although this may have been a polite spin on the refusal of many of his men to follow. As at Ichinotani, the arrival of the Minamoto from an unexpected quarter, coupled with arson by their landing forces, persuades the Taira that they are under attack from a much larger force. Consequently, the Taira take to their boats once more, and only realize the small extent of Yoshitsune's force once they have a clear view from the shore.

The ensuing Battle of Yashima is loaded with poetic juxtapositions of the Minamoto and Taira – since Yoshitsune has the land and the Taira have the sea, both are literally in their element. A salvo of arrows from the Taira ships decimates Yoshitsune's men, who huddle around to protect their leader. The bow, that ancient weapon that has played such a huge part in the samurai arsenal since the earliest times, appears several times in famous stories of the

Battle of Yashima, in anecdotes that first emphasize the ritual nature of courtly combat, then the bitter realities of war, and then the strange priorities of samurai protocol.[23]

In the first incident, the Taira offshore send a silent challenge to the Minamoto. A lavishly decorated Taira boat punts towards the shoreline with a teenage princess standing at the prow. She is either holding a long pole or stands before a mast without sails – in either version, the pole/mast is topped by a fan, decorated with a bright gold rising sun against a red field. She then waits.

The Minamoto decide that the fan is a challenge. Some versions of the story even suggest that it has been taken from a shrine sacred to the Taira, and that its fate will also exercise a sympathetic magic on the battle itself. If the Minamoto can hit the fan with an arrow, the day is theirs.

The challenge is also a trap. The Taira clearly have learned enough about Yoshitsune's foolhardy nature to think that he will take the shot himself, and thereby bring himself within range of the Taira's own archers. Advised that it is he who is the target and not the innocuous folding fan, Yoshitsune orders one of his underlings, Nasu Yoichi, to take the shot.[24]

With deep reluctance, Yoichi accepts the challenge. He prays to Hachiman for guidance, and he vows to commit suicide if he shames his side by missing. He then rides some thirty paces into the sea, as close as he can reasonably get without forcing his horse to swim. When his first arrow neatly severs the fan from its pole, both sides erupt in applause and approbation.

The second incident is not so genteel. A Taira warrior emerges on the boat and begins to dance around the pole, possibly in some sort of ritual designed to exorcise the bad luck. Yoshitsune promptly orders Yoichi to shoot him, and the archer's second arrow strikes the warrior in the neck.

This sudden, vicious and unnecessary death is greeted with cheers from the Minamoto, but ominous silence from the Taira, who have just been reminded that this is not a game. Instead, a boatload of Taira samurai make a landing further down the beach, and the Minamoto are mobilized in a battle for the sands.

Although the Minamoto are victorious, driving the Taira back into the sea, Yoshitsune drops his bow in the struggle, and can be seen in many depictions of the incident, floundering in the shallows in search of it while the battle rages around him. Later on, the *Tale of the Heike* has him explaining his sudden concern over lost property. The bow, it transpires, is embarrassingly low-powered. It only takes two men to string it, whereas the bows of mightier, taller warriors take notably more – an average samurai, suggests the *Tale of the Heike*, might require three men; a real superman, such as Yoshitsune's uncle Tametomo, might wield a 'five-man' bow. This is, however, not quite true. 'Three-man stringer' (*sannin-bari*) is a common term in Japanese martial chronicles for an *extra*-powerful bow; far from being an embarrassment, a two- or even one-man stringer seems to have been a perfectly average weapon among the samurai. Yoshitsune's discomfiture is hence either a narrator's subtle suggestion that all the Minamoto are supermen, or perhaps an indicator that the more powerful bows were commonplace among the ruling class, who had spare squires available to ready their equipment before a battle.[25]

The Battle of Yashima fizzled out late in the day and never quite restarted. Taira plans to mount a night assault were ruined by squabbles among their commanders, and the following day, the Taira fleet retreated further to the west. Although recorded as Minamoto 'victories' neither Ichinotani nor Yashima represented truly crushing blows to the opposition. Instead, they could more reasonably be regarded as skirmishes fought as the Taira mounted a gradual withdrawal to their heartland in the west. The final confrontation would not be fought until Yoshitsune had successfully acquired a fleet of his own to fight the Taira on the sea.

A month later, in late April 1185, he finally got his chance at Dannoura, a strategic strait where the tips of Honshū and Kyūshū met – the gates, as it were, to the Inland Sea. It was very plainly a last stand for the Taira; it was difficult to see where else they could go, as beyond the straits there was nothing but Tsushima and then Korea. However, merely because the Taira had taken to the wooden walls of their ships, it did not mean that they still hoped for victory. The Taira commander, Tomomori, knew the tides and currents of the strait well, and took to his ships at the first sign of the Minamoto advance. However, this time the Minamoto arrived with ships of their own. The Taira ships fanned out and edged closer, as the air became thick with clouds of arrows. The first stray shafts, launched from the largest enemy bows, began to thud into the hulls of ships on either side. Some of them bore the names of their owners, daring the best bowmen among their enemy to pick them up and shoot them back.

As the thuds of the arrows steadily increased above the splashes of near misses, one Taira commander exhorted his archers to look for one man in particular. He would be in a general's armour but plainly short, his skin pale, his teeth notably protruding. This was Yoshitsune, the architect of the Taira's demise, and a special prize to any Taira who killed him.

Among the Minamoto, Yoshitsune was also singling someone out. The shipborne nature of the Taira made it unlikely that they could ever be truly wiped out. If they ever faced defeat, they could always run to regroup or seek sanctuary among the pirates. Yoshitsune was more interested in Antoku, the eight-year-old Child Emperor, who was sure to be in one of the Taira ships. If Yoshitsune could take the Taira's nominal ruler, they would have no choice but to obey his commands.

As the battle commenced, segueing from the exchange of arrows to hand-to-hand combat, the Taira had the upper hand. The tide was in their favour, and the efforts of the Minamoto misdirected. Yoshitsune aimed his attack at the garish, highly decorated flagship of the Taira fleet, unaware that it was merely a decoy, and that Antoku and his 'court' were sequestered on a less obvious vessel.

With the turning of the tide in the Minamoto's favour, Yoshitsune also gained vital information from a Taira turncoat, who informed him of the location of the Child Emperor Antoku. Yoshitsune orders his archers to fire upon the sailors and rowers in nearby ships, ignoring the samurai entirely, but rendering the vessels dead in the water. As Yoshitsune drew dangerously near to Antoku's ship, the Taira commander announced to the tearful imperial family that there was no hope of escape. The white banners of the Minamoto were triumphant. The red banners of the Taira would fall. The great war of the two clans was finally over, and there was nothing left to live for.

Antoku's grandmother, the widow of the long-hated Kiyomori, took the Child Emperor's hand, and persuaded him to pray to Buddha with her. Then she spoke the most famous last words in the history of the samurai: 'Our capital lies beneath the waves.'

With that, she hugged the Child Emperor close to her and jumped into the sea. At the sight of her suicide, the other members of Antoku's refugee court rushed to follow him, hurling themselves over the side of the ship. Antoku's mother was only 'saved' because a Minamoto grabbed her hair with a rake as she sank beneath the sea. The imperial sword, an ancient artefact dating back to the time of legend, was lost forever, although the Sacred Mirror was saved when the courtier carrying it was pinned to the ship by Minamoto arrows. Other Taira wrapped themselves in anchor chains to guarantee their deaths, or threw on heavy armour to ensure they would sink. One samurai, glancing disapprovingly as the head of the Taira clan prevaricated, pushed his lord into the sea:

> The surface of the sea was thick with scarlet banners and scarlet pennants cast away, like scattered red leaves after an autumn storm on the Tatsuta River. The once-white waves that crashed upon the shore were dyed crimson. Masterless, abandoned ships drifted on the wind and tide, melancholy and directionless.[26]

The mass suicide at Dannoura, and the downfall of the Taira that it represented, made the entire area taboo for centuries. Japanese sailors would avoid the area to the best of their abilities, and fisherman stayed away for fear they would run into the restless ghosts of the doomed clan. Those who dared to venture close to the strait would sometimes catch crabs with strangely human faces etched into their carapaces. Believing them to be the reincarnations of Taira samurai, they threw these 'Heike Crabs' back into the sea. In modern times, eight centuries of such unnatural selection, favouring crabs with samurai images upon their backs, has turned the carapaces of the Heike Crabs into chilling facsimiles of warriors' faces, and serve as a constant reminder of the tragic end of the Taira clan.

5

THE DIVINE WIND
THE KAMAKURA SHŌGUNATE AND THE MONGOL ARMADA

In the aftermath of the defeat of the Taira, the uncontested Minamoto-backed eighty-second Emperor, the teenage Go-Toba, conferred the post of shōgun on Yoritomo. The Minamoto were hence granted the right to rule Japan in the Emperor's name, and Yoritomo set about doing so from his base in Kamakura. For Yoritomo, and for all his successors as Shōgun, the most commonly heard term was *Bakufu* – 'curtain-' or 'tent-government'. In this instance, the *baku* was a wide bolt of cloth, periodically reinforced by a wooden stake. Once the stakes were pounded into the ground, the cloth formed a long windbreaker, roughly as high as a man, which both marked out the headquarters of a general and shielded him from public view. It hence afforded him some protection from the elements, and made it impossible for distant enemies to aim an arrow at his precise location. Seated on a stool within his *baku*, a general could command in relative safety. But just as the *baku* was erected merely for the duration of a battle, and would be struck and rolled away when the army moved on, a shōgun was supposed to be a temporary appointee, granted the position in order to deal with a national emergency. But where was the emergency? The Taira were gone, their last loyal retainers scattered to obscure mountain villages in western Japan, the back of the resistance broken. Instead, in a consolidation of power sadly typical of victorious samurai, Yoritomo turned on his own people, notably the victorious general Yoshitsune.

Only three days after Yoshitsune returned to Kyōto in triumph, a letter from Yoritomo arrived accusing him of being lax in command, disobeying reasonable advice, and spurring his men onto unnecessary dangers. A shocked Yoshitsune proceeded on to Kamakura to deliver his prisoners and report, but was kept waiting for a month at the nearby town of Koshigoe. The *Tale of the Heike* includes the plaintive letter he wrote to his brusque half-brother, which was ignored. Instead, Yoshitsune was ordered to return to Kyōto, where he learned that he had been dispossessed of his lands.

An assassination attempt on Yoshitsune led him to accept the Retired Emperor Go-Shirakawa's command to 'chastise' Yoritomo – effectively a proclamation of war between Minamoto and Minamoto. However, soon afterwards Yoshitsune disappeared from sight, and his few remaining followers disbanded in a storm.

The popularity of the Yoshitsune story has obscured the fact that Yoritomo purged several other prominent leaders as well. The men who won the victory for the Minamoto clan were largely killed off in a few years, but it is the fall from grace of Yoshitsune, still in his twenties, that captures the Japanese imagination.

Unsurprisingly, Yoshitsune resolved to return to safe ground in the north of Japan, where he had once fled his Taira enemies as a boy, and where he now hoped to evade the pursuit of the Minamoto. He would, however, have to reach the north by somehow traversing the heartland of Yoritomo's power. Knowing this, Yoritomo ordered a lockdown of every provincial border, and no crossing without proof of identification.

In perhaps the most famous incident of Yoshitsune's exile, he and a handful of his men supposedly sneaked through a checkpoint at Ataka disguised as Buddhist monks. Owing to his diminutive stature and the need not to draw attention to himself, Yoshitsune is given the role of the porter to play, while his famous henchman, the towering Benkei, plays the lead. With their traditional power positions reversed, the men approach the checkpoint, one of several roadblocks set up on Yoritomo's orders. However, Benkei seems to persuade the samurai guards that the party genuinely does comprise monks, supposedly on a pilgrimage to collect promises for the rebuilding of a famous temple. In the numerous plays that have been written about the incident in the centuries since, Benkei seals the deception by unrolling a scroll and pretending to read out a subscription list of promissory donations. The men are allowed to pass, but then Yoshitsune inadvertently draws attention to himself. Thinking fast, Benkei beats the 'porter' for clumsiness, thereby convincing the guards that it could not possibly be Yoshitsune, as striking one's commander would be a capital offence.

Variant versions of the story disagree on the complicity of the guardsmen. In both the Nō play *Ataka* and the kabuki play *Kanjinchō* (*The Subscription List*), the leader of the guards realizes the deception, recognizing Yoshitsune and even seeing that Benkei is 'reading' from a blank scroll. However, he lets the men pass, considering that honour has been served, and demonstrating a common respect for Yoshitsune's predicament – *hōgan-biiki* ('sympathy for the lieutenant'), remains a Japanese term for championing the underdog.

Yoshitsune's years of wandering came to an end in 1189, when his northern host turned upon him. At the fort of Takadachi, on the banks of that same Koromo River where Emishi had once massacred invaders centuries in the past, Yoshitsune and his last handful of followers were sur-rounded by local samurai. Overwhelmed and with no means of retreat, Yoshitsune retired to the inner chambers to commit *seppuku*. Outside, the last of his men held off an attack by many dozens of enemies, until only the giant Benkei was left alive. Holding a choke point where he could easily fight off only one or two opponents at a time, Benkei and his long *naginata* unseated many riders.

At one point, the samurai halt, unwilling to approach any closer, while Benkei leans silently on his *naginata* pole, his armour bristling with arrows; the flames of Takadachi climbing into the sky behind him. None of the samurai are willing to attack, and the brooding figure of Benkei waits, unmoving, just as he once loitered on the Gojō bridge in search of a worthy foe. It is only when the breeze of a passing horse pushes Benkei over that the truth is revealed. He has been dead for some time, held up only by his armour.[1]

Haunting from beyond the grave was a recurring theme in the later tales of the Minamoto. The northern samurai who turned on Yoshitsune were themselves wiped out in a 'punitive' expedition sent to the north by Yoritomo, purportedly to avenge the death of his beloved half-brother! In 1199, Yoritomo fell from his horse and died from his injuries – popular folklore soon held that it had been the ghost of Yoshitsune or Benkei that caused the horse to rear.

The rule of Yoritomo hence lasted for only a few years after his brother won his victories for him. Nominally, the Minamoto clan remained as the holders of the shōgunal title for almost 150 years. In fact, their hold was already gone by the time of the death of Yoritomo. His two sons succeeded him, but both were very young, and hence required a regent.

So it was that the shōgun ruled in the name of the emperor, but the regent (*shikken*) ruled in the name of the shōgun. Exhausted and decimated by conquest, the Minamoto enjoyed the fruits of their victory in name only. Instead, it was the family of Yoritomo's wife, Hōjō Masako, that held the reins of power. Shaving her head in order to give the outward appearance of having cloistered herself, she gained the nickname of *Ama Shōgun* – the Nun.

Hōjō Masako (1157–1225) had been a witness to many of the events of the Genpei War. She had been born at the height of the Heiji Insurrection, and had been a child when the teenage Yoritomo was sent into exile in her father's domain. Despite Yoritomo's status as an enemy of the Hōjō clan's Taira allies, Masako had been permitted to marry Yoritomo in 1180. As the worst of the Genpei War tore central and western Japan apart, Masako and Yoritomo had been parenting their children, including two future shōguns, at the Hōjō power base in Kamakura.

With the death of Yoritomo, Masako ruled in the name of her eighteen-year-old son, and when he died in suspicious circumstances, in the name of his younger brother. When this boy died, too, Masako and her brother decided on a replacement who was merely an infant, ensuring that the role of shōgunal regent would be as long-lasting as that of similar offices that ruled in the name of the Emperor.

There were, of course, other individuals who had their own ideas. The Retired Emperor Go-Toba (1180–1239) had abdicated from the throne in 1198, and attempted to steer Japanese politics from the shadows behind his next three successors – two sons and a grandson. He came unstuck with the death of Yoritomo's second son, when he refused to collude with the Hōjō in the selection of a successor with imperial connections. The origin of the subsequent unrest was officially based in a dispute over reassignment of lands, but the hostility between Go-Toba and the Hōjō was born from the belief of each that the other was a pointless sinecure. The Hōjō saw Go-Toba as an unwelcome meddler; Go-Toba saw the Hōjō as worthless parasites, unnecessarily maintaining an institution whose *raison d'être* had sunk with the Taira.

The conflict, known as the Jōkyū or Shōkyū Unrest, for the year in which it took place (1221), first saw Go-Toba assembling a body of horsemen in Kyōto, ready to take on the Kamakura shōgunate. He did this in the guise of an archery tournament, which assembled the first recruits to his army. He also enlisted the support of the Miura clan, and hoped that once his revolt was openly promulgated, other clans with no love lost towards the Minamoto would join in. The Taira might have been officially destroyed, but there was always a fresh crop of landless lower-orders, disenchanted clan branches and embittered samurai who might be persuaded to topple an order that was unfavourable to them.

Go-Toba then issued a decree, not unlike that of his distant relative Prince Mochihito, calling on samurai loyal to the throne to disregard the authority of the Kamakura Shōgunate. However, this met with only the vaguest of attention from the samurai of the realm, and Go-Toba was disappointed to hear that even his putative Miura allies were uninterested in supporting him. In the interests of establishing the imperial family itself as a military force to be reckoned with, Go-Toba commissioned an imperial banner. By luck or by design, its base colour was a deep red evocative of the dead Taira clan, decorated with metallic representations of the sun and moon. It was the first, but not the last, time that an imperial banner would become a rallying point for 'loyal' soldiers. In theory, the intended implication was that no truly loyal subject would dare to charge an army that carried the symbol of the Emperor's own legitimacy. In practice, both in this war and in later ones, there was always a way of arguing that the bearers of the standards had borrowed, stolen or otherwise obtained their symbol through underhand means.

Back in Kamakura, the news of the decree met with a swift response. The shōgunate could not risk the possibility that the banner would be shown in too many provinces. Not waiting for an official declaration of hostilities or an advance from Kyōto, the men of the Hōjō clan dispatched three groups of samurai, in the expectation that each would accrete into an army by the time it reached the Kyōto region.

Although there were several skirmishes between Go-Toba's troops and the approaching armies, the decisive battle would be fought, yet again, at the river crossing near Kyōto that was a last line of defence before the road to the capital. Hence, 1221 saw a *Third* Battle of Uji, or rather, stretching along the length of the river from Uji all the way up to the next bridge at distant Seta. Imperial forces, comprising Go-Toba's dwindling supporters and warrior monks, held the line for as long as possible, but the Bakufu attacked at every possible weak point along the long banks. It was hence only a matter of time before the Shōgun's troops successfully crossed over and routed their enemies.

Already aware that his forces were entirely overwhelmed, a panicking Go-Toba sought sanctuary with the warrior monks of Mount Hiei, only to be told that he was not welcome. With the arrival of the Kamakura forces in the capital, the nascent rebellion was nipped in the bud. Go-Toba and his two sons were exiled. His recently enthroned infant grandson was deposed and replaced by a more malleable nephew. In effect, the Genpei War had seen a much shorter and less damaging re-run, with the Emperor himself in the role of the Taira. But now that the Emperor had been defeated, the court was firmly in the grip of the shōgunate. Moreover, the victorious forces held not just the Kantō plain, but now also confiscated lands and holdings from the losers. The Kamakura shōgunate thereby enjoyed an unprecedented hold on the heartland of imperial power, as well as the resource-rich Kantō region. To the west of Kyōto, many lands remained in the hands of lords who owed no allegiance to the Bakufu. Rather than rock the boat, the Bakufu simply left the Emperor in place as the focus of the loyalty of the independents.

In the aftermath of the Jōkyū Unrest, the Bakufu ruled Japan in relative peace for fifty years. It was only after these two generations that new troubles arrived. There were two major issues facing the Kamakura Bakufu, neither at first appearing to be anything more than a minor issue of protocol, both of which would escalate into conflicts that claimed thousands of lives.

The first, in 1272, was the death of the Retired Emperor Go-Saga, grandson of the luckless Go-Toba. This in itself was of little consequence to the Bakufu, who had assumed so much power in the day-to-day running of the country that the court often had little to occupy itself except disputes over protocol. However, Go-Saga's death drew attentions to a fatal flaw in the Retired Emperor system. It was all very well for Retired Emperors to shuffle and meddle with their successors, as they were duty-bound to obey their ancestor's command. But what if, as in this case, a Retired Emperor died without leaving clear instructions, and died leaving one son who was also a Retired Emperor, and a second son who was the incumbent? If the incumbent retired, whose son should succeed him? In terms of court protocol, was the retired brother senior, or was it the incumbent brother? If Go-Saga had been alive, he could have settled the issue with a word, but now he was gone, there was nobody of sufficient authority to pronounce on the situation.

Ironically, Go-Saga seems to have kept quiet *because* he expected the Bakufu to decide for him, as they had on every other imperial issue during his reign. Now that he was gone, the Bakufu would be unable to issue an edict of their own, as whichever candidate they favoured, the loser was sure to raise a complaint, and claim that his father's wishes were misrepresented. It was only a short step from such complaints to a full-on restaging of the revolt of Prince Mochihito. Rather than offer potential enemies the fuel to mount a resistance, the Bakufu offered an uneasy compromise that merely postponed the inevitable. When the incumbent Emperor inevitably abdicated, the Bakufu backed the succession of his son, on the understanding that when the son resigned in turn, the succession would pass to his cousin. Thereafter, the imperial succession would instead alternate between the two branches, to ensure that everyone was displeased equally. This alternation between the senior and junior lines of succession would last for another fifty years before it collapsed, but the seeds that were sown in 1272 would develop into a conflict that would eventually bring the Kamakura Bakufu down.

In the meantime, the Kamakura Bakufu had a more pressing problem. This, too, began as little more than a protocol issue, before encompassing a great conflict. In the greatest irony of all, a folktale sprang up that claimed the great hero Yoshitsune had not died in the tragedy of Takadachi fort. Instead, there were whispers in Japan that he had fled the country that betrayed him and sought sanctuary on the Asian mainland. There, he had found a willing army of new loyalists, who proclaimed him their 'Great Leader'. Under this name, *Genghis Khan* in Mongol, he had led a mighty army that had conquered much of the known world. True enough, the historical Yoshitsune and the historical Genghis Khan were roughly the same age, and both were respected by their men, but there the resemblance ends.

Across the strait in Korea, the local people had fought a long and ultimately unsuccessful war against the Mongol invaders. By the time Korea was conquered, Genghis Khan's grandson had also occupied the capital of China. A great army had seized control of much of northern Asia, and its leader, after some wrangling amongst rival generals, had now proclaimed himself the Emperor of China. Now this leader, Khubilai Khan, sent ambassadors to Japan, asking that its 'King' establish friendly relations with his Empire. His letter, courteous but clear, noted that he was the ruler of the world, and that it was in the interests of a 'small country' like Japan to cultivate friendly relations. The alternative to this vague and unspecified acknowledgement would be war. 'And who is there who likes such a state of things?' finishes Khubilai in fake chumminess.[2]

The juxtaposition of the terms 'emperor' and 'king' spoke volumes. The ruler of Japan was to acknowledge that he was a mere vassal of Khubilai Khan, or face violent consequences. Nor were the Japanese entirely ignorant of the way that Mongols behaved. If a city refused to surrender, the Mongols would massacre every living thing within it. During the peaceful reign of the Kamakura Bakufu, Mongol armies had travelled as far west as Austria, had conquered Siberia and smashed the rule of the Jin dynasty in northern China. Now Korea had fallen, too. Unless the ruler of Japan kowtowed before Khubilai Khan, Japan would be next.

According to a few smug rumour-mongers in the western regions of Japan, the letter from Khubilai Khan was not a disaster at all. It was, instead, an announcement that the hostilities of the Genpei War were just about to recommence. The Taira had not been defeated after all; instead, they had faded into the fantasy world of exotic, unknown China, and returned two generations later as the masters of a foreign armada. There was, of course, no veracity whatsoever in the bogus story – rather, it tells us a different truth: that Japan remained disunited even under the rule of the Bakufu, and that the Mongols might even find willing collaborators if someone did not manage to rally the Japanese together.

Crucially, Khubilai Khan's letter was addressed to the wrong person. It confused the title of Emperor of Japan with the position of Ruler of Japan. If Khubilai Khan had known more about the Japanese, he might have realized that the Kamakura shōgunate ruled Japan in the Emperor's name. Had he known even more about the intricacies of Japanese politics, he would have known the Shōgun was himself a puppet, and that the true ruler of Japan was the Shōgun's Regent.

At the time, the Shōgun's Regent was the newly appointed Hōjō Tokimune, an eighteen-year-old youth upon whose shoulders would rest the defence of Japan from a military force that had conquered the world. He very carefully avoided making any definite reply to the Mongols, pursuing instead a common Japanese tactic of delay, in the hope that the situation in China would change.

Part of the reason for the Japanese prevarication can be found in the long-running Korean campaign. The Mongols were no real threat until they had pacified Korea, and the battles on the peninsula stretched on for years. Even if the Mongols successfully conquered Korea, the Japanese might still hope that troubles elsewhere, the death of Khubilai Khan, or a long time spent planning might delay any actual attack. In 1271, an uprising in Korea threatened the pro-Mongol government, and the Japanese were invited to participate – however, the Bakufu refused to get involved, sure in the knowledge that if they did and failed, the Mongols would then have an excuse to attack them immediately.

By 1273, the first group of Mongol soldiers arrived in Korea to prepare for the invasion of Japan. They found a country so impoverished by its resistance to the Mongols that there was no spare food, and supplies had to be transported all the way from China. As long as Korea was unable to feed itself, it was in no position to function as a marshalling point for a Mongol armada, and the Japanese were safe.

Hōjō Tokimune put the samurai to work on a massive defensive scheme, establishing forts and walls around Hakata Bay – the natural choice for any invading fleet, and the only harbour large enough to shelter an invasion fleet from the mainland. Another year passed with no Mongol invasion. Then, pointedly when the harvest had been collected in Korea, the first signs of an enemy fleet were seen in the Korean Strait.

The first point of contact was the island of Tsushima at the midway point of the strait, now under the rule of the Sō clan. According to legend, the first clue that the defenders of Tsushima had of the approaching Mongols was the outbreak of a fire at the shrine of the war-god Hachiman outside the town. A witness claimed that the fire had broken out soon after a flock of white pigeons had landed in the grounds, a claim that was laughed off by the samurai leader Sō Sukekuni as a sign from their patron deity to prepare for defence. Those with a better knowledge of Mongol tactics might recall stories of Mongol warriors setting fires in enemy towns by using birds as the delivery systems for incendiary devices – quite possibly, the 'warning' from Hachiman was actually the first act of Mongol aggression.[3]

The massive bay of Sasunoura began to fill with a huge fleet of ships. Sō Sukekuni sent a small dispatch over to the lead ship, only to have his men beaten back by a hail of Mongol arrows. This was the first intimation that the Japanese had that their enemies would not be following the established rules of samurai combat.

A junior samurai launched a humming-bulb arrow to announce the opening of initial hostilities. Instead of answering with a volley of their own, the Mongols merely laughed at it. Instead, the enemy forces sloshed ashore and immediately began attacking the assembled samurai, with no recognition of rank or precedent. As Sō's men struggled to meet the charge of the Mongols, men fell, struck by poisoned arrows, while huge catapults launched explosive iron balls that wiped out entire platoons. Unlike the samurai, the Mongols were armed with metal shields, and advanced in a phalanx under a further hail of poisoned arrows.

It was only later in the day, when the battle degenerated into a general mêlée, that the samurai were able to fight in the manner to which they were more accustomed, in isolated pockets of single combat. But the poisoned arrows and the scrum of linked shields had permitted many thousands of 'Mongols' to come ashore – the army included Koreans and Chinese, but they were all 'Mongols' to the samurai.

One of the Sō leaders, having dispatched a giant Mongol foe, stood on top of the body and yelled at the other invaders, calling them cowards, and daring them to come and meet him in single combat. Instead, he was transfixed by dozens of arrows, three of which struck him mortally.

Sō Sukekuni led a final charge towards the place where his lieutenant had fallen, only to join him in death:

> Governor Sō, who had been commanding the garrisons, shouting to his troops and stimulating their martial spirit, and had already been wounded, now appeared on horseback leading a band of cavalry, in the quarter where ... his best general was slain ... This was the most terrible scene of all, and also the final stage of the day's battle ... The ear of heaven was deafened with the din of the Mongol drums, the earth shook at the tempest of war cries. Ah! Where is our forlorn hope that rode into the jaws of death? The shafts began to fall like raindrops of spring, and blood flowed until the field looked like a crimson sea. Where is the brave band of Sukekuni of Sō, in the smoke of the guns or the clouds of the arrows? They were no more seen in the isle; all that came into sight again out of the smoke were a few masterless horses, returning and neighing for their empty camps.[4]

True to form, the Mongols set about massacring everyone left behind – or at least a fair part of them: the fact that *someone* lived to tell this tale, and that boats reached nearby

Iki with an account of the samurai's last stand make it clear that some did escape the island alive. The last stand of Sō Sukekuni left Tsushima undefended. The women of Sō's mansion were already dying in a mass suicide, and the Mongols fell upon the suriviving men over the day that followed, putting all to the sword and burning the town to the ground. Those women that did not take their own lives were raped and taken aboard the Mongol ships as slaves and, it seems, human shields. When the armada reached the next island, Iki, off the coast of Kyūshū, the lead ships were adorned with a necklace of female prisoners, cruelly threaded together with wire through the palms of their hands, some already dead from exposure or injury, others terrifyingly still alive.

In distant Kamakura, the shōgunal Regent Hōjō Tokimune approached his favourite Buddhist priest to confess his fears of the Mongol invasion.

'Finally,' he said, 'this is the most momentous event of my life.'

The priest asked him how he planned to deal with it. Tokimune's answer was a barely intelligible scream of belligerence: '*KATSU!*' ('Victory!').

'It is true,' said the priest. 'The son of a lion roars as a lion.'

The story of Tokimune and his Buddhist confessor is well known in Japan, despite its historiographical problems. *When*, precisely, did Tokimune confess his fears, and mull over the approach of the Mongols? All retellings of the story, as plays, in novels or on television, can cut, as does this book, between the first onslaught of the Mongols and the defiant scream of Tokimune, setting him up as a quintessential samurai, facing his foes with pure fury and will for victory. However, modern commentators have read Tokimune's resistance differently, as the desperate, flailing actions of a man impossibly out of his depth, who has only avoided becoming one of history's great failures by sheer luck and serendipity. One might note, perhaps, that among the many 1980s management books and hagiographies that attempt to apply the samurai mind to the business world, not one of them dares to suggest that the answer to any problem is to simply scream at it.[5]

The narrative force is further diminished if we remember that communications were not so swift. There was no messenger arriving in distant Kamakura to blurt the news of the Mongol arrival, no reportage of the massacre at Tsushima. By the time Hōjō Tokimune heard the true facts of the Mongol attack, it was already over. For all Tokimune knew, when he 'roared like a lion', southern Japan could already be in Mongol hands.

The island of Iki lacked a large samurai contingent. The island's commander, Saemonnojo Kagetaka, was left to hold his territory with a rag-tag army of fishermen and farmers armed with rusty weapons, hunting spears and rocks. Kagetaka sequestered the men's wives and children within his castle, and mounted a strong resistance against the landing invaders. He was pushed back within his castle on the first day's fighting, but settled down for a siege, in the hope that samurai reinforcements were already en route from further down the coast.

However, he was entirely surrounded by a vast host of enemy soldiers, facing a sea of red banners – the choice of colour a mere coincidence, but sure to bolster the rumours that this was the vengeful Taira reborn. At dawn the next day the attack continued, and even as Kagetaka and his men fought Mongol troops away from a broken gate, an exploding Mongol firework set the castle ablaze. Realizing that it was all over, Kagetaka ordered one of his retainers to run for headquarters with news of the defeat, and to take his sole heir, his daughter Katsura, with him to continue his line. True to samurai form, the account of Kagetaka's last stand is taken up only partly by his spirited defence of the castle – several pages are instead devoted to the bickering among the samurai over who should stay to die an honourable death.

Sadly for Katsura, it was all in vain. Her fleeing boat sailed perilously close to the Mongols, and she died in a volley of arrows. Meanwhile, the Mongols advanced on Kagetaka, pushing their human shields ahead of them. Above the Mongol drums and the roars of the invaders, the defenders heard the pleas of the womenfolk, begging them not to hold back, but to shoot them where they stood in order to get at the invaders. As the last bastion fell, Kagetaka retired to his inner chambers, where he killed his wife and set fire to his mansion.

Four days later, the Mongol fleet reached Hakata Bay itself, the victims of its earlier victories nailed to its prows and strung from its gunnels. The samurai were ready for them – Katsura's unsuccessful guardian having nevertheless survived to tell the tale of Iki – but still unprepared for the changes in tactics. It seems that among the garbled messages of the Mongol approach, nobody had yet thought through the implications of the great Mongol war drums, which were used not merely for signalling, but to scare horses.

One of our best sources for the attack on Hakata is a series of painted scrolls, commissioned by the samurai Takezaki Suenaga as part of his submission to the Bakufu for reward and reimbursement. It offers what appears to be a remarkably honest account of the changing fortunes of the samurai defenders. Suenaga reports arriving with his men to find the Mongols landing, openly disobeying the order to wait for reinforcements. Level-headed samurai commanders, having already seen the lack of Mongol interest in name-announcing and single combat between equivalent ranks, were already trying to persuade the Japanese to stay back and take potshots at the arriving invaders. Suenaga, however, charges brashly forward, past two fellow samurai who are already carrying Mongol heads – he is clearly not the first.

Suenaga's charge meets with expected results. An unstoppable volley of arrows kills his bannerman and critically wounds another of his men. Fighting is clearly so close to the water that the sand is still wet – Suenaga's horse stumbles on the beach as the arrows keep coming. Samurai armour, of course, is largely designed to keep out arrows, and Suenaga is relatively unharmed. His horse, however, is hit several times. One of the catapult-launched explosives goes off directly overhead, peppering both horse and rider with shrapnel. As they both fall bleeding to the sand, Suenaga believes that his life is over, only to be rescued by an equally foolhardy charge by another group of samurai, which distracts the Mongols and allows Suenaga to limp back out of range.

The fighting on the beach lasted all day. One young samurai managed a lucky shock that gravely wounded one of the 'Mongol' leaders – in fact, a Korean general. By evening, the Japanese withdrew to the tree line nearby, leaving perhaps a third of their number dead or dying on the sand. There, they huddled behind a worn stone wall atop an earth embankment. The irony, perhaps, was not lost on them that this part of the defences against Mongol attack had actually been built 600 years earlier, during the great panic over an invasion from the mainland that had preoccupied some of the first of the samurai. For the historically minded, that invasion had been a long time in coming, but had finally arrived with the self-same cataclysmic force that the ancestors of the samurai had feared.

'We lamented all through the night,' recorded one warrior, 'thinking that we were doomed and would be destroyed to the last man, and that no seeds would be left to fill the nine provinces.'[6]

Unknown to the samurai, similar arguments ensued aboard the Mongol ships, where the would-be invaders had been taken by surprise by the ferocity of the Japanese defence. Unaware of how far away reinforcements might be, and in what numbers, the Mongol generals pondered how long their assault might reasonably continue. They had yet to establish a firm beachhead, although the city of Hakata was in flames. One of their leaders was barely conscious after being struck by an arrow. More crucially, the fearsome clouds of Mongol arrows, while they had decimated Japanese forces, had also seriously depleted Mongol ammunition.

In a conference aboard the Mongol flagship, the leaders of the invaders bickered over their next move. One, General Hol-Ton, sensibly pushed for a night assault, warning that unless the Mongols mounted one, the Japanese were sure to arrange one of their own. Hol-Ton was overruled, but suspecting that the Japanese would come after them at night, the other generals decided to withdraw all surviving troops to their ships, ready to put ashore again the following day.

Hol-Ton was right: the Japanese *were* planning a night assault, but not from the land. Some 300 open boats, each bearing a dozen samurai, edged close to the towering Mongol ships under cover of darkness. Twenty of the boats did not contain samurai at all, but stacks of dry grass and straw, ready to be used as fireships. The moon had not yet risen, and the only light was the distant glow of burning Hakata town. The evening was cloudy and blustery, with dots of drizzle beginning to fall, all helping to conceal the

Japanese as they neared the invasion fleet. Most crucially, the Mongols seem to have been taken entirely by surprise by the idea of a marine counter-attack.

As soon as the lead samurai were in arrow range, they began picking off the watchmen on the Mongol vessels. All semblance of stealth soon evaporated, as the samurai archers celebrated their first hits, and the troops on the armada vessels raised the alarm. Mongol drummers began frantically sounding a call to action stations, but the Japanese boats presented small targets on the dark sea, while the Mongol ships were unmissable.

The sea grew rougher, the rain beginning to spatter in heavier drops as the samurai lit their fireships:

> All at once the darkness cleared . . . as the fireboats advanced here and there towards the Mongol fleet. The numberless vessels were so brilliantly observable by the reflection of the blazing fires that they became easy targets to the Japanese archers, who could more easily escape the enemy as they floated up and down on the billows.[7]

Fire leapt through the Mongol ships, igniting some of the gunpowder supplies, preoccupying the sailors with extinguishing instead of resisting. Some samurai, desperate for glory, even clambered aboard the Mongol vessels to set fires and stab their enemies. But the sea was becoming still rougher, the rain now pelting down, dampening the fires in Hakata and aboard the ships, and adding choking, blinding smoke to the conditions at sea. Realizing that a storm was swiftly rising, the samurai retreated to their boats and rowed for the shallows, leaving the larger Mongol ships rolling at anchor, pitching dangerously in the savage sea.

At dawn the next day, most of the Mongol ships were gone. The baffled samurai emerged from their redoubt among the trees to find the rain-swept beach silent, littered with the bodies from the previous day's fighting and a jagged forest of charred driftwood. The few remaining Mongol ships on the water were already receding, sailing with a strong easterly wind, unseasonally blowing back towards the mainland. In the distance, a couple of Mongol vessels were marooned on the sands, pitched over and wrecked. Some fifty luckless invaders – accounts do not distinguish between Koreans and Mongols – were stuck on the sands with their ships, lacking armour or many weapons, and were easily rounded up.[8]

For the samurai on the front line, their battle was apparently over, and the armada had taken advantage of the rare easterly wind to retreat before it suffered further losses. The night attack and the fortuitous storm had been a success, much to the annoyance of samurai reinforcements, who arrived over the next few days to discover that there was no enemy left to fight.

The story, however, seems to have grown with the telling. By the following month, when the story had reached the court and the Bakufu, the several hundred Mongol vessels had been inflated to 'several tens of thousands' in an excitable courtier's diary. The 'reverse' wind had carried them off, and this was seen by some as a magical rescue:

> The reverse wind must have arisen [as a result of] the protection of the gods. Most wonderful! We should praise [the gods] without ceasing. This great protection can only have happened because of the many prayers and offerings to the various shrines . . . throughout the realm.[9]

For the samurai at Hakata Bay, the Mongols had been beaten back by grit and determination, with a little help from the weather. But it would seem that courtiers, priests and administrators in distant parts of Japan were keen to claim some of the credit for themselves. Takezaki Suenaga's account, a relatively contemporary source, makes no mention of divine intervention in the defeat of the Mongols, nor does any official court document in existence. The notion that the gods had come to Japan's aid was certainly a popular conceit, and is mentioned in the private diaries of some contemporary courtiers, but the concept that the Mongol invasion was an attack fought off by the power of prayer was a later idea popularized by certain Buddhist sects. It was, they began to argue, not merely the samurai who held off the Mongols. It was the weather. It was the gods themselves. The newly unified polity of Japan did not only allow the samurai to band together in the defence of the realm, it also permitted the entire Japanese nation to claim the credit. For this rumour, this consensual myth, to have any legs at all, it would need to be couched in epic proportions. The Mongol attack needed to comprise an uncountable armada, a myriad of ships. The samurai defence needed to be spirited, but desperate. But thanks to the prayers of the priests (who were soon demanding part of the reward), and the commoners, the gods had stepped in, not with a simple change in wind direction or a fortuitous typhoon, but with a 'Divine Wind', a *Kamikaze*.

As far as the Mongols were concerned, the remnants of their armada limped back into harbour in Korea, to report that the Japanese resistance had been impressively strong, and that a larger fleet would be required. The matter-of-fact way that this was stated suggests that the 1274 'invasion' fleet may have always been intended as a reconnaissance mission rather than a full-blown invasion. The Mongols, too, mentioned bad weather conditions, and notably in reports of 1274, it is the Mongols who make more of the storm than the Japanese. Quite probably, this was because it was better for the public image of the generals if they were able to blame the elements, rather than inadequate supplies or poor management, both of which would have been interpreted by their own superiors as passing the buck.[10]

Not all the invaders perished or were captured at the Battle of Hakata Bay. A nest of 'Mongol spies' was uncovered in Kyūshū, and was later found to largely comprise Chinese sailors shipwrecked after the disaster. Preying on local people as little more than bandits, they were rounded up and massacred by vengeful samurai.[11]

So, too, were the hapless members of a new delegation from Khubilai Khan, who arrived in Kamakura with a golden tablet bestowing the title of 'King of Japan' on Hōjō Tokimune. He reacted to this 'peace-offering' with indignation, and had the envoys executed at a place called the 'Dragon's Mouth' (*Tatsu no Kuchi*).

Neither side doubted that there would be a rematch. While the Japanese redoubled their efforts to fortify the coastline near any harbour likely to shelter a second invasion force, Khubilai Khan attempted to drum up support in China for an even larger fleet. This time, the armada truly was of massive proportions. One group of ships was assembled in Korea, while a second battle group was assembled on the River Yangtze, where Marco Polo witnessed the preparations of '15,000 ships . . . all belonging to the Great Khan and available to carry his armies to the isles of the sea.'[12]

In Japan, the samurai had wisely reinforced the coastal batteries, so that now there would be no opportunity for the Mongols to retake Hakata town. News arrived from the mainland that southern China had finally fallen to the Mongols, which not only freed up Mongol forces for a renewed assault on Japan, but also increased the likelihood that they would arrive with ships purloined from the defeated Song dynasty.

They arrived in 1281 in two waves. The first proceeded directly from Korea, following the course of their predecessors, taking Tsushima and then Iki. Their orders were to wait there until a second, even larger navy arrived from the Yangtze, but they tired of waiting and headed for Hakata. There, they found the new walls blocking any attempt to land troops. Despite having the whole of the Japanese coast to choose from, the Mongols were obliged to put ashore at Hakata, in a prolonged landing operation with no cover and no chance of forming a beachhead. Having trouble even making it past the high-water mark, their conquest was limited to a small island in Hakata Bay, where they quartered some of their horses.

Skirmishes continued for five weeks, divided between Mongol landings and counter-attacks by Japanese flotillas. Takezaki Suenaga was back among the defenders, and seems to have spent much of his time unsuccessfully trying to barge his way onto one of the Japanese boats that were taking the fight to the Mongols. His account of the battles takes no shame in his repeated attempts to bully or cajole his way onto the boats because, as far as he was concerned, such an eagerness for glory wholly befitted a warrior. Eventually, he managed to slip aboard a boat only by ordering his own men to stay ashore.

According to Suenaga's account, not even that was good enough. The oarsmen on his boat, understandably reluctant to get too close to a Mongol ship, were too timid for Suenaga, and he claims to have switched vessels midstream in order to join a team that was hungry for hand-to-hand combat. Suenaga and his fellow marines were forced to dodge stones flung from the Mongol catapults (there is, by this time, notably no mention of explosives, the Mongol supplies seemingly depleted). Taking heavy losses from Mongol arrows, they nevertheless clambered aboard ship after ship, meeting the invaders in close combat before retreating to strike once more. Fireships took their toll once more, while the Mongol-occupied island became the site of a more traditional land battle.

Meanwhile, the second, larger force finally arrived. Led by a Chinese general, and largely staffed by Chinese soldiers and sailors, this other 'Mongol' fleet wisely avoided the boxed-in Hakata Bay and put ashore thirty miles south. Two weeks of fighting followed, village by village, between hastily reassigned samurai defenders and some of the Chinese arrivals. The bulk of them, however, remained at sea in a jury-rigged floating fortress – dozens of the largest vessels, chained together and circled by a wooden walkway as a combined embarkation point for landing craft and defensive perimeter against the inevitable Japanese marine assault.

A second storm, even more powerful than the first, whipped up in late summer – as one Japanese account put it, with all the ferocity of 'a green dragon rising from the waves', filling the sky with sulphurous flames.

[The Mongol ships] were impaled on the rocks, dashed against the cliffs, or tossed on land like corks from the spray. They were blown over till they careened and filled. Heavily freighted with human beings and weighty weapons, they sank by hundreds. The corpses were piled on the shore, or floated on the water so thickly that it seemed almost possible to walk thereon.[13]

When the news reached the court, one diarist put it very succinctly: 'A typhoon sank most of the foreign pirates' ships.'[14]

A number of the troops did not die at sea, but managed to land or wreck themselves at a nearby island, where they were then slowly worn down by pursuing samurai. We know this not only because of the jubilant reports of the Japanese, but also because of the despondent accounts of a handful of survivors, who would eventually recount the story back on the mainland. The tale of the failed Mongol attack on 'Xipangu' (Japan) formed one of the high points of the diaries of Marco Polo, who had no access to Japanese sources, and hence wrote of the events entirely from the Mongol point of view:

> And it came to pass that there arose a north wind that blew with great fury, and caused great damage along the coasts of that island, for its harbours were few. It blew so hard that the Great Khan's fleet could not stand against it. And when the chiefs saw that, they came to the conclusion that if the ships remained where they were then the whole navy would perish.[15]

According to Polo's account, the Mongols had other troubles. Unbeknown to the Japanese, there was tension in the Mongol army between the nominal Mongol leader, a man called Arakhan, and the Chinese general Fan Wenhu, who was the man to whom the troops, who were mostly Chinese, were loyal. Arakhan was supposedly ill during much of the expedition, but not so ill that he did not bicker with General Fan and query many of his decisions. In fact, this 'tension' may have been Polo's garbled interpretation of a very basic difference between the two fleets. Arakhan was in charge of a direct assault, using ships suited to the sea-crossing; Fan Wenhu was in charge of a larger fleet that contained soldiers but also much more in the way of supplies. Fan's fleet came directly from the mouth of the

Yangtze, and arrived later – since each fleet relied on the other, it was possibly this division of responsibilities that led to the tensions described by Polo.

Unmentioned in any source of the period, and only really appreciated in the light of modern archaeology, was the composition of the armada that had apparently been so easily defeated by a storm. Reconstructions of the many wrecks strewn around the site of the second Divine Wind tell a tale of shoddy construction, old ships hastily and poorly repaired, and vessels that were literally falling apart at the seams before they even commenced their crossing to Japan. It seems that while there may indeed have been the towering battleships reported among the Mongol fleet, the bulk of the troop transports were old, reconditioned vessels. Worst of all, many seem to have been flat-bottomed boats intended for river transport. Circumstantially, this is not surprising – it was, after all, Marco Polo in Hangzhou who spoke of the *river* being crowded with boats for the invasion, and entirely believable that the Chinese and Koreans might have been browbeaten by their land-locked Mongol rulers into sending unsuitable boats for the long crossing. The Mongol invasion of Japan was no Dunkirk of little ships, or if it were, they had much farther to go – the Korean Strait is over a hundred miles wide.[16]

Regardless of what logistical problems the Mongols may have faced, the Japanese perspective was one of divinely assisted victory. As the years passed, the enduring story of the Mongol invasion was not one of ill-prepared conscripts, bad weather and unsuitable boats. It was instead, of course, that of two great Divine Winds that came to aid the samurai defenders at their hour of need. Japan enjoyed the protection of the gods, and her warriors were undefeated. However, we owe much of this myth not merely to the two failed invasions, but to the panic in Japan in the decade that followed, as the samurai prepared for an expected third attack.

Khubilai Khan fully intended to return a third time. While the Japanese celebrated, Khubilai mobilized Chinese businesses in a third effort in 1283, leading to complaints among Chinese merchants that their profits were being undermined by the demands to contribute to yet another invasion fleet. As late as 1285, there are records of administrators stockpiling rice and lumber for another invasion of Japan, although the long-delayed third armada never materialized. By 1286, Khubilai Khan was distracted by unrest elsewhere, and then by his own declining health. His successors at least paid lip service to the idea of conquering the rebellious Japanese, and a 'Mobile Bureau for the Subjugation of Japan' remained a key part of the occupation government of Korea until as late as 1365. However, the Mongols did not trouble the Japanese again.[17]

It is only here, with the Japanese unaware that the worst of the Mongol threat had actually passed, that we first hear of the Bakufu ordering mass prayers for victory in 1283, an order that was then extended to a national decree in 1290. Far from the modern assumption that the Japanese state had sought divine intercession during the Mongol invasions, the historical record shows that the greatest output of prayer was followed not by a Divine Wind, but by no attack at all.[18]

Modern historians cannot agree on the 'what if' possibilities of the Mongol invasion. It is, in the words of William Farris '. . . likely that a well-coordinated Mongol attack would have succeeded had nature been on their side'.[19] Conversely, Thomas Conlan suggests that the Japanese were entirely capable of fighting the Mongols to a standstill, and that the Mongol invasion of Japan would have soon suffered from the same insurmountable issues of supply that would defeat the later Japanese invasion of Korea in the late sixteenth century.[20]

The foreign tactics and weapons of the Mongols were arguably less devastating than the challenge they presented to the tradition of Japanese warfare. In all previous wars, ever since the time of the campaigns against the Emishi, loyal service to samurai leaders had been repaid to the victors, usually in grants of land. But in the case of the Mongol invasions, there were no lands to confiscate and reassign; there was little in the way of treasures to loot from the attacking ships. Consequently, even as they celebrated their finest hour, the regents of Japan saw their authority undermined, their ability to reward their samurai drastically limited. It would not be long before the rule of the Hōjō commenced on an unstoppable decline. The Mongol threat had passed, but in doing so, it freed the Japanese to fight once more among themselves.[21]

6

TWO SUNS IN THE SKY
THE KENMU RESTORATION AND THE ASHIKAGA SHŌGUNATE

The signs of trouble first appeared before the Mongol threat was even past. In 1272, Hōjō Tokimune's own brother was murdered in what appears to have been an attempt to usurp the Regency. Tokimune himself died, still in his early thirties, in 1281, believing that the Mongols were sure to return in even greater numbers. His fifteen-year-old son Sadatoki succeeded him, meaning that now the administration required proxies for the Regent of the Shōgun, himself ruling in the name of the Emperor! The two samurai ruling in Sadatoki's name were at odds with one another, and would eventually come to blows in a coup attempt in 1285.

The victor was soon ousting lieutenants and constables from the administration in favour of his own cronies, which only served to accentuate the ill feeling towards the Kamakura Shōgunate. As the Mongol threat faded it became clear that there were very few rewards to be had. Regime change came in spring 1293, when Sadatoki asserted his maturity by ordering an attack on his surviving proxy. Rather smartly, he did so in the immediate aftermath of a great earthquake, adding an element of divine approval to his seizure of power.

However, none of this removed the fiscal or logistical problems that dogged the Bakufu. The likes of Takezaki Suenaga, who had fervently fought in Kyūshū to protect Japan from the Mongols, did not see any sign of a reward until 1294, and even then they were restricted largely to parcels of land confiscated from Sadatoki's enemies. Meanwhile, the continued threat of another invasion led the administration to commandeer large areas of land in Kyūshū for government use. This might have made sense under emergency conditions, but was seen by many locals as theft by another name. Yet again, it led to accusations of cronyism against the Kamakura Bakufu.

Japan suffered from a different, subtler invasion, as inflation began to cripple some of the older domains – Chinese money, in circulation as an ad hoc local currency due to several centuries of trade with the mainland, had begun to lose its value in Japanese eyes. By 1297, Sadatoki might have wished for the simplicity of swords and arrows; his administration's new enemy was the dull, financial spectre of inflation and loan foreclosures. His decrees were aimed not at Mongol invaders, but at usurers seeking to oust feudal lords by calling in their debts.[1]

The samurai had nobody left to fight except each other. Struggling domains laid off surplus retainers, creating a new underclass of rōnin – 'wave-men' – drifting, masterless samurai with nothing to lose, and often no skills except warfare. In some cases, they united with the dispossessed retainers of those who had been disinherited in Sadatoki's purges. Before long, Sadatoki's successors faced a rising crime rate, not of simple muggings and robberies, but of bands of trained, organized bandits, operating out of remote fortresses that they had built themselves.

Meanwhile, in Kyōto, the imperial court muddled along with the unpopular compromise that had ended the Jōkyū Unrest of 1221 – the alternation of the succession between junior and senior descendants of the throne. The uneasy truce faced a new challenge in 1318 with the accession of the ninety-sixth Emperor, Go-Daigo, a strong-willed man in his thirties who resisted the power of his 'retired' predecessors. He made official decrees fixing the price of rice, and soon regarded the 'tent-government' Bakufu as an unwelcome anachronism which had no right to interfere in the running of the Japanese state.

At the time of Go-Daigo's succession, the shōgunal regent was Hōjō Takatoki, a weak-willed man more given to dances, plays and dogfights than performing the role to which he was appointed. In 1322, a dispute broke out in the far northern province of Mutsu, where two brothers of the Andō clan opposed each other's inheritance. Both sent embassies (with bribes) to the Bakufu with requests to settle the manner. Takatoki's chamberlain sent a body of troops to put the rebellion down, but the rebels defeated the government's samurai. For Takatoki, it was an irritation: a cause for the chamberlain's dismissal, and the need to send a second expedition. At the imperial court, it had a more far-ranging implication – the troops of the shōgunate were clearly nowhere near as good as they needed to be.

Before long, there were whispers of conspiracies at the imperial court. In 1324, a group called the 'Free and Easy Society', nominally a drinking club, was outed as a secret society with the stated aim of overthrowing the 'eastern barbarians' of the Bakufu. Go-Daigo denied all knowledge of it, although it comprised high-ranking samurai and courtiers, and he was sure to have been associated with it behind the scenes. In the years that followed, Go-Daigo cultivated good relations with the warrior monks of the Buddhist temples near Kyōto. Tipped off that the Emperor was assembling an army of his own, which could only have one purpose, the Bakufu moved in, not against him, but against his associates.

After Bakufu forces stormed a fortified temple in Kyōto, the administration lost its patience with its alleged superior, and informed Go-Daigo that it was time for him to step down. Go-Daigo duly 'retired' under duress, and was sent to a remote island in an attempt to prevent him from interfering further. He had escaped by early spring 1333, and made it clear that he did not regard his abdication as binding. In fact, he intended to restore himself to power, and to abolish the now unnecessary tent-government' that claimed to rule in his name. Inevitably, full-blown hostilities broke out between samurai 'loyal' to Go-Daigo, and supporters of the Bakufu, who attempted to write off Go-Daigo as a pretender. The resultant conflict would eventually be known as the Kenmu Restoration, 'Kenmu' being Go-Daigo's deliberate choice for a reign name, meaning 'built by war'. He had lifted the name from an ancient Chinese dynasty, in which imperial rule had been wrested from the control of a power-hungry usurper.[2]

Surviving accounts of combat in the period are notably different from those of previous eras. There is a sense – perhaps learned the hard way from the Mongols, perhaps simply a reflection of more realistic storytelling – that battle is nowhere near as glamorous as the old tales make it out to be. The chief war chronicle of the era, usually known by its Japanese title of *Taiheiki* (*Chronicle of the Grand Pacification*) is conspicuously less packed with detailed accounts of samurai donning armour with particular lacings, patterns or designs. There is none of the 'dressing scene' build-up to battles common to earlier tales, nor is there all that much in the way of 'name announcing' on the battlefield. Combat is instead presented as a much grittier, more brutal affair, with a much heavier emphasis on trickery, deception and surprise.[3]

The *Taiheiki* pits mounted, armoured samurai from the Kantō region (the samurai of the Bakufu) against pro-imperial forces that might be better described as guerrillas. These 'warriors of the fields' (*nōbushi*) are often depicted on foot and favouring spears over swords, a world away from the knightly samurai of the previous century. Conversely, the pro-imperial forces insist on referring to their enemies as the 'eastern barbarians', evoking the snobbery of bygone days when the warriors of the Kantō region were regarded in Kyōto as little better than the Emishi they were suppressing.

The unquestionable samurai hero of Go-Daigo's 'restoration' was Kusunoki Masashige, a man whose loyalty to the Emperor would become such a powerful icon that his statue continues to occupy the pride of place at the entrance to the Imperial Palace in modern-day Tōkyō. The descendant of Minamoto clansmen, Kusunoki was supposedly promoted within the ranks of imperial loyalists after Go-Daigo dreamt that he was sheltered (i.e. protected) by a camphor tree (*kusu no ki*). Beyond such portentous beginnings, Kusunoki also proved himself to have an able grasp of the new era's tactics. Besieged by Bakufu forces in the lightly appointed fortress of Akasaka, lacking a moat and open to attack from all sides, Kusunoki held off his attackers with judicious use of archers, and hastily improvised siege devices.

With only a few days' food and water, Kusunoki piled up his dead in a huge mound in the middle of the castle. The remainder of his men slipped away in small numbers during the assembly of the massive pyre, so that by the time it was lit, there was only a single loyalist left alive in the castle. The weeping man informed the newly arrived besiegers that Kusunoki and all his men had committed mass suicide, and the sight of the burning corpses was enough to convince the Bakufu forces that this claim was true. By the time the deception was discovered, Kusunoki was long gone.

Perhaps it is unfair to call Akasaka a fortress. Go-Daigo's forces favoured strongholds and stockades in their warfare against the Bakufu, largely because they knew they were strongly outnumbered by the Bakufu forces. Akasaka may have lacked a moat because it was never a real castle, perhaps more a fortified mansion or guardhouse. In one incident at Akasaka, the wall itself was seen to be false, or at least easy to dismantle. As Bakufu troops massed beneath it, Kusunoki's men cut ropes holding the false wall in place, and the entire edifice turns from a defensive element into an offensive one, crushing the attackers.

Although true 'castles' were not yet part of the Japanese landscape, it is Kusunoki's era that sees many elements of siege warfare coming to the fore. The *Taiheiki* has footsoldiers using 'bear-claw' rakes to pull down flimsy walls. Such devices have been mentioned before, fishing Taira from the sea at Dannoura in the *Tale of the Heike*, but now they are employed against edifices instead of people. Meanwhile, besieged soldiers pour boiling water on defenders. There is a modern fad for questioning the efficacy of boiling water against attackers, largely because the temperature of the water rapidly plummets as it falls through the air. However, the author of the *Taiheiki* seems to have already thought of this, and points to Kusunoki's men using ladles some ten or twenty feet long in order to deliver the scalding liquid right into the armour joints and exposed skin of the attackers, where it is sure to deliver the greatest damage.[4]

Such behaviour is remarkable not because it is new, but because it has not been described before as the behaviour of samurai. There is no sense here of the level playing field of earlier samurai-on-samurai conflicts – instead we see a much more pragmatic approach to battle by warriors prepared to seek any possible advantage over their foes. The samurai of this period are, at least according to their chronicles, no longer playing by the rules. Considering the large numbers of warrior monks and 'warriors of the fields' on the imperial side, we might presume that the ranks of the samurai have become permeable once more, dropping their pretentions of class and heredity, and admitting common men again. This is probably why we see a transformation in Japanese armour design in the period. Armourers seem to have accepted that not every warrior would be fighting on horseback with a bow. They reduced the box-like shape of the original samurai armour in order to make it less unwieldy on foot. They also discarded the former fixed skirt, designed to protect the thighs of mounted men, in favour of separate skirt pieces. The box-like shapes returned, not on the shoulders but on the thighs, intended to protect a footsoldier from the down-ward slices of swords, *naginata* and the hybrid weapon known as a *no-dachi* – best described as either a short-hafted *naginata* or a long-hilted sword.[5]

The *Taiheiki* also sees widespread mention of *seppuku*. Whereas it was previously couched as a strange practice limited to warriors from the Kantō plain, it now seems to have become a common tradition, even among the imperial supporters largely drawn from western Japan. Accounts in the *Taiheiki* of numerous warrior suicides conform to our modern idea of what *seppuku* was – one or more cuts, perhaps in a cruciform shape made in a ritual disembowelment, often with an officially-appointed second standing over the suicide with a sword, ready to strike a mercy blow.

Seppuku in the *Taiheiki* is often committed to avoid capture – a strange decision since part of its intention is to ensure a slow death, not a swift one. Other warriors are seen stabbing themselves, or stabbing each other in suicide pacts. But the period also appears to introduce a new practice that would become a recurring motif in all samurai: that of following one's lord in death. *Junshi* – literally, 'a martyr's death' – first achieves prominence in this era. We have already heard of suicides of women in the northern campaigns to avoid captures, and of the tragic mass suicide of the last of the Taira at Dannoura, but at the time they took place, those deaths were reported because they were extraordinary. In the *Taiheiki*, we get our first taste of *junshi* not as an uncommon, rare act, but as something that is all but expected of a samurai whose lord has been defeated. The custom seems to have achieved prominence with great rapidity, such that at the aforementioned Siege of Akasaka, Kusunoki was able to fake the mass suicide of his men, and to present it as a reasonable story to his enemies.

Notably, siege warfare is a constantly recurring theme in the *Taiheiki*. No sooner has Kusunoki fled from Akasaka, than he has retaken it, ready for a second siege in the same place when the Bakufu soldiers come after him once more. Later on in 1333, having escaped a second time, he is hemmed in at still another fortress, Chihaya, a short distance to the south, supposedly outnumbered a thousand to one. At Chihaya, Kusunoki continues to decimate the enemy with trickery. He sneaks out under cover of darkness to place armoured dummies at the base of the wall, and then has his men create a racket at dawn. This leads the besiegers to think that the imperial forces have sallied forth for hand-to-hand combat; they rush to engage the dummies, discovering too late that they have been had, just as heavy boulders rain down on their heads from the real soldiers, still safe behind the walls. The enemy tries cunning tactics of its own, engaging 500 carpenters to build a bridge, which they then lower across a gap between a ridge and Chihaya's walls. This is dealt with in an unsurprising manner – set aflame by the defenders in a stirring scene, as the bridge collapses, taking the attackers with it.

If the rules changed on engagement, armour and weapons, they also seemed to change on respect. Common to many military traditions is the dehumanizing of the enemy. We have already seen how the Emishi were regarded as subhuman until they were assimilated, and how Chinese and Koreans were all written off as 'Mongols'. However, at times of conflict between samurai and samurai, previous accounts have often been kind to both sides. The *Tale of the Heike* only had one villain in the shape of Kiyomori, and he was arguably dead before the bulk of the battles were fought. His shadow lurks in the background of the Genpei War as its true instigator, whereas the impression is strongly suggested that both Minamoto and Taira are good folk, steered into conflict by powers beyond their control. Not so in the *Taiheiki*, which often characterizes the men of the imperial faction as true, loyal servants of the Emperor, and the forces of the Bakufu as corrupt, evil usurpers.

Perhaps the chroniclers of the conflict felt able to do this because of the way that the conflict was ended. A third side entered the fray, with behaviour that any other generation of samurai would have found contemptibly treacherous. However, since the third side effectively won, its behaviour has been refashioned and reinterpreted as an act of over-arching, supreme loyalty. 'Loyalty', to a higher purpose, to the Emperor and not his underlings, is hence a constant refrain in the *Taiheiki* because it is the only argument that permits the victors to finish their story with any semblance of being on the moral high ground.

Tiring of the wild goose chase against Kusunoki, the Bakufu resolved to send an army directly after Go-Daigo himself, and to hence nip the Kenmu Restoration in the bud by depriving it of an emperor to restore. The man they sent to do it was Ashikaga Takauji (1305–58), another distant cousin of the Minamoto, and a veteran of the sieges of Akasaka and Chihaya. Marching at the head of his army, Ashikaga waited until he was safely out of Bakufu-friendly territory before announcing that he had no intention of attacking Go-Daigo. Instead, he was prepared to declare his loyal service to Go-Daigo, and to prove it, he arrived in Kyōto and killed the local Bakufu official.

Ashikaga was not the only turncoat. Realizing that many of the Bakufu's soldiers were loitering pointlessly in the fields around Chihaya Castle in the ongoing attempt to starve Kusunoki out, and that the next biggest Bakufu army had just switched sides, yet another Minamoto descendant, Nitta Yoshisada (1301–38) decided not only to declare for Emperor Go-Daigo, but also to do so by marching on Kamakura itself. Nitta advanced on Kamakura in three columns, the first of which was wiped out by strong Bakufu resistance. The others, however, approached Kamakura from an unexpected direction, marching across the sands at low tide. Unsurprisingly, such an act of betrayal required supernatural approval, and folktales of Nitta's march have him praying to the Sun Goddess for her aid in bringing down the usurpers, and then throwing his sword into the sea to part the waters. The last of the Hōjō regents committed suicide during the attack, along with an estimated 6,000 of his faithful followers.[6]

The reader will perhaps have already noted that many of the architects of the downfall of the Bakufu were themselves relatives of the Minamoto, who might arguably have regarded the Hōjō family as usurpers, not of the authority of the Emperor so much as of the authority of the Minamoto clan that had originally been appointed as shōguns. If so, this was neither the first nor last time in Japanese history that a coalition of victors celebrated their achievement before turning on each other when it became clear that they had different priorities.

Ashikaga and Nitta seemed to want a return to the situation of a century beforehand, when Minamoto clansmen ruled on behalf of the Emperor. Hence, they were expecting to see their names high up on the lists of new appointments and fiefdoms bestowed by Emperor Go-Daigo. However, the Emperor had set his sights on an even earlier precedent; Go-Daigo did not want a shuffling of prominent clans, but a true restoration of imperial authority, such that Japan had not seen for several centuries, if ever. The very name he chose for himself, Go-Daigo, which I have used anachronistically to refer to him before his reign was over, was a reference to a historical precedent: he called himself 'Latter Daigo', in reference to the original Daigo (r.897–930), who had legendarily been the last to rule without the interference of regents or proxies.

Go-Daigo seems to have been ill-prepared to deal with the consequences of his victory. He parcelled out rewards to many of his samurai supporters, but, in the opinions of many others, nowhere near enough. Already set on restoring imperial authority, he ordered the construction of a new imperial palace and levied extra taxes to do so, leading some samurai to question how on earth the new order benefited them at all. Ashikaga Takauji was particularly resentful, he seems to have been expecting to be appointed to a high-ranking feudal office, preferably that of Go-Daigo's new shōgun. He was, after all, a Minamoto, like the shōgun of old, Yoritomo, whose post had been usurped by the Hōjō family. He had, after all, personally destroyed the Hōjō family's hold on Kyōto, and installed himself in a prominent Kyōto palace, the Rokuhara, setting it up as his new administrative office. He had, in other words, been acting for some time as if the post of shōgun were already his.

Instead, Ashikaga fumed while Go-Daigo appointed his own six-year-old son as the nominal governor of the two northernmost provinces of Mutsu and Dewa – the region where the earliest Minamoto had first won honour. The final straw came when Go-Daigo announced that another of his sons would be the shōgun.

Go-Daigo may have had honourable intentions – to wrest control of the country from the military clique that had dominated it for so many centuries, and return the country to civilian rule – but civilians were in no position to fight angry soldiers. When a scion of the Hōjō family initiated a new rebellion, it was Ashikaga Takauji who had to put it down. This he did, but having chased the rebels out of Kamakura, Ashikaga proclaimed himself as shōgun, and launched into a new campaign against the 'traitor' Nitta Yoshisada. Nitta, of course, had done nothing wrong, but his alleged betrayal allowed Ashikaga to announce his newfound opposition to Emperor Go-Daigo without openly switching sides.

The war recommenced once more, this time with Ashikaga fighting for the shōgunate (his own shōgunate), against Nitta and Kusunoki, the loyal adherents to Go-Daigo's cause. As Ashikaga fell on Kyōto, he accompanied his movements with a call to all 'loyal' samurai to adopt his call. The decree forced clans all over Japan to declare their allegiances to the Emperor or the shōgunate, initiating new conflicts all across Japan. Two neighbouring domains in distant Kyūshū each discovered that the other had chosen a different side, and launched into immediate hostilities in the name of a squabble several hundred miles away.

The great decisive battle, however, was fought in 1336 on the coast of the Inland Sea, where the Minato River ran into the sea. The Ashikaga were advancing from the east in two groups, one on land and the other by sea. The imperial loyalists had no navy to speak of, and, crucially, a new command structure that did not favour the wily Kusunoki. Had Kusunoki been in charge, as he had been at the smaller skirmishes of the Kenmu Restoration, he would have certainly run for the hills, hoping to stretch out his enemy's lines of communication, and deprive the seaborne contingent of any advantage. In fact, he even had a hill in mind, suggesting that Go-Daigo should seek refuge on Mount Hiei, where the defending samurai could draw on warrior monks for reinforcements, and where the Ashikaga forces could be lured into street-by-street fighting after they entered Kyōto. That is how he summarized his recommendations to Go-Daigo, only to have the Emperor bloody-mindedly order him to make a stand at the Minato River. Go-Daigo, it seems, appreciated his loyal samurai, but had not truly understood how they had won their earlier battles.

In the earliest extant text of the *Taiheiki*, in a highly critical passage excised from later editions, Kusunoki archly observes that:

The scheme to achieve victory by deceiving a numerically superior enemy apparently does not suit His Majesty. Instead, he issues a decree calling upon peerless warriors to throw themselves against this great foe, which is the same as ordering them to go to their deaths.[7]

However, true to his claims of loyalty to the Emperor, no matter what, Kusunoki Masashige achieves immortality by following the order anyway. The *Taiheiki* has him bidding a fond farewell to his ten-year-old son, bluntly telling the boy that they are unlikely to meet again in this life.

The ensuing Battle of Minato River saw Kusunoki, as he had expected, hemmed in by the Ashikaga forces, some of whom made an amphibious landing behind Kusunoki's lines. Kusunoki's personal entourage of 700 warriors was worn down to just 73, but even when an avenue of escape opens before them, the *Taiheiki* has him resolutely refusing to leave. Wounded in eleven places, an exhausted Kusunoki retreats to a peasant's house with the last of his followers, where they chant ten Buddhist prayers for their own souls. As his men kill themselves all around him, Kusunoki turns to his brother Masasue and asks him how he would like to be reincarnated. Famously, Masasue replies that he would like to be reborn seven times over, and that each time he would return to fight the enemies of the court. Kusunoki heartily agrees, and with the stout cry of 'Shichisei Hōkoku!' ('Seven Lives for the Fatherland') the brothers stab each other and collapse 'onto the same pillow'.[8]

Kusunoki's sacrifice, as he already knew, was in vain. The Ashikaga army entered Kyōto. Ashikaga forcefully informed Go-Daigo that his 'retirement' still stood, and ordered him to hand over the sacred treasures of the Empire to a new Emperor. Go-Daigo appeared to do so with great reluctance, and stole out of the capital before the

Ashikaga faction realized that they had been had. The 'sacred treasures' were fakes, and once Go-Daigo was safely out of the capital, he stated once more that rumours of his retirement were greatly exaggerated. The Ashikaga refused to play along and duly enthroned their own candidate – Japan now had two Emperors.

Many Japanese historians seem to regard this event with momentous awe, as if the earth itself might split asunder at any moment. That is certainly how it would have been regarded by any expert in court protocol – Emperors ruled with the mandate of heaven, and essentially possessed a divine right to rule. There could be only one. It therefore followed that if there were two claimants, at least one of them was a liar. It was incumbent upon all samurai to offer their loyalty to the right Emperor, and to remove the pretender.

As the oft-cited Chinese aphorism held: 'There can be no two suns in the sky, nor two emperors on the throne.' And yet Ashikaga's act was not as radical as it is often depicted. In fact, there had been two claimants to the throne ever since Go-Daigo had proclaimed his own retirement null and void. Go-Daigo's son-in-law, Emperor Kōgon, was an Ashikaga puppet ruler for the two years preceding the Ashikaga victory, and the new pretender, Emperor Kōmyō, was Kōgon's younger brother. Moreover, this was far from the first time that Japan had enjoyed the doubtful benefit of two rival Emperors. After all, the poetry and narrative of the Genpei War tended to forget to mention that when the doomed Child Emperor Antoku slipped beneath the waves at Dannoura in 1185, his 'successor' Go-Toba had already been on the throne for two years. What marks the enthronement of Kōmyō out in Japanese history was not that there was an argument over the succession, but that the conflict was not easily papered over after a few months of fighting. Instead, the impasse endured for several decades, with the Northern and Southern Courts each insisting the rightful heir was theirs. The uneasy compromise of the alternating imperial houses now flourished into open competition. Samurai in search of an imperial house to which they could declare undying loyalty now found themselves in the unenviable position of having to choose between two. The period is remembered today as the South and North Courts (*Namboku-chō*), and lasted from the enthronement of Kōmyō in 1336 until the eventual, messy resolution of the crisis in 1392.

The long-term winners were the Ashikaga family, with Ashikaga Takauji gaining the coveted title of shōgun from the Northern Court. The Ashikaga shōguns would dominate the imperial court for the next 200 years, for the era usually known today as the Muromachi Period, after the location of their mansion in Kyōto. Conspicuously, the Ashikaga clan's Muromachi residence, the 'Palace of Flowers', was twice the size as the residence of the Emperor they claimed to serve. Nor were the Ashikaga shōguns unafraid of taking the initiative. The third Ashikaga shōgun, Yoshimitsu (1358–1408), was not above re-opening Japanese trade with China, describing himself in communications with the Ming Emperor as the 'King of Japan' and a vassal subject of China. We might recall that only a century beforehand, Japan had been prepared to go to war with Khubilai Khan when he used such terminology. Now, the Ashikaga did so with impunity.

The influence of the Southern Court gradually dwindled over many hard-fought campaigns, although it was widely understood that the Northern Court was merely a mouthpiece for the Ashikaga. At the time, the Northern Court believed itself to have 'won', although since 1911 opinions have changed, and it is now usually regarded as a pretender regime. But since everyone was descended from earlier emperors anyway, this was all largely moot. The last of the southern emperors abdicated in 1392, leaving the field clear for his northern rival to rule alone. The hundredth Japanese Emperor, Go-Komatsu, hence has two dates of enthronement, depending on where one stands with regard to the conflict. Either he came to power in 1382, when he was crowned by the Northern Court, or in 1392, when the Southern Court stopped complaining.

Although there were many great battles and noble sacrifices on both sides, the long conflict began to take on a more symbolic, political aspect in the outlying regions. In particular, Kyūshū and the Kantō plain devolved into semi-autonomous areas, left to run their own affairs while the main conflict centred on the piece of land between Kamakura and Kyōto. Meanwhile, many of the middle-ranking samurai houses grew progressively disenchanted with the standoff, which often cost them dearly. A rival court could dish out honours and promotions, but if a clan accepted them, they would be painted as collaborators if the enemy court then rose to prominence in the same region. Exasperated with such wildly swinging changes in fortune, some houses began to play both sides of the conflict, with different branches supporting opposite sides, in order to ensure that land and wealth could remain in the family, come what may. Hence, we see one branch of a clan being 'deprived' of its wealth, which is then handed to the other branch in recognition of services rendered. In fact, in some cases the 'services' only existed on paper, and both branches had no so much fought a war as staged a wargame:

> One party would erect a fort or stockade in a strategic position and provision themselves to maintain it; the other would raise a similar structure in the immediate

neighbourhood. In the encounters between the two garrisons, sword wounds were exceedingly rare, although there were occasional accidents in the exchange of arrows. The party whose provisions gave out first would retire. Thus when the recruiting agents appeared, the opposing chiefs could urge that they were too closely pressed at home to be able to spare any men for distant expeditions.[9]

The Shibuya clan, for example, cunningly divided into northern and southern factions, staged mock battles, and then filed mock reports. Vetted and approved by commanding officers, the Shibuya samurai made sure to mention how well their 'enemies' were fighting. Such notes on battle prowess, confirmed by reports of the opposing side, were enough to convince Ashikaga Takauji, who sent approving acknowledgements. When Ashikaga samurai eventually arrived in the Shibuya clan's home province to fight a real battle, the supporters of the Southern Court 'deserted' and their lands were given to the 'victors', their Shibuya kinsmen.[10]

If patience wore thin among the samurai participants, it was arguably even thinner among the peasantry. The presence of two rival authorities, each granting itself the right to grant pardons, adjudicate in legal matters and levy taxes, was sure to create trouble with the subjects at a grass-roots level. Some, like the cunning Shibuya, learned to play the system. Inevitably, there were those who lost out, with loans defaulted, disputes resolved in a rival's favour, or taxes levied twice by contending collectors. By the fifteenth century, the traditionally docile peasantry had become increasingly fractious, and rose up in a number of revolts and protests; familiarity with two emperors bred contempt even in the imperial capital. Kyōto was attacked by peasant protestors on numerous occasions, first in impromptu riots, and then in what appear to have been meticulously plotted uprisings. In one notable incident in 1457, armed peasants clashed with 800 mercenary samurai who had been hired to protect Kyōto moneylenders. Notably, the peasants won.

The hold of the Ashikaga shōgunate was slipping. Never as powerful as the Kamakura shōgunate, facing a country collapsing with each decade further into regionalism, the Ashikaga's claim on being the Emperor's chosen suppressor of troubles slowly wore away. It is perhaps unfair to call this a 'failure' of the Ashikaga – a system is hardly a failure if it endures for over a century – but the very nature of the Ashikaga shōgunate's foundation, in opposition to the Kamakura Bakufu, forever tied it closer to the weaker power base of the imperial capital. While the Ashikaga Shōguns enjoyed the courtly life, 'lesser' lords in the outlying regions enjoyed growing autonomy, over domains that were justifiably mistaken by foreign observers for small kingdoms in their own right. It was only a matter of time before some perceived slight or injustice provoked these lords into conflict. Should the Ashikaga fail to settle matters, their rule would be over.

Inevitably, war broke out once more, largely in a repeat of the standoff that began the Genpei War. Again, two rival houses, this time the Hosokawa and the Yamana, manoeuvred for control of capital politics. Again, they came to blows within the capital itself, in what is now known as the Ōnin War (1467–77, named after the year in which it broke out), a prolonged episode of urban conflict that saw much of Kyōto reduced to ashes. The first signs of trouble began as suspicious fires and disappearances. Men of both rival clans were seen fortifying their houses, replacing paper screens with wooden shutters, and laying on extra guardsmen and water pails to ward against fire.

After the first month of fighting, northern Kyōto was an ashen husk of burnt-out buildings. The capital was carved into tiny, petty strongpoints, barricaded at crossroads, with fighting raging from city block to city block. In fighting for control of the 'glorious city', the samurai had destroyed it, turning it, in the words of one heartbroken Ashikaga official, into 'the lair of foxes and wolves', a blasted heath picked over by darting birds:

The city thou knew
Is become a barren moor
With rising skylarks
And falling tears.[11]

The havoc of the Ōnin War was a fitting end to an era. For centuries, Kyōto had been the epitome of class, the courtly paradise to which the samurai had aspired. Now, after many false starts, they had destroyed it. Although Kyōto would be rebuilt, and would remain the residence of the emperors for many centuries to come, it had lost its allure to the samurai. Although the emperors remained officially in charge, their personal circumstances were straitened beyond all expectations. By 1500, when the retired 103rd Emperor Go-Tsuchimikado (r.1428–64) passed away, his court could not afford to bury him, and he lay 'in state' (in fact, in a storeroom) for a month. Nor could the court find the money to pay for his successor's coronation, which was delayed for twenty years. This was partly as a result of extremely low finances, and partly as a result of the other priorities for spending in the rebuilding of Kyōto. But also, one gets a sense that the court itself had given up on protocol in the sixteenth century, disheartened and heartbroken by the damage wrought by the samurai.

The Ashikaga shōgunate remained at least nominally in charge for another century, although after 1490 the

Muromachi Period gave way to a new name, the *Sengoku Jidai* (Age of the Country at War), for over a hundred years, up to 1603. The name seems deliberately intended by Japanese historians to evoke the 'Warring States' period in Chinese history, and some English-speaking historians do follow their lead in calling this the Warring States period of Japan. However, these are hardly states – local lords might have enjoyed sway over areas the size of European dukedoms, but the Emperor was still the nominal, distant authority, huddled in genteel poverty amid the blackened ruins of Kyōto as the capital slowly regained its footing.

There are two keywords for the Country at War period. One is *daimyō*, literally 'great names' – the new breed of local lords, each supreme in his own domain, constantly jockeying for position. The other is *gekokujō*, 'the low dominating the high' – a reference by many disinherited members of the old order to the rapid, brutal social mobility of the time. Japan entered one of its periodic purges of noble houses: once-great names sank with the declining fortunes of their families, and entire clans were wiped out. The emperor, of course, was powerless to intervene, and the shōgun unable to fulfil the conditions of his title. The country would not stabilize again until a single individual could gather together the fragmented clans and domains and unite them all, thereby allowing for the proclamation of a new shōgunate. The rise of such an individual would take a century, as the small clans fought and merged to form bigger clans, until eventually all Japan was split into only a handful of rival factions, fighting to determine who was the true ruler.

Two rival warlords, Uesugi Kenshin (1530–78) and Takeda Shingen (1521–73), entered in a dispute so formalized that their 'war' became more like an annual event. Their rival armies met at the river confluence of

Kawanakajima in 1553, 1554, 1555, 1556, 1557 and 1563, for camp-outs and fights that would sometimes last for weeks. This was no bloodless sports-meet like some of the battles of the rival Emperors' period – every occasion saw multiple deaths. But nor was it the relentless total war of other periods. Instead, it was a remarkably gentlemanly affair. The two warlords, both admirers of classical literature, gleefully referred to themselves as the 'dragon' and the 'tiger', two traditionally antagonistic martial beasts, and conduct on the battlefield was usually reminiscent of the most genteel encounters of old. On one occasion, when Takeda's supply of salt was cut off by the Hōjō clan, Uesugi sent supplies of his own, with the courteous comment that he fought with swords, not salt.

Their most famous encounter was at the fourth battle of Kawanakajima in 1556, where Uesugi's assault made it all the way to the command post of Takeda himself. Uesugi personally charged on his horse past the windbreak curtain and into the Takeda inner sanctum, his sword drawn. The shocked Takeda, not having time to grab a sword, held him off with his metal *tessen* (a general's fan usually used for signalling), until one of his spearmen stabbed Uesugi's horse. The two generals were dragged apart, and the battle raged on, but it is remembered today largely for the moment when the leaders of the two armies came directly to blows.

Such incidents were increasingly rare in the sixteenth century, as changes in military technology were altering the face of the battlefield once more. Foreign traders in the south of Japan had introduced the Japanese to the concept of the matchlock gun, and the new weapon had swiftly caught on. The samurai were not unfamiliar with gun-powder – they had, after all, suffered dearly from its use in the Mongol invasion – but the concept of a portable, light arquebus that could be carried by a single soldier was new to them. The first guns had arrived in the early 1540s on the island of Tanegashima, a remote outpost just off the south-west coast of Japan. There, Portuguese sailors had demonstrated their arquebuses to the enraptured local warlord, who ordered his master swordsmith to make as many copies as he could. The swordsmith was initially stumped by the technology required, but after legendarily selling his daughter to another set of Portuguese traders in exchange for further lessons, he was soon churning out reasonable facsimiles of the Portuguese guns. The Japanese began calling the weapons *tanegashima*, after the place of their 'discovery'.

Some samurai were aghast at the idea of the gun. An arquebus was expensive, it required fiddly maintenance and was useless without dry powder and spare musket balls. Nor was it as accurate as a trained archer. There were, undoubtedly, those who thought that the arquebus would come and go just as the fabled *ōyumi* had done in ancient times.

However, times had changed. Japanese smithing technology was more than adequate for making new arquebuses, and hence these new devices were not fated to slowly dwindle and fall apart. Moreover, while a musket was undoubtedly expensive to manufacture and difficult to maintain, it was a veritable bargain compared to the cost of training a skilled archer. Bows, too, required expert maintenance, and were nowhere near as durable. While it took years to train an archer to reach the best of his abilities, the merest peasant could be trained up to make the best of his arquebus within days. In the years since the Mongol conquest, the role of archers had diminished, but so too had that of swordsmen. Modern samurai armies still had mounted warriors among the officer class, as in days of old, but increasingly relied upon far greater numbers of footsoldiers (*ashigaru*). Samurai armour that has survived from this period often has a tell-tale dent in the metal breastplate, where the armourer has pronounced it fit for purpose by test-firing a gun directly at it.

Takeda Shingen, the crouching 'tiger' at perpetual war with the 'dragon' Uesugi, was at the front of the queue for the new weapons, purchasing 300 of them in the year before his one-on-one fight at Kawanakajima. By 1571, he was prepared to declare that arquebuses had forever altered the nature of warfare in Japan:

> Hereafter, guns will be the most important weapons. Therefore decrease the number of spears [in your armies] and have the most capable men carry guns. Furthermore, when you assemble your soldiers, test their marksmanship and order that the selection of [gunners] be in accordance with the results.[12]

However, Takeda Shingen was not to be the main beneficiary of firearms. In fact, according to one of the many stories surrounding his death, they may have even been responsible for his own early demise. Depending on who one believes, he died, aged forty-nine, either of disease in his camp, perished from an old war wound or was shot by a sniper. It was this most popular of the explanations that featured as part of Kurosawa Akira's film *Kagemusha* (1980), which drew its inspiration from the last days of Takeda's life, and apocryphal musings about his clan's actions in the aftermath.

Despite his rapid rise to prominence, Takeda was himself defeated by the underlings of a warlord destined for superior greatness. Oda Nobunaga (1534–82) had had a wayward youth, born to a small landholder in Owari province, and growing up with a reputation for erratic behaviour. Nobunaga (he is usually written of in history books with his first name, not his surname) even gained the nickname of 'the Fool of Owari', with erratic behaviour that reached its peak at his father's funeral. Supposedly, the anguished Nobunaga picked up the incense tray and hurled it at the altar – an act of such great impropriety that one of his father's retainers saw fit to chastise him by committing *seppuku*. However, before long the young warlord had righted his errant ways. Nobunaga was a huge fan of the new *tanegashima* weapons, and soon put them to use in a meteoric rise to power.

He was aided in his ascent by a man of even lowlier origin. Toyotomi Hideyoshi (1536–98) had been born into a peasant family, sent away to a monastery by his parents, but absconded and joined a samurai army as a footsoldier. Stealing enough money to buy himself a suit of armour, he soon turned up in Nobunaga's army, again as a footsoldier, but swiftly rose through the ranks.

Nobunaga's first great military achievement was the Battle of Okehazama in 1560, when he faced an oncoming army led by the warlord Imagawa Yoshimoto. Greatly outnumbered, Nobunaga rejected the suggestion that he should fortify a local temple and wait his besiegers out in the style of the legendary Kusunoki. Such tactics might have worked in the days of the Southern and Northern Courts, but in the time of the Country at War, Nobunaga evaluated his chances of holding out for more than a week as slim at best. Instead he gave the impression that he had fortified the temple by planting large numbers of banners around it. Leaving only a skeleton crew to man this 'main camp', he then led the bulk of his forces, some 1,500 men, in a sneak attack on the Imagawa camp.

The Imagawa samurai had not expected any trouble, and

were passing the early summer day with celebrations of their recent advances. There was drinking and dancing, which was only quelled by the onset of a sudden, severe rainstorm. The Imagawa samurai took their celebrations indoors, unaware that Nobunaga's men were sneaking up during the storm. As the rain let up, Nobunaga unleashed his attack – so close to the camp and with such surprise that many of the Imagawa did not even notice. Many, including Imagawa himself, assumed that the shouts and screams and occasional gunshots were the noise of renewed, exuberant celebration. It was only when Imagawa himself, tiring of the noise, came out of his tent to order his men to keep it down, that he found himself facing not a party, but an attack.

Even then, he seems to have been caught unawares. Two samurai rushed towards him, and Imagawa seems to have barely registered that they were intent on killing him. He feebly batted away the first, and lost his head to the second. Nobunaga's assault had been brilliantly targeted. By luck or judgement, the main force of his attack had fallen on the Imagawa command post, and killed almost all of the enemy officers. The remaining samurai, leaderless, soon surrendered. Or rather, they joined Nobunaga's own army, one leader being very much like another in this period.

One of the turncoats who signed up with Nobunaga was a man who would eventually be known as Tokugawa Ieyasu (1543–1616). He became a powerful ally of Nobunaga through the 1560s and 1570s, and would form and break alliances not only with Takeda, but also with Takeda's sworn enemy Uesugi, amongst many others.

Nobunaga coveted an official appointment for himself, and associated himself with the dying embers of the Ashikaga Shōgunate. In 1568, he allied himself with Yoshiaki, younger brother to the murdered thirteenth Ashikaga

Shōgun, and entered Kyōto in support of Yoshiaki's counter-attack against his murderous cousin, another Ashikaga. Needless to say, while Ashikaga Yoshiaki may have been restored to power, he had little to do beyond the completion of ceremonial functions. Like the emperors before them, the Ashikaga shōguns were now little more than puppets, and Yoshiaki would be the last of their line. Although Yoshiaki did not officially resign his post until 1588, the Ashikaga shōgunate was effectively dead by 1573. Nor did Nobunaga suffer any rivals within Kyōto, declaring war on the vast Buddhist temple complexes that ringed the city, and putting many of the warrior monks who might have otherwise opposed him to the sword.

It was the beginning of a new era in more ways than one. In terms of Japanese history, Nobunaga's entry into Kyōto marks the official end of the Muromachi era and the onset of the brief Azuchi-Momoyama Period, named after the location of the castles of Nobunaga and his successor Hideyoshi, and for their dominance of Japanese politics from 1568 to 1603. The period also saw the arquebus achieve true dominance on the battlefield, most notably at the Battle of Nagashino in 1575, when Nobunaga and his ally Tokugawa Ieyasu rushed to the aid of a supporter besieged by the son of Takeda Shingen. Expecting a cavalry charge from Takeda's men, Nobunaga set up a wooden stockade on the top of a small ridge. Or rather, he set up several overlapping stockades, with paths through them that would allow his own men to dart in and out should the need be required, but would force any attacking cavalry into a path through the obstacles that left them exposed to gunfire. Nobunaga heavily outnumbered the Takeda forces, but crucially had almost as many gunmen as Takeda had horsemen. He also had them organized so that they would fire in shifts, with one group reloading as the other took aim.

It was a hot, damp June day, and Takeda reasonably assumed that his cavalry would be at an advantage, and that many of Nobunaga's gunners would find that their powder was wet. His horsemen approached the shallow stream that divided their forces, with Nobunaga's men ominously silent behind their stockade. Takeda assumed that this meant his prediction was correct, but he was much mistaken. In fact, Nobunaga's men had carefully kept their powder dry, and were simply waiting until Takeda's men were at a range where bullets could reasonably be expected to penetrate their armour.

Takeda Shingen's prediction about the future of guns on the battlefield came true with devastating force. Despite the continuing pitfalls of arquebuses – poor aiming, occasional unreliability and long reloading times – the sheer numbers of Nobunaga's gunners, and the efficient marshalling of three alternating lines, soon put an end to the Takeda cavalry, which was decimated by a continuous succession of volley after volley of lead.

The year after his victory at Nagashino, Nobunaga commenced work on his new home, Azuchi Castle outside Kyōto, near Lake Biwa.It was a fortress with a new method of construction that seemed to recognize changes in both technology and power. This was no temporary stockade like the strongpoints of old – Nobunaga clearly intended to use his castle as an impregnable, long-term residence, as a place of both repose and respite, but also of powerful defensive properties on the approach into Kyōto.

Azuchi Castle was deliberately placed out of sight of Kyōto itself, away from the periodic threats of city fires. Eschewing the usual practice of locating fortresses at the base of a mountain, Nobunaga built Azuchi on a broad plain, affording ample sight of any approaching enemies. The central keep had a tall watchtower, unusual for the time, but ideal for both observing the approach of others, and for affording a better range with firearms. The castle walls were made of stone, another rarity, and were around twenty feet thick, sure to hold off an assault made by contemporary samurai armed with *tanegashima* firearms.

All these aspects served to mark an over-arching assumption on Nobunaga's part, that while there might still be trouble ahead, the nature of conflict had progressed from the small- and medium-sized skirmishes of the preceding century. Azuchi seemed to have been built as a prediction that the last act would be just as bloodthirsty, and involve participants dug in for the long haul, fighting to preserve ever-larger domains, with a new emphasis on castle towns. Nobunaga was right in all these predictions, although he would not live to see them come to fruition.

His unexpected nemesis was one of his own generals Akechi Mitsuhide (1528–82), who had fought loyally for Nobunaga's armies in the past. The precise reason for Akechi's grievance remains a matter of debate among Japanese historians. There are stories that Nobunaga was a cruel and vindictive superior, who would taunt and tease Akechi, and once even grabbed him in a headlock and drummed on his head. Such an anecdote points to other injustices – Akechi seems to have been annoyed at his constant reassignment from one domain to another, and that he was aggrieved that Nobunaga would exclude him from certain councils of war. It is widely understood that he had been nursing a grudge ever since Nobunaga had executed prisoners to whom Akechi had personally guaranteed safety. Such reversals were not uncommon in samurai warfare, but Nobunaga's purge had inconveniently left several relatives of the victims alive, and in time they had carried out their revenge by murdering members of

Akechi's own family. In later generations, when the story was retold in plays and novels, all these various incidents were combined, and Akechi was given a predictable rationale – that of 'loyalty' to a higher power. Nobunaga, it was claimed, had committed gross acts of hubris by attacking Buddhist monasteries and committing 'atrocity after atrocity'. As his most prominent English-language biographer observes, his achievement was 'different in scope, though not in kind' from that of his competitors.[13]

Whatever the cause, Akechi had his reasons. In 1582, Akechi was ordered to proceed with his army to reinforce another of Nobunaga's generals, Hideyoshi, who was laying siege to one of Nobunaga's few remaining enemies. Instead, Akechi announced: 'The enemy is in Honnō-ji', referring to a Kyōto temple where Nobunaga was currently quartered. Akechi's forces took Honnō-ji in a surprise attack and Nobunaga, supposedly already wounded with an arrow, committed suicide in the burning buildings. His body was never found.

Akechi's act was soon punished. Hideyoshi and To-kugawa Ieyasu, suspiciously absent at the time of his attack, were soon out for revenge. Even as Akechi's men hunted down and slew Nobunaga's relatives in Kyōto, Hideyoshi was already on his way, having suddenly made peace with his rivals and departed for Kyōto. Traditionally, it is understood that Hideyoshi received a secret communiqué informing him of Nobunaga's death. The more suspiciously minded might instead speculate that the 'secret communiqué' arrived before the attack on Honnō-ji, and that Akechi either hoped or already believed that Hideyoshi would be a co-conspirator.[14]

Instead, Hideyoshi attacked Akechi's forces just outside Kyōto. Akechi fled the battlefield by wading through the rice paddies, but was set upon by peasant looters and

murdered for whatever he had on him. His 'reign' as Nobunaga's successor had not even lasted a fortnight, and he
would sometimes be known disparagingly as the 'Thirteen-
Day Shōgun'.

It was Hideyoshi who reaped all the rewards. Being of
such humble birth that he did not even have a family crest,
Hideyoshi adopted the gourd as his personal symbol. The
image was a reference to an incident from his younger days,
when in 1567 the thirty-one-year-old Hideyoshi had scaled
the walls of a castle at Inabayama, and signalled his ascent
to Nobunaga's army by waving a gourd from the summit.
For this climbing feat, or perhaps his allegedly simian countenance, he gained the nickname 'Little Monkey' (*kozaru*),
but also the notice of Nobunaga. The gourd was hence a
symbol not only of Hideyoshi's long service to Nobunaga,
but of his humble origins and practical military experience.
In later life, Hideyoshi's standard would be a massive,
golden gourd up-ended on a pole. He would add another
smaller gourd for each of his victories, until his standard
gained the nickname of the 'Thousand-Gourd Tree' (*Sen-
naribyōtan*).

Hideyoshi's campaign against the enemies of Nobunaga
did not end with the death of Akechi. It encompassed any
of Akechi's allies, any remaining adversaries and any
members of Nobunaga's family who did not accept that
Hideyoshi was now in charge. Tokugawa Ieyasu briefly
opposed him, before accepting Hideyoshi as his master.
Through battle, betrayal and treaty, Hideyoshi had united
all of Japan. Nobunaga had managed perhaps a third of the
task, but Hideyoshi built on his predecessor's achievements
to become the military master of the entire country.

Hideyoshi would not, however, be shōgun. Instead he
was adopted into the ancient Fujiwara clan and 'accepted'
the post of imperial regent (*kampaku*) from the Emperor in

1585, along with the Toyotomi surname, which gave him noble status. As the 1580s proceeded, Hideyoshi continued to consolidate his unprecedented position as the military master of all Japan. Firearms had proved to be a magical catalyst in unifying the country. But for it to stay unified, Hideyoshi would need to kick away the various 'ladders' that had permitted people like himself to make such a rapid ascent. He would need to take dangerous weapons out of the hands of a large proportion of the Japanese population, send the farmers back to their fields, and find a way to keep the samurai occupied without fighting each other. He also saw it as his duty to scrub a new threat from Japanese shores before the rhetoric of loyalty to a 'higher purpose' took on a troublesome, foreign taint.

7

THE FAR WEST
EUROPEAN CONTACTS AND THE KOREAN CRUSADE

Guns were not the only thing that had arrived from the West. First the Portuguese, then the Spanish and then the Italians sent Christian missionaries, determined to spread the Bible to the Japanese. Exotic and alien, Christian belief achieved virulent proportions in Japan, with such large number of converts that Japan effectively became the largest non-European diocese in the world by the end of the sixteenth century.

The rise and fall of the missionaries during the period 1549–1650 is often known as 'Japan's Christian Century', a problematic term.[1] In the south-west, in particular on the island of Kyūshū, there was a strong upwelling of interest, particularly after missionary orders stopped targeting the poor, sick and needy, and adopted the Buddhists' strategy of preaching to the upper classes, in the hope that their subjects would follow their lead. This led to a couple of generations of Japanese nobility with Christian names, as converts adopted baptismal names from the distant West – amongs others, we see a Dario Sō in the ruling clan of Tsushima, a lord André of Arima, and the zealous lord Bartholomew of Ōmura, who briefly granted Jesuit missionaries authority over the harbour town of Nagasaki.

Sometimes these conversions were genuinely devout, such that missionaries pronounced Japan as the most fertile ground in the world for seeding the Gospel. On other occasions, it was more pragmatic, with local lords accepting baptism in the hope that it would also bring European traders, guns and technology into their realms. Japan undoubtedly gained Christian believers of outstanding devotion, as shown by the many martyrdoms of the seventeenth century, but also many half-hearted 'converts' created by lordly fiat. In other parts of Japan, Christianity flourished in accordance with other foreign fads. Hideyoshi himself was once spotted wearing a crucifix, not as a sign of his belief, but as a fashion accessory.

The first Christian missionaries were mistaken for emissaries from yet another Buddhist sect. The guns they supplied, however, made the likes of Hideyoshi worry about the power that Europeans might be able to unleash. Strangely for a nation reared on reincarnation and noble suicide, Japanese non-Christians also reacted badly to the notion of a heavenly paradise, regarding it as an empty promise sure to sway believers into selfless acts. Selfless acts were all very well when pursued in the name of Hideyoshi or the Emperor, but the concept of the Pope was harder for the samurai to swallow. The translation into Japanese presented the Pope as a distant God-King with uneasy similarities to the meddling Retired Emperors of old – he had no official, temporal power, but still out-ranked kings and emperors; he was a humble priest, but was able to sway armies. In short, he came to be regarded as something of a threat: missionary preaching about the Bishop of Rome started to make the Pope sound like a new force in Japan's volatile political mix – an alien potentate from the same place that had provided Nobunaga with the regime-changing, enemy-toppling *tanegashima* firearms.

Signs of Hideyoshi's consolidation of power can be seen in several edicts of the 1580s. In 1587 he decreed that Christian missionaries were no longer welcome in Kyūshū – a deliberate attempt to prevent the Jesuits in particular from meddling in local politics by providing arms to local lords. Another edict, in 1590, organized a census and forbade resettlement without prior permission. It effectively hunted down any newcomers in Japanese villagers and forced them to return to their hometowns, and was the first true example of the martial law of the samurai being applied in a time of peace. In the decades that followed, Hideyoshi's successors would refine this localized rule of law until Japan was an impregnable police state.

The census came on the heels of another edict that called for a *katanagari*, literally 'sword hunt', to ensure that only samurai and approved personnel possessed swords. This covered not only swords, but also axes, spears and many types of knife. Hideyoshi's sword hunt was not the first, by any means. There had been several by previous rulers, with the most recent being declared by Nobunaga only a few years earlier. But Hideyoshi's decree served multiple purposes. Its alleged purpose was the acquisition of sufficient quantities of metal to make a massive statue of Buddha. However, the statue project required nowhere near the amount of metal collected. Instead, it helpfully disarmed potentially fractious peasantry as well as monks, and represented the first steps of a separation of samurai and subject that would come to fruition over the next two generations. It also concentrated thousands of confiscated weapons in the arms of the authorities, shortly before Hideyoshi announced his next great enterprise – he intended to invade China.

Considering his successes in Japan, he believed such a gargantuan venture to be easily within his grasp, and indeed, so he claimed, as easy as 'for a mountain to crush an egg'. Announcements of his plan were sent to neighbouring countries (although notably not China), accompanied by demands for nearby countries to pledge homage to him. The Ryūkyū Islands acknowledged his rule and sent a gift. Hideyoshi's envoy to the Philippines, however, met with a different response, as he diplomatically neglected to translate the most demanding passages of the letter. Consequently, the baffled Spaniards sent a 'gift' of their own – a globe of the Earth clearly marking the vast immensities of the Spanish empire, and making Japan's peripheral position abundantly obvious. Such subtleties were lost on Hideyoshi, after his underlings had carefully rephrased the Spanish reply in the obeisant manner of a cowering envoy. Similar confusion attended the proclamation of the Italian Jesuit priest Alessandro Valignano from India, which Hideyoshi was allowed to misconstrue as a pledge of fealty from the entire sub-continent.

Meanwhile, the King of the Ryūkyū Islands, now a vassal of both China and Japan, secretly forwarded Hideyoshi's letters to the Chinese Emperor. It was the first that the Chinese had heard of it, and immediately caused them to question why the Koreans had not brought it up themselves. The Koreans, in fact, were frantically trying to ameliorate Hideyoshi's plan, as they had already worked out that any conflict between China and Japan was sure to be fought largely in Korea.

Hideyoshi's brusque demand that the Koreans pay him homage lost a little in translation. This was largely down to Sō Yoshishige, whose clan ruled Tsushima, and through whose hands the message passed en route. Sitting at the midpoint of the strait between Japan and Korea, Tsushima had long profited from its position as the gateway between the two cultures. The Sō clan enjoyed an official monopoly on trade, and cannot have wanted to see a massive mobilization that was sure to put ships and sea-routes in the hands of lesser clans – such as the upstart Matsuura clan of Hirado, long suspected of smuggling and piracy in the strait that undermined the Sō's dominion. Furthermore, the Sō were far more familiar with the power and strength of the Koreans – the Sō emissaries toned down the belligerent rhetoric, softening Hideyoshi's demand for 'tribute' to a suggestion of a 'goodwill mission'. Such subtle diplomacies bore little fruit when the Sō decided to distance themselves and send someone expendable. Unfortunately, they also sent someone very rude – a brusque, middle-aged samurai from the Tachibana clan who demanded five-star treatment everywhere he went and repeatedly lampooned the Koreans' short stature. Despite all the prevarication, Hideyoshi's letter shocked the Koreans with its arrogance – using a personal pronoun reserved only for emperors. Nor were they impressed with the inference that Hideyoshi was the 'King' of Japan, since that rather implied that he had killed his predecessor, and that the Japanese Emperor was of no consequence. When the embassy was sent home empty-handed, a furious Hideyoshi executed the rude ambassador and removed Sō Yoshishige from office. His replacement Dario Sō, was soon back in Korea with a second letter, in which Hideyoshi boasted that he had been conceived by a beam of divine radiance, and that a fortune teller had prophesied that he would rule the world. With this in mind, he intended to invade China; he would go there through Korean, and he hereby invited the Koreans to join forces and share the spoils.[2]

Caught very much in the middle, Dario Sō may have even tried to send a signal to the Koreans when he presented them with some arquebuses. Although the Koreans were familiar with cannon, they had never seen such readily portable firearms. If Sō had hoped thereby to inform them of what kind of weaponry the Japanese had to hand, his hint fell on deaf ears.

A return Korean 'goodwill mission', pointedly ignoring much of Hideyoshi's bluster, only made matters worse. Heads literally rolled on Tsushima when the Korean nobles stopped off en route and found Dario Sō's hospitality wanting. They already had him pegged as 'young and fierce', and rightly regarded him as perhaps the best of an extremely hot-headed bunch of warlike neighbours. Ironically, the Koreans' reaction to their audience with Hideyoshi was not that dissimilar to the shocked disapproval of Kyōto courtiers at the first appearance of samurai in their midst. Kept waiting for four tense months, the Koreans were eventually admitted to an audience where, instead of providing a lavish banquet as protocol demands, Hideyoshi merely passed around some rice cakes and a communal bowl of *sake*. He then reappeared in everyday clothes, cradling his infant son, who helped proceedings not a jot by choosing that moment to urinate on him.

The Koreans were left with the misleading impression that Hideyoshi was a buffoon who posed no threat at all, while Hideyoshi may never have realized that they had not actually offered him the 'homage' he had demanded. Inevitably, as the months of embassies, letters and replies wore on, the subject of the Mongol invasions came up, along with the baffling assertion that an invasion of China would be Hideyoshi's tardy revenge. As ever, the Koreans found this all ludicrous – they were vassals of the Ming Emperor, whose ancestors had famously cast the Mongols out of China in the fourteenth century. Hideyoshi was hence 'avenging' himself on an entirely different regime. Eventually, an honest Korean reply called his idea 'the most reckless, imprudent and daring of any which we have ever heard'; it also reasserted Korea's loyal vassal status towards China, although by this time the Chinese Emperor was already wondering why he had not been informed of Hideyoshi's plot.[3]

Dario Sō evacuated his clan's compound in the Korean harbour town of Pusan in early 1592, sure that war was now inevitable. Yet again, Kyūshū was the site of major operations. The main point for embarkation was the port now known as Karatsu, eight hours' sail from Tsushima, from which it was only another six hours to Korea itself.[4] Hideyoshi's loyal underling Katō Kiyomasa put thousands of conscript labourers to work on a massive double-moated, walled fortress.

Hideyoshi's recruitment recognized that contribution to the war effort was cheaper for Kyūshū-based rulers than for rulers coming from farther afield. Hence, the bulk (52 per cent) of the manpower for the army and the labourers that supported it was drawn from Kyūshū itself. Obligations thinned out the further east one went from Kyūshū, with fiefs supplying either less men and matériel, or in the case of Hideyoshi's greatest allies, none at all thanks to special incentives. By luck or by design, this created a massive military force, partly comprising many of Hideyoshi's former enemies, pointed at a foreign target. The total nationwide mobilization for the Korean invasion project was 335,000 men, although only 158,800 of them were intended for Korea.

Hideyoshi's strategy reflected his years of local combat experience. Of the nine 'Korean' regiments, the first three were almost entirely Kyūshū men, and would spearhead the assault and rush north for Seoul as swiftly as possible, armed with colour-coded maps that reduced Korea's eight internal provinces to a deadly rainbow of objectives. Regiments four to seven would follow behind at a more leisurely pace.

Hideyoshi's plan allowed for a Chinese/Korean counter-attack. His eighth and ninth divisions were to be held in reserve on Japanese soil, and were not intended to go any further than Tsushima, where they would be moved by the transport fleet when logistics allowed. A further 75,000 men, not counted among the Korean numbers at all, comprised soldiers from Hideyoshi's allies in the north and east, who would be posted to Kyūshū for defensive purposes only.

Hideyoshi was playing a long game. As in his conquest of Japan, he kept the newest vassals in the front line to take the brunt of the damage. He intended, when Korea was pacified, to use Korean troops against Beijing, and when Beijing was his, to recruit the Chinese against southern China. He still hoped, as late as April 1592, to receive a message from Dario Sō that the Koreans had relented, agreed to join Hideyoshi's putative China campaign, and hence removed the need for his arrival in Korea to end in bloodshed.

When Hideyoshi ran out of patience, he gave the order to attack. Carried on horseback by messengers, it flew far ahead of him, as he began a leisurely journey in its wake, part of a long train of retainers and servants, accompanied by pomp, ceremony and sixty-six banners, one for each of the Japanese provinces he ruled.

The leaders of the three landing regiments were all young, enthusiastic samurai. Katō Kiyomasa (1562–1611) was a distant cousin of Hideyoshi who had been blooded as a teenager. He had risen rapidly from a glorified lord of the manor in 1576 to the lordship of Kumamoto Castle by 1580, with suzerainty over half the province and a samurai complement in the thousands. Half of his regiment comprised his own men; the rest were troops provided by two neighbouring lords. Katō was eccentric, even by samurai standards – in battle his helmet was a three-foot-high metallic hat, like a shark's fin. Rare for the Japanese, he also favoured wild and piratic facial hair, claiming that his beard helped cushion the rubbing of his helmet straps. Katō was a staunch Buddhist of the Nichiren sect and led an army that largely comprised fellow Buddhists. Despite his youth – he was only thirty at the time of the invasion – he was a notorious martial purist, and had no time for the niceties of poetry, fine foods or clothes. Katō was early to rise at 4 a.m., practised with horse, sword and bow every day without fail, and shunned any form of 'hobby' unless it was a wholesome outdoor pursuit or transferable skill like falconry, deer hunting or wrestling. He reserved particular ire for theatres and dances, and recommended that any samurai 'who practises dancing – which is outside of the martial arts – should be ordered to commit *seppuku*'.[5]

Hence, Katō was sure to disapprove in all sorts of ways of his fellow generals. The twenty-four-year-old Damian Kuroda (1568–1623) was, as his name implied, a Christian.[6] He was also a cultured member of the gentry, proud of his ability in poetry and unafraid of championing the need for a true samurai to master not only the martial arts, but also management, empathy and protocol. His father Simeon Kuroda had been a Christian convert and strategist within Hideyoshi's army. Damian had first donned armour at the tender age of nine and hence was an experienced samurai despite his young years. He had been appointed as the lord of the Fukuoka region of Kyūshū only three years earlier, after his father fell out of favour with Hideyoshi. Simeon had renounced his Christian faith; Damian, however, had retained his religion, which only heightened tensions between him and Katō.

It is the third of Hideyoshi's front-line commanders, however, that interests us the most. Augustin Konishi Yukinaga (1558–1600) was a merchant's son who had risen swiftly through the ranks. He had been among the besiegers of Ōta Castle in 1581, and is listed as a commander of the *suigun* – the 'marines' or waterborne commandos. This put him in the thick of the fighting around the increasingly waterlogged castle, particularly during enemy counter-attacks. As a young samurai in the invasion of Kyūshū he had won crucial victories for Hideyoshi, for which he was rewarded at the age of thirty with a fief of his own, largely comprising the Amakusa archipelago, stretching to the west from his mainland residence, Udo Castle.[7]

Konishi was also a Christian. His parents had been baptised in 1560, making them early adopters of the religion as it swept through the upper classes of western Japan. Konishi himself was not baptised until 1583, and does not seem to have internalized many Bible teachings in his younger days – his behaviour towards his foes, for example, does not display any remarkable difference from that of his non-Christian colleagues. However, unlike more easterly gentry, who may have regarded Christianity as little more than a fad or fashion, Konishi had both family connections and local contacts. He had strong connections to the Sō clan that ruled Tsushima, as his daughter Maria was married to Dario Sō. His regiment was a veritable army of crusaders, as shown by the number of baptismal names among the commanders. Augustin brought 7,000 men from the Amakusa region. His son-in-law Dario Sō commanded another 5,000 from Tsushima. Protasio Arima, the ruler of the Shimabara peninsula that sat at the far end of Konishi's realm, arrived with another 2,000 samurai. Sancho Ōmura, whose father Bartholomew had been the very first lord to accept baptism, led another 1,000 men, alongside non-Christian rulers from other parts of Kyūshū. In fact, only one commander in Augustin Konishi's regiment was not a Christian convert – Matsuura Shigenobu from the seafaring coastal domain of Hirado.[8]

Many of the soldiers led by these commanders were Christians themselves; some merely by fiat, converted en masse at the order of their lord, others by genuine belief. A cynic might suspect that this was what Hideyoshi was hoping, and that the Korean invasion was designed to funnel an entire generation of young, unwanted samurai, many with unwelcome connections to the foreign mission-aries, into a campaign that took them out of Japan.

It is, however, unfair to credit Hideyoshi with quite so much deviousness. One did not need to be an evil schemer to see that the Korean invasion was a natural progression from the unification of Japan. The conquest of Kyūshū, it was hoped, was the final culmination of centuries of squabbling among the Japanese, dating back to the Genpei War, and further back to the pacification of the north. But with Japan now supposedly at peace, and with all lands and fiefs assigned, the samurai engine continued to run. Far from wishing his vassals a quick death on the Korean frontier, it is more likely that Hideyoshi hoped they would win new victories, and carve out new lands for themselves that kept them occupied away from the Japanese heartland. The alternative would be to turn against each other, and repeat the cycle of vendettas and skirmishes once more.[9]

The invasion force did not just have foreign-influenced

beliefs. They also bore foreign-influenced technology. Horses and bows, those ancient symbols of the samurai lifestyle were often only seen among the officers. Arguably, the bulk of the army did not comprise 'samurai' at all, but rather their lower-class adversaries, the *ashigaru* footsoldiers. These men could be armed with swords or spears, but most wielded arquebuses – the terrifying *tanegashima* firearms that had proved to be so instrumental at Nagashino.

Factionalism at the Korean court left the defenders only half-prepared. The highest-ranking officers were kept in Seoul at the King's pleasure when they could have been acquainting themselves with the future battlefields of the south. Many commissions were political, and hence did not reflect actual military talents. A new policy invited recommendations for promotion on merit, but came too late for many participants in the opening skirmish.

Even when it was understood that the Japanese were on their way, Korean preparation reflected a distinct lack of appreciation of how far the Japanese had come technologically. In many ways, the Koreans were equipped after a fashion that would have been familiar to the Japanese of the seventh century. They wielded straight, double-edged swords or long spears. Their bows utilized an innovative 'firing tube' that allowed smaller, lighter arrows to be discharged, and hence increased their range. However, the devices were fiddly and required long periods of training. Korean firearms were limited to old-fashioned Chinese cannons and mortars – devastating but in short supply. Their Japanese opponents were backed by thousands of footsoldiers wielding portable muskets that required minimal training.

Pusan, on the south-west tip of Korea, was known to be the most likely point of contact. A countryside signal-fire system supposedly made it possible to appraise Seoul of any events within four hours, but the intermediate beacons were often left untended on their remote mountaintops. On the morning of 23 May 1592, the commander of the Pusan garrison was out hunting deer when he saw the shadows of the vast armada looming out of the thick sea mist. One of the few functioning beacons (manned because it was a lighthouse) soon confirmed his suspicions.

Ironically, the Koreans had 150 warships, which could have made short work of many of the Japanese transport vessels, as they were poorly protected. There were admittedly some reinforced boats among the Japanese armada that were designed as floating forts, but Hideyoshi's fleet was arriving without the Portuguese warships that he had rashly assumed might be provided by his foreign allies. Nor was it accompanied by the dozens of purpose-built warships that Hideyoshi had earmarked for protection. Rather than wait for these vessels to sail up from the Inland Sea, Augustin Konishi had gambled that his landing would take the Koreans by surprise before they could mount a proper defence.

He was right. Instead of launching an immediate attack, the Korean commanders merely filed their reports and waited for orders to come back down the line of beacons – the original estimate of '90 ships' approaching soon climbing into the hundreds, and showing no sign of letting up even by sunset.

It was, then, hardly a 'surprise' attack. The Japanese ships waited at anchor until just before dawn the next day, when the assault began in earnest. Dario Sō led the attack on Pusan, sloshing ashore at the head of a group of Tsushima samurai – pointedly not the musket-wielding footsoldiers, but old fashioned men with swords. Sō was in the vanguard because the territory was known to him. He had visited

Pusan many times as a trader, and knew the town layout well enough. He led his forces straight for Pusan Castle while Augustin Konishi's men struck out along the coast towards a fort at a nearby rivermouth. They carried a huge stuffed bag on a pole as a banner – a reference to Konishi's pharmacist father – and several large crucifixes.

Dario Sō gave his erstwhile trading partners one last chance, yelling at the defenders of Pusan Castle that if they joined the planned attack on China, there would be no need for them to fight. When they refused, he launched his attack on the fortress, letting loose the footsoldiers and their firearms. The pre-attack parley, it seems, was merely cosmetic by this point. In the massacre that followed, wave after wave of footsoldiers attacked with deadly salvos of musket balls, and swordsmen waded through the dwellings within the castle walls killing men, women and children, 'and even dogs and cats'. The raiders reported that their human victims begged repeatedly for mercy in a language that they assumed to be Chinese. As far as many of the lower-ranking soldiers were concerned, the attack on 'China' had already begun. One wonders how many of the soldiers appreciated how many miles away their ultimate objective was.[10]

The landing forces took Pusan with minimal casualties, despite the bloodbath among the enemy. Augustin Konishi experienced similar successes at his objective. Meanwhile, to the east, the commander of a coastal fortress fled to the north, pausing only to scuttle his ships. A second Korean admiral, seeing the smoke in the distance, also began scuttling his fleet, only to be reminded that he would be executed if he retreated. He therefore resolved to make a stand, even though he had just destroyed all but four of the ships that might have turned the tide of the battle.

Tactically, the Japanese generals had scored a textbook victory. Strategically, they were pig-headed and fiercely competitive. With Hideyoshi, their commander-in-chief, still dawdling through his Japanese domains towards the coast, there was no overlord to rein in their excesses. According to their orders, Augustin Konishi was supposed to fortify his beachhead, send word of his success back across the strait, and await the arrival of Katō's second wave. Instead, he lingered for barely a day before striking out north, determined to race Katō to Seoul.

When Katō Kiyomasa finally waded ashore on 28 May, delayed by unfavourable winds, he discovered that his Christian rivals were already on the march. This made him almost as angry as the Koreans, and he immediately set out on a second road, also with the ultimate aim of reaching Seoul. Damian Kuroda was not far behind, landing west of Pusan. After delaying only to take a small fort and execute its defenders, Kuroda set off on the northward route that he had been assigned.

By the time the disabled beacon system had ground into action and properly reported the Japanese invasion four days later, the three racing samurai armies had already covered a quarter of the 450 kilometres that separated Seoul from Pusan. Augustin Konishi, taking the straightest route, found towns deserted or token resistance at strategic strongpoints. But even these brave stands soon collapsed before the onslaught of the arquebuses.

Back in Seoul, the Korean defence finally got underway. By virtue of the heavily mountainous terrain, the Koreans knew that there were only three major routes to Seoul. Each of the generals was taking one of the routes, largely in order to ease the logistics of keeping an entire regiment supplied. This meant that the Koreans could at least predict the towns through which the samurai were sure to pass.

Augustin Konishi next met resistance on 3 June, when he ran into General Yi Il, an optimistic warrior who had hastily augmented his small cavalry force with a band of some 900 peasant conscripts. Scandalously, Yi Il had executed a messenger for daring to suggest that the Japanese had already made it halfway to Seoul. On realizing that he had been telling the truth, a more contrite Yi Il waited on horseback at the front of his men, proudly holding his banner on a hillside. If he had been expecting some sort of ritualized combat, with announcing of names and escalating duels, Yi Il was in for a surprise. The first he knew of the Japanese approach was when one of his scouts suddenly tumbled from his horse, the sound of a gunshot slapping through the air a millisecond behind. Konishi's forces materialized from out of the forest gloom, and then began to advance slowly on Yi Il's forces.

At only a hundred paces, Konishi's musketeers opened up in a phased series of volleys that allowed one platoon to reload as the next continued to advance and fire. Fifty paces further, and Yi Il's men were dying all around him. The untrained peasantry, unused to the brutal attrition of battle, turned and ran. So too did Yi Il, who eventually turned up, armourless and on foot, at the next defence point, where he reported the hopelessness of the situation to his colleage, General Sin Ip.

Sin Ip responded with a suicidal move. He chose to wait for Konishi on a plain beside the South Han River near Chungju, with the hill of Tangumdae to his right. The location left no possibility of retreat, although it has been presumed by generations of scholars that Sin Ip was well aware of this, and chose to give his men no opportunity to flee in order to ensure that sheer desperation forced them to make a stand.[11]

By this time, Katō and Konishi had met on the road, in a tense reunion. Incensed that Konishi had disobeyed orders, Katō announced that *he* would be the first man into

Seoul. Refusing to recognize Katō as his superior, Konishi announced that *he* would be first. Hearing of Sin Ip's stand at the river, Katō decided to let the hot-headed Konishi have his day, and waved him on in the hope that Sin Ip would teach him a lesson.

The Battle of Chungju was a dismal rehash of the defeat of Yi Il. Konishi's arrival presented a terrifying sight – he had deliberately spread out his forces thinly, so that the appearance along the ridges of so many banners made the defenders assume that there were many more unseen soldiers. Japanese guns made short work of the Korean footsoldiers, but Sin Ip, who had carefully chosen flat ground where he could use his horses, led his cavalry in a brave charge straight at the Japanese lines. The arquebuses, however, were just as good against mounted men, and the charge of the Korean knights never reached the Japanese front lines.

In the wake of the Battle of Chungju, Konishi's Christian soldiers collected 3,000 heads. They were lined up for inspection, as was traditional, but the samurai had already realized that they had more pressing priorities for their porters than carrying so many heads home. Furthermore, they expected to be taking many more heads at many more battles. In Korea, with lines already stretched to their limit, horses in shorter supply, and logistics more worried about bare essentials like food and ammunition, samurai found the old-fashioned head-count method of assessing their battle prowess to be out of date. Instead, once the enemy heads had been confirmed as those of enemy soldiers, the noses were hacked off and sent back to the rear pickled in barrels. From June 1592 onwards, many more thousands of Korean noses were brought back to Japan where, all tallies made, they were eventually shovelled into a pile in an obscure corner of Kyōto and covered with earth. Now known, in misguided euphemism, as *Mimizuka* (literally, 'the Hill of Ears'), the grisly memorial to the Korean wars is still to be found just to the east of the Kamo River, not far from a children's playground. It is perhaps Japan's least popular tourist attraction.[12]

Rivalry between the generals soon arose once more. Fuming at Augustin Konishi's success, Katō Kiyomasa arrived in the worst of his many bad moods. He deliberately baited Konishi in their strategy meeting, pointedly suggesting he take a road that was marked with a pharmacy. When Konishi suggested that they settle who would take which road by drawing lots, Katō scoffed that such a method was a natural suggestion for a tradesman. Konishi angrily reached for his sword, and was only restrained from attacking his colleague by the intervention of their seconds-in-command.[13]

Chungju had been the last place where a significant Korean force had stood between the Japanese and Seoul. Consequently, as the Koreans evacuated Seoul, the Japanese armies had an unimpeded progress towards the capital. Their greatest obstacle was the Han River. Konishi's force crossed it at its southern branch, just north of Chunju itself, and approached the city's east gate. Katō had more difficulty, as he did not have to cross the river until substantially closer to Seoul itself, where the river was now half a mile wide and swollen with spring floodwaters. There were no bridges and remarkably few boats – legend holds that the Koreans had destroyed all river shipping to impede the enemy advance, but rumours persisted that Augustin Konishi had done so himself in order to delay his rival.

Many Korean soldiers fled at the first terrifying sight of the Japanese, particularly when Katō ordered a cosmetic but compelling firing of the arquebuses across the river.

Without any resistance from the defenders, Katō's men felled trees to construct rafts, and crossed the river the following day. However, to his further irritation, he was forced to do so in sight of new soldiers on the city walls – Konishi's men, defiantly hoisting their medicine-bag standard, had walked into the deserted city scant minutes ahead of him after a lieutenant had levered open a floodgate in the wall. In an additional embarrassment, Katō's men were initially refused entry to the south gate by Konishi's officers.

The state of Seoul at the time of its capture is a matter of some controversy. It was, and still is, widely believed that the conquering Japanese committed untold acts of vandalism in Seoul, razing many of its fine palaces to the ground. But although they certainly burned many towns in the south if the inhabitants offered resistance, Seoul had already been evacuated. It seems more likely that the fleeing Koreans themselves carried out the destruction of several royal palaces in the city, as the Japanese would surely have much preferred to keep Seoul intact as their new base of operations.[14]

It is certainly notable that many residents had returned to the city within a couple of weeks of the Japanese conquest, and were encouraged to go about their business as if nothing had happened. Japanese propaganda asserted that the population of Seoul had been 'saved' from their supposedly oppressive King, and atrocities were kept remarkably to a minimum (by samurai standards), with only the burning at the stake of a few 'looters' and 'agitators'.

Ironically, only one palace remained standing, and that the Japanese unquestionably burned down themselves. Hideyoshi's nineteen-year-old nephew, Ukita Hideie, arrived in town a few days behind the conquerors, after a march up country from Pusan. Nominally in charge of the feuding generals, Ukita took up residence in the surviving Chongmyo Palace, only to leave after a few days, reporting suspicious deaths, illnesses and apparitions among his men. As far as the Koreans were concerned, the invaders got what they deserved by quartering troops on a sacred royal site. To the Japanese, it was a minor irritant, and one that was answered with an act of rash arson.

Back in Japan, an ecstatic Hideyoshi crowed that his armies had performed beyond even his own expectations. Nearing sixty, the old soldier was already ailing. The symptoms suggest untreated diabetes – his eyesight was failing him and his appetite had faded. He had been bereaved by the loss of his infant son and half-brother in a short space of time. Leaving the regency in the hands of his nephew, he now plotted for the subjugation of China, which would surely commence as soon as his generals had secured the north Korean border. Drunk with his success, he even wrote of a new plan for the next generation to take samurai banners all the way to India, while he planned a quiet retirement for himself at a castle in Ningbo – which, perhaps with the aid of the globe he had been sent by the Spanish, he seems to have regarded as the epicentre of a Chinese–Korean–Japanese empire.

However, the taking of Seoul, a mere twenty days after the army came ashore at Pusan, was to be the high point of the Japanese war effort. New troubles arrived, starting with Hideyoshi's tardy realization that the Japanese home islands were not entirely subdued. Even as he argued with his generals about whether he should risk a crossing in typhoon season to inspect his new Korean possession, word arrived of a rebellious army led by a Shimazu lord. The pretender was swiftly spirited away and executed by his own clan, but the news was enough to make Hideyoshi listen to his warier underlings. Hideyoshi began to doubt if he could trust the most powerful of his fellow lords not to usurp his authority while he was away. Nor was he necessarily persuaded by the Shimazu clan's claim to have policed its own rebels.

Meanwhile, in Korea, Hideyoshi's armies were hundreds of miles from friendly territory, kept alive by ever-stretching supply routes. The expectation that the locals would welcome the Japanese as liberators was ludicrous; all the more so as new arrivals looted and raided the population. Regardless of what intentions Hideyoshi may have had for incorporating Korea within Japan, the obvious language barrier and immediate supply shortages was turning the south of the country into a long series of raids and lootings.

To make matters worse, the Korean counter-attack was in the hands of one of the greatest admirals in history. Passed over in promotion, victimized for valour, Yi Sun-sin (1545–98) was a former cavalry commander, once demoted to common soldier by internal politics, who had risen rapidly through the ranks in the years before the arrival of the Japanese, and was now his country's last, best hope. After carefully biding his time, he arrived off the coast at Okpo in mid-June at the head of a fleet of true warships – where the Japanese were lucky to have two shipboard cannons per vessel, Yi's fleet often had up to twenty guns per vessel.[15]

Yi's exploits are worthy of a book in themselves. In a brief history of the samurai, it is necessary merely to observe the cataclysmic effect that his arrival had on the invaders. Yi terrorized the south coast of Korea, sinking or irreparably damaging dozens of Japanese ships.

There were, undoubtedly, seafaring Japanese who might have put up a better fight. The men of the Matsuura, for example, were sure to be better at naval combat, but 3,000 of them were marching as footsoldiers in Augustin Konishi's army. There were, of course, also Japanese warships intended to protect the transport vessels, but nowhere near enough, and nowhere close enough to Yi's predations. In June alone, Yi sunk forty ships of the Japanese navy – perhaps 5 per cent of the total. He was back soon afterwards, not only with warships, but with 'turtle ships' – named for the spiked, armoured roofs over their decks – creating havoc among the Japanese commanders. As on land, the Japanese lacked the presence of a single unifying figure, and fleets with allegiance to disparate lords were unable to cooperate sufficiently in resistance against the Japanese. Admiral Yi himself became a rallying point among the Koreans, his personality deemed so crucial to battle that he once even struggled through a skirmish with a bullet in his shoulder, refusing to let his men see him fall.

The campaign of Admiral Yi did not merely revitalize resistance in the south, it presented a dangerous threat to the ongoing victories in the north. For the first time in history, samurai armies were fighting far from a home base. Even in ancient times, during the pacification of the north, a sanctuary had always been only a few miles away. With the victories of Admiral Yi, samurai suddenly found themselves hundreds of miles from home, not sharing a common language with any locals, and unable to call upon any clan or family associations for help. Even as Hideyoshi celebrated on Kyūshū, the vanguard armies were danger-ously far to the north, with the supply lines thinning out every day.

Rested for two weeks in Seoul, the antagonistic com-manders Augustin Konishi and Katō Kiyomasa continued their march north. They encountered little opposition until they reached the Imjin River – an imposing natural barrier that marks part of today's border between North and South

Korea. Waiting on the opposite bank, on a flat plain with ample room for manoeuvre, was a force of some 10,000 Korean soldiers.

The Japanese advance, which more than one previous author has reasonably called a blitzkrieg, ground to an immediate halt. The defenders had secured all the available boats, and enemy forces were so overwhelming that there was no chance of crossing under fire on rafts or a pontoon. Never ones to give up flogging a dead horse, the Japanese generals tried yet again to persuade the Koreans that they were on the same side, and invited them to join in their march on China. The opposing armies stared each other down for ten tense days, until the Japanese made a show of breaking camp and turning back for the south.[16]

It was only then that disorganization among the Koreans made its presence felt. Clear heads among the Koreans suspected that the Japanese departure was a trap, but after baiting by other officers, brashly took up the challenge to cross the river in pursuit. There, predictably, they were ambushed by repeated salvos of Japanese musket-fire from the cover of the forest, and then pursued to a desperate last stand on the riverbank while the rest of the army watched aghast. The opposing Korean general turned away from the sight of the massacre and – sources differ – either fled alone or ordered a general retreat. The result was the same either way: the Koreans fled and the Japanese crossed the Imjin River, with a clear route ahead of them to the rump government in the northern city of Pyongyang.

Uncharacteristically, Katō Kiyomasa left the assault on Pyongyang to Augustin Konishi, and took his own forces on a prolonged campaign to secure the north-east. We can only assume that, once again, he assumed that the Koreans would prove to be harder to beat than they had so far proven to be. Konishi arrived on the bank of the Taedong

River, within sight of Pyongyang, and sent yet another request for negotiations. Within the city, chaos reigned, as the populace reacted with deep mistrust of the Korean King's decision to abandon the city and run even further north. On two boats roped together midstream on the river, representatives of the opposing forces attempted to reach an agreement. The Koreans, however, refused point blank to entertain the Japanese claim that their intentions were benign. Notably, despite the loss of more than half of the kingdom to invaders, the Koreans refused to turn on the Chinese Emperor to whom they had sworn allegiance.

A night attack by the Koreans across the Taedong scored heavy casualties against Konishi's men, but backfired at dawn, when Damian Kuroda arrived with reinforcements, and the retreating Koreans found that their civilian boatmen had fled from the approaching Japanese. In an understandable but terrible error, the retreating Koreans instead took advantage of the seasonally low waters of the Taedong to wade back to safety, thereby informing their enemies of all the locations where a keen enough enemy might ford the Taedong.

Another Korean retreat commenced, with the customary destruction and concealment of matériel to prevent it falling into Japanese hands. After the Japanese forded the river, they literally could not believe their luck. The gates of Pyongyang lay wide open before them, but Augustin Konishi and Damian Kuroda first climbed a nearby hill to peek over the walls in search of waiting ambushers. There were none. Pyongyang was in Japanese hands, as was its plentiful rice barns, which would sustain the Japanese advance for months to come.

Even as Konishi occupied Pyongyang, however, the supply problems returned. The rice was a bonus, true enough, but everything else had to cross hundreds of miles of mountainous terrain. The simplest solution would be to send the Japanese transport fleet along Korea's west coast and up the Taedong River to Pyongyang. Konishi was so sure that this would work that he even dashed off a taunting letter to the retreating Korean King: 'The Japanese navy will soon be arriving with reinforcements of 100,000 men. Where will your Majesty flee to then?'[17]

However, Konishi was either misinformed or uninformed about the victories of Admiral Yi, who by mid-August had successfully slaughtered 9,000 Japanese at sea, sunk many ships, and effectively walled off the sea-route to the north. This left Konishi's regiment reduced by illness, attrition and casualties to a mere 20,000 men. Conquering an undefended city like Pyongyang would still 'cost' Konishi a battalion, which would have to be left behind to garrison the new acquisition. With each step north, his army dwindled, even as it marched closer to the border with China. The Korean King had already begged the Chinese Emperor to send a relief force, and there was no telling when it would arrive.

Konishi's first presentiment of danger came on 23 August, when a Chinese force attacked the north gate of Pyongyang in the middle of a heavy rainstorm. Taken by surprise, the samurai held the walls with heavy casualties, until they realized that the attacking 'army' was actually significantly smaller. Accordingly, they fell back, luring the Chinese into Pyongyang itself, where the battalion of Chinese was hacked apart in street-to-street fighting.

It was, claimed Konishi, a Japanese victory. But his men suffered enough at the hands of a few hundred Chinese for him to know that there was trouble ahead. Riding back to Seoul for a conference with the teenage commander-in-chief Ukita, Konishi advised a plan of strategic withdrawal. When the inevitable Chinese counter-attack came in force, the Japanese should hold each town for as long as possible, before retreating south to the next strongpoint. It was Konishi's way of acknowledging the unpleasant truth – without better supply lines, he was overextended in the north, and might as well make the Chinese suffer similar supply problems as they advanced.

Japanese supply problems got significantly worse on 6 September when the strategic city of Chongju fell to 1,000 Korean irregulars and a single battalion of 500 soldiers on loan from an unconquered province. The Japanese garrison turned out to be unexpectedly small, and fled when hostilities were broken off by a rainstorm. Now it was the Koreans who entered a town without any defenders. Early in October, Damian Kuroda found strong resistance at the town of Yonan, where the locals set wood fires at the base of their stone walls to prevent Japanese from getting close with siege ladders. All the citizenry came to the aid of their hometown, holding off the attackers with sticks, stones and even 'soap powder' thrown in the eyes of the samurai.

An envoy from the Chinese met with Konishi and his lieutenants at Pyongyang on 4 October, where he was told the outrageous lie that the Japanese only wished for friendly relations with China. He countered with one of his own, which was that he would take their offer back to Beijing, but would require a fifty-day armistice in which to do so. Remarkably, the Japanese agreed to this, effectively postponing any further advances until the following spring. Inadvertently, this bought vital time for the Chinese, who had been delayed putting down a revolt on a distant border, and would now be able to muster ample manpower for a counter-attack into Korea.

Communications being as slow as they were in the sixteenth century, none of this information was available to the combatants in the south. Even as Konishi and the

Chinese agreed to a ceasefire, counter-attacks did further damage to Konishi's support network. On 5 October, Admiral Yi took the fight to the Japanese, sailing within sight of Pusan itself and sinking 130 Japanese ships (a quarter of the navy), many of them at anchor. The former Korean capital of Kyongju, perilously close to Pusan, fell to the Koreans a week later. Reading between the lines of the Japanese scramble to leave the town, it would seem that yet another small garrison was overwhelmed, and, in this case, additionally spooked by the Koreans' use of a *pigyok chincholloe* ('flying striking earth heaven thunder'). This mortar-launched, fizzing cannonball landed amidst the Japanese, who gathered around to look at it scant seconds before it exploded in a cloud of deadly shards.[18]

The last battle of 1592, in the southern city of Chinju, saw the Japanese edge in technology significantly blunted. For the first time, the Koreans fought back with arquebuses of their own – presumably captured from Japanese soldiers or stores.

By 1593, the rot was setting in. Hideyoshi's own ardour appears to have cooled. He had stopped talking about a Ningbo Palace, and now seemed prepared to settle for somewhere outside Kyōto. Meanwhile, in Korea itself, the Japanese were forced to abandon outlying conquests in order to reinforce the flimsy central supply route. After five months in Pyongyang, Konishi stopped agitating for reinforcements, as he no longer had the rice to feed them, even if they arrived.

The only commander with any long record of consistent success, Katō Kiyomasa, had successfully pacified much of the north-east, but met with heavy losses on an attempt to take the battle against the Jurchens in Manchuria. With 39 per cent of his army now stuck in garrisons or recuperating, Katō received the annoying order to return to the south.

Complaining that he was being penalized for the failures of lesser generals, he turned back towards the south.

By now, the countryside was alive with guerrillas, and many Korean monasteries had dedicated their own fighting monks to the cause of throwing the Japanese out. Konishi, in particular, felt isolated in the north. Pyongyang was still his, but the countryside around it was unsafe. On 5 February 1593, Konishi faced an army of 6,000 Chinese that had marched to Pyongyang and now raised a banner before the city walls, announcing that they would kill everyone who did not immediately surrender. Although his men beat the Chinese back in fierce fighting around the city's north gate, he lost 2,300 men and significant quantities of his supplies. The Chinese General Li Rusong scored his success in part because he refused to distinguish between Korean residents and Japanese occupiers, and killed 'enemies' indiscriminately. He made Konishi an offer he could not refuse. Observing that the Chinese had ample forces to conquer Pyongyang at the next assault, and that Konishi was far from home, he gave him the chance to flee. Konishi, who had been spoiling to leave Pyongyang for months, took his chance, and led his men out the south gate and across the frozen Taedong River in a silent, bitter retreat. They left their wounded behind.

Konishi's retreat towards Seoul was a series of further blows to his confidence. To his great annoyance, he found that the nearest garrison had already evacuated – instead of waiting for his order, they had abandoned their posts, taking much-needed supplies with them. Garrisons further to the south were more loyal, but were ordered by Konishi to follow his lead. By 17 February, Konishi had rolled back the Japanese front line to Seoul itself.

Li Rusong gave Konishi plenty of time to leave, but soon followed behind, reoccupying the abandoned fortress towns on the way. He was, however, unmotivated to take the battle to the Japanese. Even though the Chinese Emperor had suggested that the way to deal with the Korean problem was to pursue the Japanese out of Korea and onto Japanese soil itself, General Li was reluctant to engage the 20,000 Japanese in the Seoul area. His men were diseased, his own lines of supply were now stretched, and the Japanese had had more time to dig in at Seoul. Furthermore, Li Rusong had arguably performed his most crucial strategic duty already, pushing the Japanese back from the Chinese border. As had already been suggested at several earlier impasses along the march south, he would prefer it if the Koreans now finished the job themselves. Fearing just such an attitude among the inhabitants of Seoul, the Japanese put every Korean adult male to the sword.

Two cunning moves by the Japanese turned back Li Rusong's advance. In an act of awful ecological destruction, the Japanese burned all the fields around Seoul, destroying all the available fodder for Li Rusong's cavalry. This alone killed off 10,000 horses in the week following the Chinese arrival in the south. Word that Katō Kiyomasa was on his way south was the final straw. Unwilling to take the risk that Katō might block off a Chinese retreat, Li Rusong elected to turn back.

This was, it should be noted, precisely the sort of apocalypse that the Koreans had hoped to avoid. A war between China and Japan was now being fought solely on Korean soil, and Korean non-combatants were suffering considerably more than either army. Korean guerrillas successfully torched a Japanese grain barn near Seoul, ensuring that if the locals could not have the food, nobody could. Pestilence spread from the rotting corpses of men and beasts in Seoul's streets, and the blockade at the coast was now so effective that the samurai generals now wrote to Hideyoshi and pleaded with him not to arrive with the 200,000 reinforcements at his disposal. Food was now the most crucial ingredient.

The Koreans knew this, too, and hit the Japanese where it hurt. The invincible Admiral Yi received orders on 7 March 1593 to target Japanese transport and supply vessels. He conducted a series of raids in the spring, before temporarily disbanding much of his fleet so that his sailors could return home to their farms to plant their fields.

On 9 May, envoys from the Chinese arrived in Seoul with an ultimatum – face the overwhelming 400,000 soldiers of the Chinese army, or hand over their hostages and retreat to the south. Unknown to the Chinese, Konishi had just received an order from Hideyoshi to fall back to Pusan. However, determined to save face, Konishi demanded to hear a guarantee of peace from accredited envoys from the Chinese Emperor. With no accredited envoys to hand, the Chinese swiftly created some by dressing up two officers in impressive robes.

Augustin Konishi agreed to hand over the hostages – two royal princes who had fallen into Katō Kiyomasa's hands, and whom Katō had already refused to give up. He also agreed that Hideyoshi would be recognized as a vassal 'King' of Japan of an equivalent rank to the ruler of Korea. This decision, which was carefully kept from Hideyoshi for as long as possible, was a cataclysmic climbdown from Hideyoshi's plan of but two years earlier to become the ruler of all of East Asia. It turned the Korean war into a Chinese chastisement of Japanese upstarts, ending with the Japanese leaders' acknowledgement of the Chinese Emperor as their lord and master.

The negotiations were an outrageous pack of lies on all sides. The Chinese had nowhere near 400,000 soldiers in north Korea – instead they had only a tenth of that number. Konishi was not empowered to speak on behalf of Hideyoshi. Meanwhile, the false envoys suggested that the Japanese might be allowed to keep much of southern Korea for themselves, although they neglected to mention this to either the Koreans or the Chinese.

Konishi and his regiments pulled out and headed to the south, taking as much loot and captured womenfolk as they could, in a celebratory procession that made the retreat to the south look more like a carnival. The Koreans and Chinese reoccupied the devastated Seoul, little of which was still standing after the multiple changes in fortune over the last year. To add insult to injury, unknown raiders from the Japanese army not only broke into the tombs of a former Korean king, looted the grave goods and burned the body, but also left a commoner's corpse behind in royal robes, presumably in the hope that the Koreans would be duped into offering royal honours to an undeserving stranger – a strangely intricate prank.

Back in Japan, Hideyoshi was either deluded or duped, or both. His underlings had managed such a careful spin on the news of the retreat to Pusan that Hideyoshi genuinely seemed to believe that his men had scored a great victory, and that envoys on their way from Pusan were going to deliver 'an apology' to him on behalf of the Chinese Emperor.

Chinese envoys, real ones this time, arrived on Kyūshū in late June, where they were received by some of Hideyoshi's generals, including Augustin Konishi. In a tense exchange, made all the more frustrating by the need to communicate solely in written Chinese, the envoys demanded to know why the Japanese forces had not yet entirely quit Korean territory. Fortunately for all concerned, Hideyoshi was all but illiterate, and was entirely unaware that the ambassadors for the mainland were not paying him homage, but chastising him for his hubris. Meanwhile, when Hideyoshi ordered a punitive strike against Chinju, it was Konishi himself who tipped the Chinese off that Katō Kiyomasa was on his way to level the city. This seems not to have been necessarily aimed at annoying Katō, but at ensuring that the town was deserted when the Japanese arrived.

Katō Kiyomasa was determined to take Chinju, to tear down its walls, to fill in its wells and massacre its inhabitants, as a lesson to any other Korean cities that dared to hold out. The people of Chinju either did not receive or did not appreciate Augustin Konishi's warning, and stayed walled up in their town, the local garrison's numbers swelled by many thousands of refugees. So it was that when Katō, Konishi and Ukita pitched camp around the city, there was no longer any way out.

The siege of Chinju was bizarrely fought more over architecture than ground. In late July, Japanese attempts to raise a mound and siege tower, so that they could shoot over the walls, were matched by a Korean tower-building exercise inside the city. The Koreans won, by getting cannons on their own tower ahead of the Japanese, and blowing up the rival siegework.

A second Japanese attack aimed at dismantling the city walls, literally stone by stone, as shielded engineers picked and hacked at the lowermost stones under a hail of missiles from the defenders. Heavy rain brought a temporary respite to the guns and cannon, but also further undermined the weakened walls. After several days of siege, a portion of the city wall collapsed, and Katō's men poured through the gap. Some of the Korean soldiers threw themselves off the wall. Others made a stand, but to no avail – the Japanese killed every living thing in the city that had resisted them, and then levelled the area during a massacre that cost an estimated 60,000 Korean lives, many of them women and children.

Most notable among the defenders of Chinju was Non-gae, a *kisaeng* (entertainer, roughly equivalent to the Japanese geisha), who enticed one of the celebrating samurai over to her, grabbed him in a bear hug, and then leapt to both their deaths in the river below.[19]

In the month that followed, Hideyoshi's negotiators and the Chinese envoys, now back in Korea, carefully twisted the words and terms of the treaty. The Koreans themselves were given no say in the negotiations, which, once all the bluster and misdirection was cut out, now seemed to revolve largely around whether the Japanese could keep the southern part of the Korean peninsula for themselves, or whether they would leave. The 'negotiations', mostly comprising the long wait for letters and envoys to travel to Beijing and back by the circuitous land route, would lead to three years of waiting, and a cessation of hostilities.

Augustin Konishi had carefully dismantled all of Hideyoshi's outrageous demands, and now finalized his deception by forging a letter from Hideyoshi himself, in which the ruler of Japan humbled himself and his country before the greatness of the Chinese Emperor, and begged to be invested as a king – in other words, as a vassal of China. Hideyoshi himself was entirely unaware of this, and believed that the Chinese had agreed to stay out of Korea while Hideyoshi began a renewed campaign that would bring the peninsula firmly under his rule. 'We regard Korea', he decreed, 'as part of our domain, the same as Kyūshū.' However, the same decree shows an indication that Hideyoshi was dimly aware of trouble in the ranks, with an order for the men in Korea to stop complaining, as they were currently working less hard for the war effort than many of their compatriots back on Japanese soil.[20]

In the meantime, however, the Korean King was back in Seoul, the harvests were soon collected in the north, and the survivors of the Japanese invasion were able to make preparations for a new counter-attack. The Korean authorities were fully aware of Konishi's forgery, and suspected that it would only be a matter of time before the deception was uncovered and the war recommenced. The Koreans now took musketry seriously, and trained specialized units designed to deal with samurai opponents armed with arquebuses.

There was also in-fighting on both sides. Continued shortages, outbreaks of disease and a distinct lack of loyalty to Hideyoshi's cause led many Japanese to desert. Some sneaked back to their farms in Japan, although several thousand actually defected to the other side, and would live out their days as Koreans. Meanwhile, rival commanders among the Koreans attempted to slander the achievements of Admiral Yi, while among the Japanese, Konishi tried to blame Katō for atrocities like the rape of Chinju. Katō countered in 1594 by informing Hideyoshi that Konishi had shipped a Jesuit priest to his fortress in Korea in order to say Mass for his Christian soldiers and attend to their religious needs. According to one Jesuit observer, Konishi had advised his fellow Christians to keep a low profile in Japan, partly because Christianity was still out of favour, but mainly because the Christian samurai appeared to believe that Hideyoshi's days were numbered:

Don Austin [i.e. Augustin] and the other Christian Lords in Corea wrote frequently to them, to recommend Prudence and Moderation in their Conduct, adding by way of Reason, that in a Storm it was more advisable to carry few Sails, than spread all with Hazard of sinking . . . What yet still farther oblig'd them to moderate their Zeal, was the Prospect of a suddain change upon *Taycosama*'s [i.e. Hideyoshi's] Death, who possibly could not hold out any Time; besides, that he himself too was much abated of his former Severity against the Christians . . .[21]

All the while, Hideyoshi busied himself back in Japan on the construction of his new castle, and on a sudden obsession with Nō theatre that even extended to amateur dramatics. It was only in October 1596, when Chinese envoys arrived to present him with gifts from China, that the deception unravelled. The three years of lies almost ended at the first meeting, when neither Hideyoshi nor the envoys would kneel before the other. But it was not until the following day, when Hideyoshi finally had the envoys' two edicts translated, that the whole inconvenient truth finally came out. The first ornate scroll cheerfully invested Hideyoshi as the 'King of Japan' and expressed the strong hope that he would be obedient to the ruler of China. The second chastised him for attacking Korea, but congratulated him for realizing the error of his ways and withdrawing all his troops (several thousand of whom still remained in Pusan). It added an unexpected coda to the effect that no Japanese should ever step in Korea again, and that neither Hideyoshi nor his descendants should dare to send trading ships to China, where they were likely to be sunk on suspicion of being pirate vessels.

Hideyoshi's reaction was explosive. He tore off the crown and robes that had been presented to him by the envoys, and flung them to the ground.

[He] flew into such a Passion and a Rage that he was perfectly out of himself. He froth'd and foam'd at the Mouth, he ranted and tore till his Head smoak'd like Fire, and his Body was all over in a dropping Sweat.[22]

The envoys were ordered to leave Japan immediately, and it was only the intercession of several confidantes that stopped Hideyoshi ordering Augustin Konishi to commit *seppuku* in atonement.

The irate Hideyoshi now ordered a renewal of hostilities in Korea. He no longer gave any indication of wishing to conquer China. He merely wished to punish the Koreans for their alleged participation in the deception. The generals of the first invasion were sent back to Korea and ordered to harry the three southernmost provinces.[23]

But even as the Japanese prepared to return to the fighting in Korea, a seemingly insignificant event off the coast of Japan was about to provoke Hideyoshi into an all-new war, this time against his own people.

8

NO MORE WARS
THE TOKUGAWA IN ASCENT

The ship was called the *San Felipe*, a galleon out of Manila, whose voyage had been shadowed by ominous portents. Her crew had nervously noted the presence of a comet in the sky overhead, and, as they neared the coast of Kyūshū, were dealt another superstitious scare at the sight of lights in the sky. The *San Felipe*'s real problems, however, were much less magical. She was simply overloaded with too much cargo, and sailing right into a typhoon. Dismasted and rudderless, the *San Felipe* was lucky to make it to a safe harbour on the south coast of Shikoku, where, as the disgruntled crew helped a local warlord tow her to port, she split along her seams and sank in shallow water.

As her cargo of brightly coloured silks billowed out into the waters, the *San Felipe* was besieged by local fishing boats, whose crews began reeling up the cargo. At first grateful for the help, the pilot of the *San Felipe* soon changed his tune when he realized that they were not retrieving the silk on his behalf, but salvaging it for themselves. In the heated arguments that followed, the pilot treated the local lord to a brief history lesson on the Spanish Empire, noting that Spain extended her borders by first sending in missionaries to soften up the next generation, and then orchestrating a takeover once the Christian armies were large enough:

> He told them that this was done with the Help of Missioners, whom his Master sent to all Parts of the World, to preach the Gospel of Jesus Christ, for so soon as these Religious had gained a sufficient Number of Proselytes, the King followed with his Troops and joining the new Converts, made a Conquest of the Kingdoms.[1]

So soon after the embarrassment with the Chinese envoys, with the Korean campaign in tatters and with the likes of Augustin Konishi already incurring suspicion, it was the worst possible thing for Hideyoshi to hear.

The persecutions against Christians were renewed, and were no longer restricted to the missionaries, but also to their flocks. Christianity fell far out of favour with the ruling elites, so much so that anyone with a Christian name was advised to repudiate it. Apostasy became the only sure way to get ahead, and the most zealous of Christian-hunters introduced new inquisitions and tests. The most notorious was the *fumi-e* (the 'trampling Image'), an icon of Christ or a saint, on which a suspected Christian believer was ordered to place his or her foot. Those that refused were often tortured or killed. It was, to say the least, an inhospitable environment to which many of the Christian samurai returned from Korea.

By the end of 1598, Hideyoshi was dead and the Japanese had quit Korea for good. They returned with slaves, some artisan prisoners of war (who became the foundations of the Satsuma-ware industry and revitalized pottery), rare books and sundry other items. They left behind tens of thousands of their own dead, even greater numbers of dead Koreans and Chinese, and at least 3,000 deserters. In years to come, among many mildly contemptuous names for the folly of the campaign, it would become known as the military operation that began with a dragon's head, but ended with a snake's tail – an allegory of arrogant attack and dishonourable retreat.[2]

Korea would take decades to recover. China's Ming dynasty, having squandered almost 1,000 tonnes of silver in its own operation, would arguably never quite recover, and began a slow, spiralling decline that would end with regime change in 1644.

Hideyoshi's own order would persist in some form or other for many years. Some of the institutions and reforms he introduced would last for centuries, but his own immediate organization already showed signs of collapse. There were signs of trouble among the council of regents and commissioners assigned to watch over Hideyoshi's heir Hideyori. Some lords returned to their own domains to deal with pressing local issues. Others intrigued at the Osaka castle where Hideyori was in confinement. In 1599, the death of the powerful Maeda Toshiie left a power vacuum at the council that no other lord could fill. Lines were soon drawn between two factions of warlords. On one side was Tokugawa Ieyasu, the most powerful lord remaining, backed by Damian Kuroda, Dario Sō and Katō Kiyomasa, among others. On the other side was Ishida Mitsunari, backed by Augustin Konishi and others.

It was an interesting division of allegiances. Ishida had a long military career, but in the less glamorous world of supplies and logistics. Consequently, much of the old guard regarded him as a samurai in name only, and flocked instead to the banner of Ieyasu the career soldier. Ishida gained support from many of the surviving Christians, although most of the apostates who had already given up their religion were welcomed into Ieyasu's forces. Meanwhile, Ieyasu gained support from an unexpected quarter, when he impounded the cargo of the *Liefde*, a Dutch merchant ship that had run aground in Kyūshū. Among her many chests of cargo, the *Liefde* had carried 19 cannons, 500 muskets, 5,000 cannonballs and 300 chain shot. Her English navigator, William Adams (1564–1620), met Ieyasu on several occasions, and was treated cordially but suspiciously. He would eventually become one of Ieyasu's henchmen.

The news of a 'revolt' by Ishida in the western provinces came as no surprise to Ieyasu in May 1600. Although there were several other skirmishes and sieges worthy of note, the most infamous and decisive battle between the two factions did not occur until 21 October that year, at a critical crossroads called Sekigahara.

Conditions were a test of martial resolve. A great storm the night before kept both sides awake as they listened to the rain pounding against their tents. They, at least, were the lucky ones, as many of the lower-ranking samurai were stuck out in the open, protected to some extent by sedge raincoats that gave them the appearance of haystacks on legs.

Hilltops close by were occupied by either side. Down in the valley, Ishida's men toiled miserably on the construction of trenches, ready to repel an expected assault by Ieyasu's supporters. Much of the Sekigahara plain was 'fields', although in Japan such a simple statement is misleading – even after harvesting, these 'fields' were actually rice paddies, likely to accumulate unwelcome depths of water after a hard night's November rain.

In the small hours of the morning, the storm slackened, turning into a thick fog so impenetrable that the first shots of the day were fired when two groups of rival samurai literally bumped into each other. There were shots in the dim morning light, shouts and the ringing clashes of swords before the commanders on both sides ordered an immediate withdrawal. Both sides feared that the clash had been a planned ambush. It was only as the rising sun burned off the mist that the samurai in the valley could truly see who was where.

The forces drawn up were not anonymous. Banners displaying the distinctive crests of each house made it abundantly clear who was where. The triple hollyhock leaves of House Tokugawa; the stark, bold swastika of House Hachizuka; the black dots of House Terazawa; and the nine stars of House Hosokawa – they were all prominently visible among Ieyasu's forces. Among Ishida's forces there were many more cruciform designs in evidence – the stark cross with cross-bars of Augustin Konishi, and the cross within a circle of Kyūshū's Shimazu clan.

It was the Tokugawa who attacked first. Contrary to his instructions to wait for orders, Ii Naomasa, leader of the 'Red Devils' cavalry squadron, charged straight at the enemy. The identity of the attackers was unquestionable – Ii's helmet was topped by a giant pair of horns, and his armour and the armour of all his horsemen was unmistakably scarlet.

Ii's decision was yet another manifestation of the samurai's eternal desire to be in the front line. The honoured position had actually been promised to one of his allies, who now hurled abuse at Ii's Red Devils as they galloped past. Ii's excuse, ready to hand when the fighting was over, was that he was merely going out to 'check' the disposition of enemy troops, and had no intention of engaging them. This, of course, was news to the enemy, who charged out to meet him, initiating battle by default.

The Red Devils cut a wide path through the enemy, wheeling to avoid a second concentration of troops and scattering back towards safety. Not to be outdone, Ii's thwarted allies opened fire with their arquebuses, finally let loose after a long night struggling to keep their powder dry in the rain. Soldiers with firearms accounted for perhaps 10 per cent of the samurai on the field at Sekigahara – an immense change in military custom since the first arrival of the *tanegashima* only a few decades before.

Hoping to end the entire war with a swift, surgical strike at Ishida himself, samurai from the Kuroda and Hosokawa clans charged straight for their enemy's command post. The fighting was particularly bitter here, often pitching Christian against former-Christian, with soldiers who had once fought side by side during their career now hacking at each other, calf-deep in watery mud. Casualties in this part of the battle were not limited to the usual sword- and bullet-wounds: hapless warriors were also trampled and drowned.

Ishida tried to turn the tables by bringing up his big guns. Five massive artillery pieces, intended for siege warfare, opened up from behind his lines, throwing up great plumes of mud and water. Despite the loud noise and value to morale, the cannons were of little practical value on the flat plain. Far more damage was done to the Tokugawa by the first of Ishida's reserves, as they obeyed their orders to charge down the hillside into the flank of the Tokugawa.

'Ally and foe pushed against each other,' wrote one participant. 'The musket fire and the shouts echoed from the heavens and shook the earth. The black smoke rose, making the day as night.'[3]

There were, however, *three* sides to the battle at Sekigahara. There were already tensions between Ishida and some of his men, and intrigues behind the scenes that led some to drag their feet. At 10 a.m., a messenger from Ishida's command post rode over to the Shimazu lines and demanded that they enter the battle. Instead of immediately coming to the aid of his supposed superior, the Shimazu leader took offence at the messenger's attitude – he had, apparently, not even got off his horse before delivering the command. Ishida himself rode over to the Shimazu to make amends, but was told instead that everyone had their own battles to fight. For some reason, the Shimazu were not entering the battle at all. For all the commanding position and tactical advantage that their presence offered, they might as well not have been there at all.

The samurai of the Kobayakawa clan were similarly reluctant to get involved. They and the Shimazu had been intended as the 'crane's wings' of Ishida's big battle plan, ready to charge in to deliver a devastating blow from either side when Ishida demanded it. But neither the Shimazu nor Kobayakawa wing followed their orders. Their communiqués and refusals strongly implied that Ishida was overreacting, and that despite heavy losses on his front line, it was still too early for the devastating charge from the flanks.

This deception might have given the relatively inexperienced Ishida pause for thought, but it did not wash with the veterans in the thick of the fighting. Augustin Konishi himself sent a message up the hill to Kobayakawa Hideaki, pleading for him to do the right thing. Konishi, perhaps, was too concerned with the heat of the moment to think through what this might suggest. His fellow commander, Ōtani Yoshitsugu had more time for reflection, and began to suspect the worst. A crippled, half-blind leper, Ōtani was not an active participant in the battle, but was carried in a palanquin amidst his men. He was therefore forced to ask for constant reports on the state of the battle, and had formed more of an objective overview than Konishi. It was hence Ōtani who properly digested the information that in the middle of all the chaos, no enemy forces were attacking Kobayakawa at all – it was almost as if Kobayakawa had already made some sort of deal with Ieyasu.

If so, if Kobayakawa had marched to his location, set up camp, and suited up for battle in the firm knowledge that he was actually already on the other side, then Ishida's forces were about to suffer a brutal reversal of fortune.[4]

We can never know what Kobayakawa's precise intentions were at the beginning of the day. He seems to have accepted offers from both sides. He seems to have conspicuously marched with Ishida, after having already promised aid to Tokugawa Ieyasu. Still unsure of where Kobayakawa would place his allegiances, Ieyasu sent some musketeers over to take some potshots at his men. Spurred into making a decision by the threat of attack, Kobayakawa made his choice, thereby sealing the battle, and with it the future of Japan.

Kobayakawa gave the order to attack his own side. As Ieyasu watched in approval, the Kobayakawa samurai charged down the hill, straight for the flank of the hard-pressed troops of Ōtani Yoshitsugu. But Ōtani was blind, not stupid. He had already ordered his musketeers to expect trouble from that direction, and they opened fire on the ambushers.

Kobayakawa's men fell in their hundreds, tumbling down the hill towards their new enemies. The sight, however, of the surprise attack, galvanized several other wavering units, who also committed themselves to the battle on the Tokugawa side. Ieyasu himself, seeing that the 'crane' now only had one wing, committed some of his own reserves, and Ishida's line began to buckle. Sheer weight of numbers overwhelmed the foresighted Ōtani musketeers, and as Kobayakawa's samurai hacked a path towards him, the leper General Ōtani committed *seppuku*.

Such an option was not available to Augustin Konishi, who fought a grim last stand against impossible odds:

> This Great Hero seeing his Men in a Rout, and no possibility of rallying again, threw himself into the Midst of the Enemy's Troops, slaying on every Side, and bearing all down before him, till wounded from Head to Foot, and overpowered by Numbers, he was forced to yield to Fate, and surrendered himself Prisoner . . .[5]

The Shimazu, who had been waiting all this time, were now surrounded on all sides by Tokugawa soldiers. If they had been waiting for the chance to switch sides like Kobayakawa, they had waited too long. Instead of surrendering, Shimazu Yoshihiro ordered his men to punch their way out through the Tokugawa lines and run for safety. This suicidal move, requiring a large body of Shimazu troops to volunteer for certain death by covering the retreat, saw the Shimazu successfully hack their way out to safety. Ii Naomasa, the infamous Red Devil, was among the samurai who tried to stop them, and suffered a bullet wound that would fester and, it was said, ultimately kill him.

By 2 p.m., Tokugawa Ieyasu could be sure that he had won. He had watched the whole battle from his camp stool, clad in his armour but with only a silk rain hood over his head. It was only now that he called for his headgear and strapped it on, rising to his feet ready to claim the field. As he did so, he muttered a phrase that became an enduring aphorism for remaining wary when the trouble is supposedly over: 'At the moment of victory,' he said, 'tighten the straps of your helmet.'[6]

The battle lines at Sekigahara had solved for Ieyasu the problem of redistributing lands among faithful samurai. Unlike Hideyoshi, he no longer had to seek new acquisitions in Korea to settle his troops. Instead, he was able to forcefully redistribute the landholdings of the eighty-seven lords who had opposed him. Those defeated rebel leaders who had not already died on the battlefield were invited to commit suicide. Only Augustin Konishi refused, proclaiming that suicide was forbidden in the Bible. He met his end after sending a message to his Christian wife Justa, that:

> What I earnestly recommend, and that which most concerns you, is that you serve God faithfully, and love him with your whole Heart. The Prosperity and Advantages of this world are but temporal and transitory. On the contrary, the Joys of Heaven are constant, eternal, and never to have an End.[7]

It is only here, after all the deceptions, betrayals and murders of Augustin's long military career, that we are afforded a glimpse of the depth of his Christian faith. The Christian historian Crasset has Augustin led to the scaffold with the two unbelievers Ishida Mitsunari and the Buddhist warrior monk Ankokuji Ekei – flanked, as it were, like Jesus at Golgotha. He is seen asking for a priest (which is denied to him by his captor, the apostate Damian Kuroda), praying with a rosary, and ultimately bowing three times to an image of the Virgin Mary. Only then was his head hacked from his shoulders in three bloody strikes.

His eldest son was executed a few days later. Augustin's adopted daughter Julia, a Korean orphan he had brought back from the war, lived out the rest of her days on an island in exile. Another son disappeared from the record, and was rumoured to have survived as a Buddhist monk under an assumed name. Augustin's daughter Maria, married to Dario Sō, was disowned by her husband during the new cold climate of anti-Christian feeling, and fled to Nagasaki. Along with many other formerly 'Christian' lords, Dario chose the aftermath of Sekigahara to renounce his Christian faith.[8]

In the fourteen years that followed, Ieyasu consolidated his hold on the other lords. Ieyasu's career as Regent was short-lived by his own choice – like many emperors and shōguns of old, he 'retired' so that some hapless underling could remain mired in ceremonial while he continued his politicking in safety.

In 1603, Ieyasu arranged for his seven-year-old grand-daughter to marry the ten-year-old Hideyori, although this dynastic marriage does not seem to have lessened the growing enmity between then. The standoff between Hideyori and Ieyasu was characterized by misinformation. In his distant Edo base, Ieyasu was told that Hideyori, the master of Osaka Castle, was weak-willed and effeminate, a deliberate deception that lulled Ieyasu into a false sense of security.

Ieyasu also pushed Hideyori into building schemes in honour of his departed father, seemingly intended to drive the young lord into bankruptcy. Hideyoshi's Great Buddha, built with all the requisitioned swords, had been destroyed in an earthquake in 1596. Hideyori's supporters' attempt to rebuild it had reached as far as the neck when a freak fire ruined the enterprise. Work resumed, along with the casting of a great ceremonial bell bearing the legend *Kokka Ankō*: 'Peaceful and Prosperous Country'. Unfortunately for Hideyori, the slogan included the characters for the name 'Ieyasu', and split them in a manner that Ieyasu found to be insulting. He also took umbrage at the wording of an innocuous poem that mentioned the 'setting sun' – the man who had faced thousands of foes in battle was now apparently so thin-skinned that he could not bear the thought of a symbol of the fading west (i.e. Edo) juxtaposed against the moon rising in the east (i.e. Osaka). As was his wont, he tried to reshuffle the feudal lords again, letting it be known that he wanted Hideyori to quite Osaka for another fief where he did not enjoy so much support. Hideyori responded that he lived in Osaka, and would die there, too, and Ieyasu began operations to grant him his wish by force.[9]

It is worth noting that Hideyori, the alleged dastardly plotter, was barely out of his teens when the sexagenarian warlord Ieyasu commenced his bid for power. Ieyasu did nothing to stop rumours that Hideyori was plotting against him and hoarding supplies for a revolt. Hideyori appears to have had no such intentions – in fact, he had recently returned a quantity of gunpowder to the English factory at Hirado because he had no use for it. We know this because Ieyasu bought the powder himself, along with some high-quality English cannons.[10] However, Hideyori had certainly attracted a sizeable quantity of hangers-on with a grudge against the Tokugawa. When the growing rift between him and Ieyasu became known, many thousands of samurai, dispossessed or lordless after Sekigahara, flocked to his standard.

The campaign usually known as the 'Siege of Osaka Castle' incorporates both the surrounding of Hideyori and several minor battles fought on the periphery, in a campaign that stretched from November 1614 into the following year. Ieyasu fought dirty, trapping Hideyori and his men within their fortifications before ordering his cannons to be trained not on the keep, but on the residence of Hideyori's mother within the castle grounds. With several female casualties, Hideyori's mother pleaded with him to sue for peace – Ieyasu was her uncle, but members of the defending forces with longer memories recalled Ieyasu's reputation for going back on his treaties when it suited him. However, Hideyori was persuaded, and a treaty was drawn up, signed by Ieyasu in blood. Only the most gullible of observers thought this was anything more than a delay in hostilities. Even the Jesuit priests regarded it as a cunning ruse by Ieyasu to smash certain castle defences by diplomacy instead of force:

> As it's rare in Japan for a War to end till one of the Parties is entirely lost, this Peace in Course was not like to last, nor indeed was it in [Ieyasu's] Design to keep it; being resolv'd to surprise his Enemy at unawares, and attack the Place when out of Posture of Defence.[11]

During the negotiations, Ieyasu alluded to an idea that would come to characterize his clan policy for centuries to come. With the settling of differences between himself and Hideyori, there would now be no more wars. It was hence unnecessary for Osaka Castle to have such wide-ranging defences. Although this idea was not incorporated into the text, it was soon made reality. During the process of 'departing', Ieyasu's troops approached close to the castle walls and filled in the outermost moat. Feeble protests from Hideyoshi's side were ignored, and in the weeks that followed, the 'no more wars' was forcibly restated. In other words, if he attempted to dig out the moats, he would clearly be preparing for combat, and the only possible foe would be Ieyasu. Hence, any attempts to refortify Osaka would be seen as an act of war, and an invitation for further hostilities.

A second, 'summer' campaign erupted in 1615, and ended after several skirmishes with the Battle of Tennōji, near Osaka Castle. It was widely believed by all present to be the last battle that would ever be fought on Japanese soil. Hideyori had an army in front of the castle, an army sneaking up on Ieyasu's flank, and a further force inside the castle. He planned to ride forth from the castle, his father's distinctive gourd standard held aloft, at a moment when his forces had the upper hand, presumably hoping to remind the assembled samurai that all this was being fought in the name of the order that the late Hideyoshi had established.

The nature of samurai combat had changed remarkably from the traditions of the medieval period. Now there was no exchange of arrows as an opening display, nor was there any thought of challenges to single combat. Instead, troops marched close enough to each other for the first line of footsoldiers to commence firing with their arquebuses. Strangely, even the habitual horsemen left their mounts behind on Ieyasu's advice. The Battle of Tennōji was fought largely on foot, devolving into an ugly scrum as each unit of gunners became too enmeshed in hand-to-hand combat to properly reload.

Only one part of the old tradition remained. There was still a certain power in the distinctive armour of known commanders and celebrities. One leading member of Hideyoshi's forces, a samurai named Sanada Yukimura who had been instrumental in Hideyoshi's small number of victories, supposedly faced Ieyasu in single combat and dealt him a savage spear-thrust in the side before the two were separated. Sanada limped away from the fighting to rest, exhausted, on a stool. As he crouched, panting in a brief respite from the violence, he heard an enemy soldier challenge him. He looked up and wheezed something non-committal, only to find that the man had come up close. Sanada was grabbed by the head and executed where he sat. It was a far cry from the ritualized combat of the olden days, although as we have repeatedly seen, the olden days were not entirely as the songs and poems depicted them, either.

The news that Sanada's head had been taken was itself a powerful weapon in Ieyasu's victory, although it alone was not enough to turn the tide. Straightforward losses, the failure of the sneak flanking manoeuvre to pay off, and the fact that the fighting was soon close to the walls of Osaka Castle all played their part. By the end of the day, Ieyasu's cannons were in range of the castle. The central keep was in flames the following day, and Hideyori was found to have committed *seppuku*.

Ieyasu did not long survive his victory at Osaka; he died in 1616. According to some sources, he died after the wound dealt him by Sanada refused to heal; according to others, he died of plain old age. But unlike previous warlords, Ieyasu's hold on Japan was sure. His legacy left the Tokugawa clan in control of 20 per cent of Japanese land, and with a system of hostage exchange and obligation that locked the second rung of landowners securely into the Tokugawa clan's axis.

Just as Hideyoshi had once collected swords, the Tokugawa Shōgunate collected guns, rounding up most of the muskets in peasant hands and locking them in castles. The castles themselves were carefully controlled. Each district was permitted to have only one true castle, which was to be the residence of Ieyasu's feudal appointee. Each lord maintained both a standing army of direct retainers and a subsidiary force of underlings who brought their own troops. However, no lord could move his forces across the borders of his domain without the authority of the Shōgun. Hence, the power of the samurai was turned almost entirely inward, for use in police actions, tax collecting and law enforcement. Other fortifications were decommissioned and dismantled, with the intention that each area would have a single strongpoint – one that was already in government hands.

Lords who knew what was good for them renounced their Christian sympathies. No Japanese lord dared to raise a Christian banner after the siege of Osaka Castle. Dario Sō, who cast off his Christian belief and Christian wife as a gesture of loyalty to the Tokugawa, was the example for the other lords to follow. Japan's Christian heartland, the Nagasaki–Shimabara–Amakusa crescent on Kyūshū, saw all its overlords become apostates. The last generation of footsoldiers, those who had fought in Korea, Sekigahara and Osaka – particularly those who had fought on the losing side – were no longer samurai at all. Instead, they were termed *kinōbushi* – 'soldiers returning to the land' – and were left to eke out existences as humble peasants. Many returned to their home domains, once Christian enclaves, now under the harsh rule of new appointees under strict orders to stamp out Christianity and keep their former enemies in line.

As a case in point, Matsukura Shigemasa (1574–1630) was a young soldier from central Japan, one of the last to climb up through the ranks. He won plaudits and a small fief at Sekigahara. Fifteen years on, at the end of his active military career, he fought under Ieyasu at the siege of Osaka. For this he was promoted into a challenging post. He was awarded Shimabara, the old estates of the lords of

Arima, a notorious Christian heartland, and home to many of Augustin Konishi's old troops. Matsukura was infamous for his persecutions of the Christians, against whom he employed inquisitors and informants. He also taxed them harshly, in part because of his own social aspirations. Determined to be regarded as a major lord, Matsukura deliberately miscalculated the productivity of his realm, assessing his annual rice quota as many times higher than the region's average yield. This gave him clout in Edo, but also forced him to back up his claims by meeting his boasts with sufficient tithe. It was his farmers who paid the price, taxed even further into the ground to meet unrealistic expectations.

Furthermore, after the imposition of the 'one-domain, one-castle' rule in 1618, Matsukura imposed even heavier demands on his people. Finding the extant castles in the region to be too small for his grand ambitions, he began building a super-fortress at Shimabara. The new castle was truly massive, drawing corvée labour and onlookers from all over the district. Matsukura's men ripped up ancient megaliths on the shore, and dragged rocks from decommissioned forts elsewhere. It incorporated seven wells within its grounds, and was far enough inland to avoid sea-based cannons. On a clear day, a watchman in his tower could see not only a vast swathe of Matsukura's territory, but across the strait to the neighbouring islands of Amakusa.

A message from the Shōgun Hidetada, Ieyasu's son, summed up the government's concern that Matsukura was taking things a little too seriously. 'Please use moderation in building the castle. There will be no more wars.'[12]

Matsukura died as his castle was completed. His son, Matsukura Katsuie inherited a pointlessly expensive military fortification, and a population on the edge of starvation. One of his neighbouring lords wrote: 'Districts are destitute, and because they could not farm or harvest, people have left their lands to find temporary work away from home. The fields have fallen into ruin.'[13]

In the 1630s, the peasants pushed back. Bad harvests, strong tax and victimization simply for once being a Christian region all took their toll. In 1637, a fight in southern Shimabara over tax collection escalated into a full-blown riot. By the time Matsukura's first group of samurai rode out to put the uprising down, they faced several hundred armed farmers. Matsukura, along with many of his underlings, had made a fatal error, confusing simple peasants with *kinōbushi* veterans who had nothing left to lose. He faced a group of rebels led by men of his father's generation, old soldiers who had fought hard in Korea and against Ieyasu. Far from Edo, many had even avoided the gun collectors, and still retained their old arquebuses.

The precise origins of the revolt are confusing. Accounts differ as to whether it was a spontaneous uprising or a rebellion that had long been planned by a group of persecuted Christians. The nominal leader was Jerome Amakusa Shirō, a teenage messiah, the son of an underground preacher and the figurehead of an uprising that soon swelled to encompass Shimabara and the entire Amakusa peninsula. The true leaders, perhaps, were half a dozen old warriors in their fifties and sixties, whose connections had united the veterans, disaffected peasantry and persecuted Christians of the area.[14]

The Shimabara Rebellion was arguably the last conflict of the original samurai era. Its participants were the last to remember a real war and real battles. The Christians involved were the last to remember the glory days of the foreign missionaries. The government response to the Shimabara Rebellion was the last test of the new Tokugawa system of control, and met with brutal, desperate success.

The rebels achieved limited early victories within their own domain, laying siege to a surprised garrison at Shimabara Castle, and looting the surrounding area. Non-Christians were forcibly conscripted into the army, and proclamations were issued to neighbouring domains, in the hope of stirring further trouble. Only the Amakusa islands, Augustin Konishi's old fief, responded with any enthusiasm. The tide of rebellion was held off at the other borders, thanks to severe clampdowns and brutal suppression.

The Shimabara rebels enjoyed a brief respite while the neighbouring lords waited for government approval to cross their own borders. Punitive forces from several neighbouring clans lurked, ready to pounce, but required the Shōgun's authorisation to do so. This, in turn, required the news of the revolt to travel to Edo, and for the order to suppress it to travel back. The first lords to hear of the uprising were hence the last who were permitted to mobilize against it, and did so ahead of further forces marching down from the south. This was to cause a certain tension among the government forces, as the closest neighbours rushed to score a decisive victory in the few weeks they had before far larger forces of allies arrived.

In Edo, the authorities reacted to the uprising with cold calculation. With Matsukura's behaviour already a matter of some concern, it was widely understood that simple poverty and deprivation was a far more likely cause for the revolt than a resurgence of Christian belief:

When talking at Edo Castle about the cause of the riot, the chief retainer of the Ōmura clan, Hikōemon, was asked whether Christians habitually had such uprisings. Hikōemon said that he doubted the insurrection was because of Christians. 'During the civil war era,' [he said], 'there were many Christian lords, but they never started riots. To tell the truth, I am now 70 years old, but I was once a Christian soldier myself.'[15]

Despite this level-headed assessment, the Shōgun resolved to use the pretext of the Shimabara Rebellion to kill off the problem of Christians once and for all, by killing off all the remaining Christians.

When the uprising faltered at the edges of Nagasaki and Kumamoto, the rebels retreated to Hara on the Shimabara peninsula. A decommissioned castle from the old days, Hara was an island connected to the mainland by a tidal marsh. As thousands of government troops occupied the nearby headland, the rebels waited within their hastily refortified base, numbering some 37,000 men, women and children.

Some of the early samurai arrivals decided to take the castle before the latecomers could share the credit. They were beaten back in a turkey-shoot as they attempted to scale the snaking pathways onto the heights of Hara:

Among [the defenders] were four or five hundred bowsmen able to hit even the eye of a needle, and some eight hundred musketeers that would not miss a boar or a hare on the run, nor even a bird in flight. On earthen parapets they set up catapults to hurl stones at the approaching enemy. Even the women had their tasks apportioned to them: they were to prepare glowing hot sand and with great ladles cast it upon the attackers, and also to boil water seething hot and pour it upon them.[16]

A second attempt to take the castle on 14 February 1638 saw the commander of the attacking forces killed in the assault. He had rushed into action in the hope of taking the castle before higher-ranking lords arrived on the scene and relieved him of his command, and contemporary chroniclers framed his decision as a form of indirect suicide. In either case, the inexperienced local commander was practically forced into 'ordering' the attack by his fractious and belligerent troops. In fact, the orders from the Shōgun, confident that the rebels were bottled inside the castle with a limited food supply, were simply to starve out the besieged Christians, and hence avoid any undue risks. Risks, however, were the samurai's staple, and the younger soldiers in particular demanded the chance to take the castle on. Even on the occasions of coordinated assaults, the siege of Hara Castle contains numerous incidents of samurai accidentally attacking too early, or taking feints too far, becoming genuine assaults.

Tachibana Muneshige, an old soldier in his eighties, was unequivocal with the bloodthirsty junior officers:

> This castle will be difficult to take in a single assault. If you press an assault, you will incur many casualties and that will be against the Shōgun's will. The best plan is to stop their supplies. Even if you wish to attack, you should wait.[17]

For making such a statement of the blazingly obvious, Tachibana was accused of cowardice by a younger officer. The arrival of Matsudaira Nobutsuna, the highest-ranking samurai present, put paid to matters. Only sixteen at the time of the Siege of Osaka Castle, Matsudaira was of the new breed of samurai who had barely seen a real battle. More used to Edo politics, he nevertheless reiterated the Shōgun's command, and ordered that the samurai should show that most unwarlike of virtues, patience:

> I have been educated in a peaceful time and have acquired no military renown; still I have come hither, commissioned

by the Shōgun, though my plans may differ from yours, and may appear to you extremely foolish, yet in the matter of taking the castle, follow my instructions. Our recent failure to take the castle was merely because the conspirators stake their lives on its defence . . . This is not an ordinary conflict. In this there is no difference between soldiers and farmers, because firearms are used. In my judgement, since this castle was fitted up in haste, there is no great store of provisions in it. Food will give out in not more than one or two months. From present appearances, when food is exhausted they will try to escape from the castle with eagerness. Should we attempt to take the place by storm, there is no doubt that many lives will be lost. Therefore, merely fortify the camp with pickets, and build towers from which to discharge your guns, and when the time to attack comes, I will give the word of command.[18]

Hara Castle held out for another six weeks, while its denizens slowly wasted away, bickered over their fate, and held off occasional 'mistaken' assaults by samurai who had carefully misheard Matsudaira's command. In particular, the samurai of the Hosokawa clan developed a reputation for cunning ruses, with attempts to tunnel underneath the castle wall, to blow up its foundations, and even to hurry along the castle's fall by hunting down relatives of the defenders and parading them in front of the battlements.

The *Rijp*, a ship provided with extreme reluctance by the Dutch East India Company, arrived in March to provide help to the besiegers. The presence of the Dutch was greeted with a mixed reception – some of the samurai appreciated a gesture that demonstrated the Dutch claims to abide by the Shōgun's laws even extended to firing on their 'fellow' Christians (as Protestants, the Dutch had merrily stamped on the *fumi-e* and continued to encourage the Japanese to regard the Catholics as their enemies).

Many more, however, were frankly embarrassed that the samurai needed to call on foreign help. A sarcastic comment to this effect was also made by the besieged rebels, and when a Dutch artilleryman was killed in an explosion, it presented the samurai with a reasonable excuse to permit the Dutch to leave once more.

Espionage also played a part. One faction of veterans within the castle intrigued with old war buddies among the besiegers. Arima Naozumi, who had once been the Christian lord Michael Arima, announced to his fellow samurai that an old acquaintance from the Korean days had contacted him from within the castle and was ready to switch sides. Whether this was true or not (and on the evidence available, it seems to have been), discovery of this conspiracy caused further division and demoralization among the ranks of the rebels within the castle.

The rebels made one desperate raid against their besiegers, before the castle fell to an assault from all sides in April 1638. During the assault, there were, true enough, echoes of the samurai of old: there was jostling, shoving and even blows exchanged over who got to be the first into each inner keep. Once inside, however, it was far from the samurai's finest hour. Defenders were weak and emaciated, and now offered little resistance. The samurai attackers nevertheless hacked and slashed their way across a vast encampment of men, women and children, many of them too weak to stand. As the castle was engulfed in flames, it became difficult to tally the number of the dead, but estimates place the rebel headcount in the tens of thousands. The massacre of the denizens of Hara Castle was intended as a final holocaust to deal with the Christian problem in the south, and a brutal message to any other disgruntled former soldiers who might be tempted to stand up to the government.

In the aftermath, Matsudaira was forced to report that, despite the Shōgun's orders to stay out of trouble, the besieging samurai force had taken casualties of 13 per cent due to foolhardy attacks and accidents. The last 'battle' of the samurai had been the simple butchery of thousands of feeble civilians. One of the besiegers was ordered to commit *seppuku*, after he had been caught claiming that the hacked-off nose of a fallen comrade had belonged to a rebel enemy. It is perhaps not surprising that so many accounts of the samurai era prefer to end with the Siege of Osaka, which was at least a battle between well-matched warriors.

However, the fall of Hara Castle was a chilling indicator of how attitudes would change during the era of Tokugawa rule. Now that all the samurai were nominally on the same side, and now that there were no more wars, to a certain extent they turned instead on those who they were supposed to be defending. The consolidation set in motion by Hideyoshi, and continued by Ieyasu, found its final fruition with Ieyasu's immediate successors. Christian belief was a capital offence, movement outside one's home domain was strictly regulated, and obedience to the samurai order was enforced on pain of death. In theory, at least, a samurai could draw his sword and strike down anyone who did not offer him the correct degree of respect. In practice, this was often tempered by the likelihood that such a loss of control would also cost the life of the angry swordsman.

The draconian order was kept in place by numerous edicts, not least a series of prohibitions on foreign travel and foreign contacts, which came to be known as *Sakoku* – the 'Closed Country'. Already in force by the time of the Shimabara Rebellion, Sakoku forbade foreigners from freely entering Japan, and even the Japanese gene pool – half-breeds being exiled in the 1630s. Sakoku created a wall of fear around Japan, and obligated domains on the coast to keep a constant watch against unwelcome foreign intruders. Among these were occasional parties of Christian missionaries, defying the death penalty to land on Japanese shores to administer to dwindling populations of secret, hidden Christian believers. One of the last missionaries to be caught was himself of Japanese descent – Father Mancio Konishi, believed to have been the grandson of Augustin Konishi, raised in Macao, ordained in Rome, and executed in Japan in 1644.

Sakoku is a problematic term in Japanese studies. There is a modern fad for quibbling with it, pointing out, for example, that while Japan may have been closed, it was hardly 'open' in the preceding years. It is also customary to point out that Sakoku, in the words of one scholar, 'had many holes', and was permeable in several places. After all, there were still official trade ties in Nagasaki, where a small number of licensed Dutch and Chinese merchants were permitted to drop anchor at their respective ghetto-islands.[19]

There were other unofficial links abroad. In Tsushima, the Sō clan continued to quietly maintain trade ties with the 'hermit kingdom' of Korea. In Kagoshima, the Shimazu clan maintained an informal suzerainty over the long chain of the Ryūkyū Islands, which allowed them indirect access to traders from China. In the far north, as the Matsumae clan settled in a trading post on the northernmost island of Ezo, the precise location of the northern border was fuzzy and open to reinterpretation. There was also an opportunity to gain access to goods that had been walked across the winter ice from Siberia. Japanese subjects continued to appear in the strangest of places. Some were found fighting as mercenaries in south-east Asia. Others, the descendants of exiles, cropped up in Macao or Goa. With the fall of the Ming dynasty in 1644, there were rumours of Japanese mercenaries fighting on behalf of the Ming resistance, although they remain unsubstantiated.[20]

Such cavils, however, often misdirect the reader into assuming that Japan enjoyed rich and varied contacts with the outside world. In fact, for all but a handful of individuals on the periphery, life in Japan during the Tokugawa period was resolutely inward looking.

The Tokugawa system classified the feudal domains in terms of their loyalties to Ieyasu – in particular, the allegiances of a particular clan's samurai at the Battle of Sekigahara in 1600 would largely determine the way their descendants were treated for the next 250 years. The wealthy domains of Owari, Kii and Mito were bestowed upon the descendants of the favourite sons of Ieyasu, and formed collateral branches of the Tokugawa family, with strong support for any incumbent shōgun. So, too, did the other 'Related Houses' (*Shinpan*), some twenty domains ruled by other descendants of Ieyasu. Beneath them in the hierarchy were the 'Hereditary Lords' (*Fudai Daimyō*), loyal vassals of the Tokugawa, and the descendants of lords who had pledged their allegiance to Ieyasu before the Battle of Sekigahara. Many of their domains were quite small, but strategically crucial, straddling important river-crossings, harbours and mountain passes. The lowest-ranking feudal administrators were the 'Outer Lords' (*Tozama Daimyō*) who had only pledged allegiance to Ieyasu after the opening charge of the Battle of Sekigahara. These included many of those who had switched sides at the last moment, but was also a polite spin on those houses that had been forced to surrender. Although many of the Outer Lords were shuffled, demoted or otherwise edged into obscurity, there were several distant domains whose rulers would remain powerful. In particular, the southern domains of Satsuma, Chōshū and Tosa would nurture their grudge against the Tokugawa for the next two centuries, and would eventually be instrumental in the Tokugawa's final fall.

For the Japanese peasant, the farming year was interrupted by occasions of corvée labour, and by the annual New Year's festivities, which included forming a line to trample on a picture of a Christian icon. After a time, the inquisitions that terrorized the Christian enclaves of the south were imposed upon the entire country. Movement was highly regulated, and difficult between domains without the correct paperwork. Nor was it easy to even move faith – every subject had to provide proof of membership of a Buddhist temple. This not only demonstrated a lack of corruption by Christian belief, but also a lifelong obligation of donations and ceremonies. Abbots came to expect the donations from their flock, and to regard any change of sect or allegiance as suspicious. There were even cases of corrupt priests blackmailing their parishioners with threats to 'expose' them as Christians.

For the samurai, now a hereditary class, movement was somewhat freer. This was largely because of the intricate system of attendance and obligations imposed on feudal lords, requiring them to spend alternate amounts of time in Edo and in their home domain. When not in Edo, a lord was obliged to leave his wife and/or heir in in his place, in a thinly disguised hostage system. Although the frequency varied – depending on the size of domain, distance from Edo and status of the lord – the Japanese roads were regularly thronged with huge processions of samurai, mounted guards, lords in their palanquins and dozens of porters carrying the baggage. Either heading to or from Edo, these snakes of people created a massive domestic travel industry of wayside inns, hot-spring resorts, entertainers, hawkers and prostitutes.

The samurai class performed many of the functions that

we would now associate with the civil service. They worked as clerks in their lords' storehouses, and as night-watchmen. They trained the next generation of warriors and, when in Edo, performed numerous bodyguard or corvée functions either for their lord when he was in residence, or as part of their lord's obligation to the incumbent shōgun. For this, they were paid in rice.

Beyond the peasants, clergy and samurai, a fourth class occupied a very strange position. Merchants, traditionally regarded as the lowest class, with a status only one above the 'untouchable' butchers and leatherworkers, enjoyed unprecedented success during the long period of peace. Urban centres attracted merchants who were able to profit from the disposable income of the richer samurai, selling them tableware and artistic artefacts, home comforts and nightly entertainments. As the generations passed, many of these profiteers amassed more wealth than the classes that supposedly sat above them on the social scale. While the samurai toiled for their lords on dull tasks, it was the merchant class who began to patronize the theatres, restaurants and brothels. As the merchants prospered, inflation began to erode the value of the samurai's rice stipend.

The rules of the samurai class reflect their bizarre position in Japanese society after the 1630s. There were, as the shōgunate had repeatedly claimed, 'no more wars,' although there were occasional peasant uprisings to put down. One gets a sense, even as early as the Shimabara Rebellion, of the young samurai spoiling for the chance to put their martial prowess to use after years and years of training for no actual purpose. The martial arts themselves, repeatedly and obsessively studied but no longer applied, began to lose some of their practical qualities. During this period, we see the resolutely realistic '-jutsu' suffix of military training replaced by the usually more theoretical

'-dō'. Kendō, the 'way of the sword', develops in this period into a symbolic discipline more like a sport, in which, for the most part, participants hit each other with symbolic swords made of bamboo or wood. Kyūdō, the 'way of the bow', remained as an aristocratic hobby. Perhaps most telling of all, we first hear talk of Bushidō, the 'way of the warrior'.

Localized, clan-based and domain-specific writings by disparate figures began to coalesce into a general idea of the way that a warrior should behave, even with no wars to fight. Although they bore a strong affinity with guides for underlings written by many samurai in olden times, the formation of a code of Bushidō in the late seventeenth century and onwards often appears to have a reactive, protesting whine to it. The ailing Shōgun Tokugawa Iemitsu was moved in 1650 to order that it was the duty of all samurai to maintain their equipment to the correct standards. In the same year, he outlawed duels between idle samurai. In 1694, his successor Tokugawa Tsunayoshi ordered that the practice of the martial arts was mandatory – as if he had noticed that many of the samurai in government service were now warriors in name only. Horrified reports attested that some samurai could not even swim. Others were dressing in outrageous finery little different from that worn by merchants. Sumptuary laws attempted to re-emphasize martial virtues, but it seems that the Tokugawa era offered many temptations for samurai to forget the old ways.[21]

Matsudaira Nobutsuna, who had successfully overseen the massacre of the Christians at Shimabara, went on to become one of the five regents of the new pre-teen Shōgun, Tokugawa Ietsuna. However, unlike Ietsuna's great-grandfather Ieyasu's doomed stewardship of another young ruler, this regency proved fruitful and successful, and Ietsuna went on to rule Japan in the Emperor's name from 1651 to 1680. When he died, still at the relatively young age of thrty-nine, a new succession crisis almost arose, when an underling dared to propose that the post of shōgun should not automatically be conferred upon a Tokugawa heir, but on an imperial appointee. After all, that would be what one might expect if the shōgun truly were a servant of the emperor. However, this idea was swiftly quashed, and Ietsuna's younger brother Tsunayoshi was put in charge. Conflicting reports about the new shōgun's secluded, scholarly upbringing have been inferred by some to mean that he was something of a simpleton, and certainly thought to be malleable by that ever-recurring Japanese group, the shadowy figures behind the throne.

Tsunayoshi was not quite the Caligula of the shōgunate, although some of the stranger events in his reign did point to the dangers of putting the wrong man in charge of a draconian dictatorship. During the twenty-nine years of his reign, some 1.4 million *koku* of feudal lands were confiscated and reassigned, demonstrating either a remarkable number of incompetent feudal lords, the settling of some old scores or, most likely, intrigues in the Shōgun's name by the inner circle that claimed to serve him. Insinuations persist that Tsunayoshi was a homosexual, not uncommon among the samurai in this period, but chiefly worth mentioning here because of the further allegation that he was under the thumb of his young lover, the minor noble Yanagisawa Yoshiyasu.

It is, then, difficult to assign blame precisely for the most infamous decrees of Tsunayoshi's reign, his Edicts on Compassion for Living Things. According to Tsunayoshi, who was born in the Year of the Dog, the people of Edo were being remiss in their behaviour towards lower animals, and it was incumbent upon them to be nice to animals, particularly dogs. Since the word of the Shōgun was law and nobody dared to oppose him, this in turn led to several bizarre years in which stray dogs and their attendant diseases multiplied all around Edo, while the populace were forbidden from interfering. In one case, a man was executed for striking a dog, while an eventual scheme to round up the dogs and take them to the countryside led to the construction and maintenance of 50,000 kennels in the suburbs. Such madness led to the characterization of Tsunayoshi as the 'Dog Shōgun'. His successor and nephew Ienobu was mercifully saner.

However, Tsunayoshi was not entirely surrounded by charlatans. His uncle, Tokugawa Mitsukuni (1628–1701), the lord of Mito domain, was a competent politician who oversaw the authorship and assembly of the *History of Japan* (*Dai Nihon Shi*). Commenced in 1658, and not truly finished until 1906, although most of the chapters were completed in Mitsukuni's lifetime, the *History of Japan* was designed to rectify what Mitsukuni saw as the shortcomings in earlier historical accounts.

There were, of course, many war chronicles and historical novels, but when it came to true court records, Mitsukuni wrote off previous efforts as mere 'chronologies'. Instead, he conceived his *History of Japan* in imitation of Chinese classics such as the *Shiji* by Sima Qian, and the works of the neo-Confucian scholar Zhu Xi. He was aided in this venture by the presence of refugee Chinese academics among the writers of his 'Mito School'. Fleeing the collapse of the Ming dynasty in mainland China, they brought an emphasis on moral education through history, and the framing of the *History of Japan* was to exert an influence long after Mitsukuni's death. The Shōgun, as all acknowledged, had been the de facto ruler of Japan since at least the time of Oda Nobunaga. Nobody had ruled Japan at all during the great civil wars, but previously authority had resided in earlier shōguns. The *History of Japan*, while acknowleding the participation of various samurai in the formation of the Japanese state, clung resolutely to a Chinese model, asserting the idea that it was the Emperor who was always in ultimate control, and that the actions of his samurai were always undertaken out of loyalty to his wishes. This, of course, was by no means the first time that anyone had claimed this – it had been a popular rallying cry for centuries. The *History of Japan* begins in 660 BC with the creation myths of the Japanese state, and concerned itself chiefly with the two millennia that followed, ending its main narrative with the resolution of the 'two emperors' problem in 1392.

Nevertheless the *History of Japan*, commissioned under the auspices of a member of the Tokugawa family, and hence presumed approved by the Shōgun himself, was to become an important book in the curriculum of future generations of samurai. Over the following decades, its assertions gnawed at the ties that bound the warrior class in allegiance to the Tokugawa. If one read between the lines of the *History of Japan*, as increasing numbers of unhappy samurai were wont to do, then there was more to the emperor than lip service to an impoverished aristocracy in Kyōto. Instead, the emperor was a viable, potent force in Japanese politics, a figure to whom all swore loyalty. Essentially, the *History of Japan* reminded the samurai that there was a higher power than the shōgun himself, and that should the shōgun ever fail in his duties, it was incumbent on samurai to assert their loyalty *to the Emperor* by defying his barbarian-suppressing generalissimo. This idea, however, was more than a century in coming. Loyalty to the emperor was a long-term, strategic matter for samurai thought; in day-to-day life, there was the more tactical question of staying alive and jockeying for position.[22]

The year of Mitsukuni's death saw one of the defining events of eighteenth-century Japan, the infamous vendetta of the 'Forty-Seven Rōnin'. As part of the endless rounds of ceremonial and courtesy calls of the Tokugawa period, Asano Naganori, the young feudal lord of the Akō domain was ordered to entertain envoys in Edo who had freshly arrived from Kyōto – still the official capital. As part of the preparations, he was instructed by Kira Yoshinaka, one of the Shōgun's high-ranking officials. The men do not appear to have hit it off, and, reading between the lines, Kira was expecting substantial bribes and honoraria from Asano, even though it was his job to instruct him. Whatever the nature of the tensions between them, Kira had mastered the art of the snide comment, and seems to have made one allusion too many about Asano's country origins. On 21 April 1701, under a covered walkway at one of the Shōgun's mansions, Kira pushed too far, and an enraged Asano drew his short sword and knifed him in the face (or shoulder, depending on the source).[23]

The wound was minor and the brawling men were soon separated by guards, but the damage was done. Regardless of claims of the right of samurai to defend their honour, drawing a weapon within the Shōgun's palace was a capital offence. Asano was ordered to commit *seppuku*, his lands were forfeit, and his followers were outcasts – rōnin. When the news reached Asano's castellan Ōishi Yoshio, Ōishi obediently shut down the castle, disbanded the soldiers, and handed the keys and manifests to the new lord appointed by the shōgunate. Where once there might have been war, the Tokugawa rule was supreme, and a lord could be unseated by simple decree.

However, while Ōishi had done his duty to the Shōgun by obeying orders, he was also determined to do his duty by the wronged lord Asano. In the company of several dozen fellow retainers (traditionally forty-seven, but possibly more), he plotted his revenge against Kira. Over the two years that followed, Ōishi gave every appearance of being a discredited samurai. He was seen in Kyōto brothels, he was publicly drunk, and he was conspicuously on the Tokugawa-era scrapheap. In a move that has often been cited as an indicator of his true nobility, he even divorced his wife and disowned his children, to ensure that they would not have to bear any consequences for his coming vendetta.

Slowly, the Forty-Seven Rōnin converged on Edo. One married the daughter of the man who had built Kira's house, obtaining in the process the plans for the inside of the mansion. Others secretly smuggled weapons into Edo. The vengeful assassins struck on 14 December 1702, in a double-pronged assault on Kira's snow-bound house. Pointedly, several of Ōishi's men were assigned to secure the porters, neighbours and servants, not with violence, but with the simple announcement that the samurai were on noble business, and that no non-combatants need be hurt.

The mansion erupted in a savage battle between Ōishi's men and Kira's underlings, which saw sixteen of Kira's men killed and another twenty-two wounded. Kira, however, had fled through a secret exit, leaving his bedclothes still warm. Ōishi bested two other retainers in a dark, secluded courtyard, before dragging the man they were protecting into the light. Beneath the warm glow of the lantern, Ōishi saw the scar left by his master's knife. He had his man.

In one of the strange turnabouts of the samurai world, Ōishi dropped to his knees and bowed before Kira, explaining who he was and humbly offering him the chance to atone for his misdeeds by committing suicide. It was only when the cowering Kira refused to respond that Ōishi dragged him up by his hair, and hacked off his head. Their job done, the samurai carefully extinguished the lamps in the house in order to avoid accidental arson, and then ran for Asano's grave with Kira's head.

As the sun rose, word spread of their action, and they made their way to the temple grounds of Sengakuji amid something of a carnival atmosphere, congratulated and fêted by the townsfolk. They laid Kira's head on Asano's grave, and then turned themselves in to the authorities – all except one, who had been sent to Asano's old domain to pass on the news.

The vendetta was an awful embarrassment for the Shō-gun's government – the samurai had behaved impeccably according to samurai tradition, but had also defied a Shō-gunal prohibition. Edo locals did not help by petitioning the Shōgun on behalf of Ōishi and his men, pointing out how true they were to the nebulously defined samurai code of honour. Eventually, the Shōgun ordered that instead of the death penalty as common murderers, the rōnin would be offered the chance to commit *seppuku* as a gesture of respect. This they did in early 1703, with the exception of the messenger in Akō, who was spared. Their act cleared the name of their late lord, restored the reputation of their many fellow retainers, and eventually led to the restoration of the house of Asano, albeit with a greatly reduced size of fief.

The men were held up as heroes by many, although one noted commentator gruffly wondered how 'true to tradi-tion' it would have been if their target had died of an illness during the prolonged execution of their two-year plan. Instead, one samurai theorist suggested that the true samurai way would have been to attack Kira on the day of the original insult. They would still have died, but the process would have been quicker and more conspicuous. Such a comment, made by Yamamoto Tsunetomo, encap-sulates the contradictions of the samurai era. Taken at face value, there often seems little difference between a samurai dispute over honour and a fight in a pub between football hooligans over who has the nicest scarf.[24]

The story was eventually adapted into a powerful drama, *Chūshingura*, 'The Treasury of Loyal Retainers', but this was only performed in 1748, two whole generations after the events it depicted. At first, it was a *bunraku* puppet show, the number of rōnin conveniently set at forty-seven so that one could be represented by each symbol in the Japanese kana-writing syllabary. It would later be adapted into a kabuki performance, and became one of the cornerstones of the kabuki repertoire. Even then, the names were changed and the setting was moved to the fourteenth century, in an effort to avoid angering the authorities. It should come as no surprise that the Tokugawa government extended its iron grip on its subjects into their entertainments. Rare indeed was the creator who was prepared to put on a play or publish a book that was critical of the Tokugawa regime. Reportage of current events was often steered into allegory, dwelling at least superficially on the distant past or exotic destinations, in order to deflect the government censor. At the time that real-world Japan was aflutter with news of the vendetta of the Forty-Seven Rōnin, the stage conspicuously occupied itself with *The Battles of Coxinga*, a garish, fantastical retelling of the fall of the Ming dynasty, and the part played in it by a half-Japanese warrior.

Chikamatsu's *Love Suicides at Sonezaki* (*Sonezaki Shinjū*, first performed 1703) reflects the samurai ethic as it was distilled into the merchant class. It features a poor merchant and his courtesan lover. He is ordered to marry another, borrows money to buy himself out of trouble, but is swindled out of his cash by an unscrupulous fellow merchant. At the edge of their wits, the lovers commit suicide, torn between the eternal Tokugawa-era standoff of Duty versus Emotion. The play was such a runaway success, and resulted in so many copycat double-suicides, that the authorities were moved to ban plays about lovers' suicides after 1723.

Although the samurai were ever present – in the streets, in the taverns, on the stage – one would be forgiven for thinking that they were ghosts of a bygone era. Japan remained, at least nominally, in a permanent state of readiness. There were 'no more wars', but the samurai class remained ever watchful for the catalysts that might trigger new conflict. They scanned the coasts for unwelcome foreign ships; they rooted out nests of hidden Christian sympathizers. And all the while, the Tokugawa clan shuffled the lords in their domains, carefully balancing the power relationships of the winners and losers at Sekigahara, making sure that all roads led to Edo.

In the far north, on a pilgrimage to see famous ancient sites, the poet Bashō (1644–94) stumbled across the ancient ruins of Takadachi Fort on the banks of the Koromo River, where Yoshitsune and the last of his followers had once made their last stand against their samurai enemies. He found an idyllic, green glade in the sunshine, broken only occasionally by patches of time-worn rubble where there had once been a building of some description. The sight moved him to write a verse on times past:

The summer grasses
As if the warriors were a dream.[25]

TWILIGHT OF THE SAMURAI
THE TOKUGAWA IN DECLINE

In the far north, on the island of Ezo, was the only place where Japanese territory still shared a land border with a foreign culture. The Takeda family, who had been most prominent in establishing colonies and suppressing unrest on the island for the last century, was renamed Matsumae, and left in charge of the island. Their true authority did not stretch much further north than the location of modern Hakodate, and was known locally as the *Wajinchi* – Territory of the Japanese. The majority of the rest of the island was *Ezochi* – 'Shrimp Barbarian' Territory, and the Matsumae clan earned much of its wealth from trade with the locals. It is unclear, but very likely, that the inhabitants of Ezo were the ethnic remnants of, or at least related to some extent to, the Emishi of ancient records. Genetically, they were clearly a different breed to the Japanese, and are today assumed to be the last remnants of a Siberian people who once inhabited the Japanese mainland far to the south, but were then pushed further and further north by the arrival of the ancestors of the Japanese from the mainland. Contrary to popular belief, they were not 'Caucasian', although they were lighter skinned than the average Japanese, often heavily tattooed, and notably hairier. Some commentators have taken this to mean that the men simply had less trouble growing beards than the average Japanese, although there is anecdotal evidence from at least one source that they were demonstrably hirsute.[1]

These people did not, of course, refer to themselves as Shrimp Barbarians. They called themselves *Ainu* ('Humans'), in opposition to their perception of another, numinous presence among the trees and mountains, the *Kamui* ('Gods'). The Matsumae clan enjoyed exclusive trading rights with the Ainu, and their mere presence began to exert powerful changes on the tribes close to their stockades. The competition for resources to trade with the Japanese often caused conflicts among the Ainu themselves. A simmering vendetta between two groups of Ainu lasted for much of the 1650s, before the chieftains Onibishi and Shakushain were persuaded to agree a truce. A decade later, in 1666, hostilities broke out once more, apparently when hunters from Onibishi's clan were allegedly caught poaching on land that belonged to Shakushain. They appear to have been led to encroach on Shakushain's turf by the constant search for live animals, skins and pelts to trade with the Japanese – the new arrivals in the *Wajinchi* had created a new demand for goods that pushed the equilibrium of the Ainu hunting system over the edge.[2]

Tit-for-tat punitive killings escalated into attacks by Ainu war bands from the rival clans. By 1668, with Onibishi killed in the fighting, men from his clan sought help from the Matsumae samurai against the 'rebel' Shakushain. Although the Matsumae sent mediators that once again calmed the unrest, it established a dangerous precedent that the clan of the late Onibishi enjoyed a special relationship with the Matsumae. When hostilities next flared up in 1669, Shakushain's tribesmen targeted not only their Ainu enemies, but also a passing Matsumae trading ship.

The conflict on Ezo was now reframed in similar terms to that of the early samurai and their interference in the relations of 'peaceful' and 'wild' Emishi 1,000 years before. By the time the news reached Edo, it was described as a 'rebellion' by Shakushain against the Matsumae.

Politically, this threatened the widely proclaimed peace of the shōgunate, and suggested that the 'barbarian-suppressing general' was lax in his duties. Behind the scenes, it also stirred up paranoia about an invasion from the Chinese mainland. The Ming dynasty had fallen to Manchu invaders in 1644, although the conquest of southern China was still underway. Just as Khubilai Khan had once occupied China and then turned on Japan, some within the shōgunate fretted that the unrest in the north was the advance guard of a Manchu invasion from the north. The Manchus, after all, were said to come from the same part of north-east Asia as cousins of the Ainu, and might be presumed to be planning an invasion from Sakhalin Island.[3]

This fear was unfounded. The notoriously land-bound Manchus never seem to have entertained the prospect of invading the inconsequential island of Japan, and Sha-kushain's uprising was a purely local event. Nevertheless, the Shōgunate took no chances and suppressed it with several thousand troops. Despite the supposed confiscation of muskets all over Japan, they still appear to have been in widespread use among the Matsumae and their Ainu allies.

Shakushain's men, however, gave as good as they got until they were surrounded by two punitive expeditions and forced to surrender and pay tribute.

After the apocalyptic conclusion of the Shimabara Rebellion, the relatively simple resolution of Shakushain's uprising seems like something of an anti-climax. Shakushain himself was killed in 1669, and with the loss of his charismatic, unifying voice, the Ainu lost an alternative vision to the trading-post relationship with the samurai on their border. The precise edge of the samurai world, its border with the lands of the Ainu, remained vague, and the island remained a wilderness frontier. Subsequent descriptions of the Ainu through to the late nineteenth century begin to bear a distinct similarity to descriptions of native Americans on their reservations – a disheartened, unsophisticated people, ring-fenced from the civilized world, and a reminder of a more savage time. Notably, there seems to have been little incentive for the samurai to spearhead active colonial efforts beyond the *Wajinchi* into Ainu lands. Instead, the Ainu hunted, fished and trapped on behalf of the Japanese, and the presence of a vast market in the *Wajinchi* gradually transformed the priorities and lifestyle of the Ainu across the border, commodifying what had once been a simple subsistence economy, and setting the Ainu against each other.

Surprisingly, the unrest in the north did not provoke the shōgunate to open up new areas of settlement on Ezo. Instead, Japan remained walled behind its sixteenth-century borders, with limited contact with the outside world, and hence little opportunity to learn from outsiders or seek their help.

The infamous 'Dog Shōgun' died in 1709 without issue, and was succeeded by his nephew Ienobu, who soon dismantled some of the stranger institutions and laws set up his predecessors. On Ienobu's own death four years later, the shōgunate fell to his infant son Ietsugu, and hence largely into the hands of the young ruler's adviser and mentor, the philosopher Arai Hakuseki (1657–1725). A prolific writer, Arai had produced an educationally motivated *Reading of History* (*Tokushi Yoron*, 1712), and a carefully compiled account of the world outside Japan, *Things Heard From the West* (*Seiyō Kibun*, 1715). This latter book comprised accounts of the continents of the world, as well as records of interviews with Giovanni Battista Sidotti (1668–1714), an Italian missionary who had been arrested after illegally entering Japan, and held under house arrest for the rest of his life.

As Regent for the Shōgun, Arai was able to put his thirst for knowledge and exceptionally bright ideas to good use. Noting the amount of gold and silver that was being squandered on trade with the Chinese and Dutch, he encouraged merchants to use barter instead of precious metals in their dealings with the foreigners. He also worked hard to codify the position of the shōgun. Realizing that times had changed since the battlefield commissions of yesteryear, Arai argued that the shōgun was as much a divinely mandated position as that of the emperor himself, and that while the emperor was undoubtedly the superior, the shōgun's role was to loyally administer the nation on the emperor's behalf. With that in mind, Arai even suggested that the shōgun be renamed the King of the Nation (*Koku-Ō*) – a suggestion that would have greatly simplified the protocols required with dealing with other countries, should the Sakoku edicts ever be repealed. His ideas, however, fell on deaf ears, and his infant charge died before reaching his teens.

The late Ietsugu had even younger brothers, who might have been installed as successors, but it would seem that none in the shōgunate wanted to revive the medieval practice of appointing impossibly young candidates and ruling in their name. Instead, the direct line of Tokugawa shōguns was declared at an end, and a substitute chosen from a collateral branch of the family, set up by Ieyasu himself in case of just such an eventuality. Knowing full well of the troubles caused by the dying out of the Mina-moto line in the thirteenth century, Tokugawa Ieyasu had nominated other branches of his family as successors ready to take power, and it was one of these, Tokugawa Yoshimune (1684–1751), who took over in 1716.

Yoshimune was a powerful man in his early thirties, already with strong administrative experience in his home domain, which he had judiciously raised out of debt following damaging fires and a tidal wave. He was resolutely practical, and found even Arai's reforms to be too airy and theoretical. In particular, he disliked Arai's Confucian-influenced drift towards ceremonial – Yoshimune preferred to spend state money on public works, not private protocol, regardless of how much philosophers thought the ceremonies improved officials' sense of propriety.

Yoshimune was arguably the best of the post-Ieyasu shōguns, aided greatly by being in power three decades, which allowed him to settle in and plan for the long term. Despite his disagreements with many of Arai's ideas, he still seemed prepared to follow Arai's implied drift towards becoming a more civilian-minded ruler, and not an ad hoc military governor. Under Yoshimune's rule, it was no longer a capital crime to appeal to the Shōgun for justice or to submit petitions of complaint or suggestion. The reign of Yoshimune also saw impressive new reclamation and irrigation schemes to open new farmland.

Notwithstanding his abilities, he inherited a state that was already teetering on the brink of bankruptcy. Although

Yoshimune publicly stated that his guiding principle was the wishes of his ancestor Ieyasu, behind the scenes he was forced to grapple with the consequences of having a ruling elite of samurai warriors after nearly a hundred years of peace. For the first time in centuries, the samurai class was expanding with no wars to thin it out; the number of retainers in the provinces was ballooning, and the inheritance of ancestors' ranks by an ever-increasing pool of descendants was placing a heavy strain on the coffers of their lords. Yoshimune limited the inheritance of ranks, particularly with regard to adoption, which, as in the days of the earliest samurai, was fast becoming a common means of nouveaux riches clambering up the social hierarchy.

Citing more pressing matters, such as famines in the 1720s, Yoshimune also began to reduce government spending on luxuries, hoping to encourage similar sumptuary reductions in the populace. He imposed a 1 per cent tax on each domain lord, but tempered this grab for finances by reducing their obligations to attend to him in Edo. In the short term, this generated more revenue for the government, but as time passed, it weakened the ties between Edo and the outlying regions. Since samurai salaries and government taxes were paid in rice, the ease on finances also worked only for as long as there was rice to be had. An insect blight in the summer of 1732 destroyed a large proportion of the year's rice crop, causing a famine among two million Japanese subjects, but also crippling the economy of samurai salaries and government revenue. Despite the proclamation of 'no more wars', food riots became a periodic occurrence in the 1730s, even in times of good harvest, when speculators began to hoard their surplus ready to cash in when food was inevitably in short supply once more. With a regime dominated by such fluctuations in price and availability, Yoshimune gained the nickname of the 'Rice Shōgun'.[4]

Japan's isolation might have cut off Christian/foreign interference, but it also left Japan to cope with natural disasters unaided. Once again, despite his self-proclaimed opposition to much of Arai Hakuseki's ideas, Yoshimune found himself following some of Arai's policies, particularly with a focus on investigating foreign technology and development. Under Yoshimune's rule, in 1720 the countrywide ban on books from abroad was lifted, affording Japanese scholars access to Chinese documents, so long as the books contained no reference to Christianity. The Shōgun also encouraged a limited coterie of experts to investigate the exotic, forbidding world of the Europeans. Called 'Dutch Studies' (*Rangaku*) after the only European nation with which the Japanese had any form of contact, this new discipline would lead to slow developments in medicine, geography and mathematics. Meanwhile, despite the official policy of no foreign contact, Japan's agriculture was diversified with the arrival of the sweet potato, which made its way into farmers' hands up the Ryūkyū Islands from China.[5]

Samurai priorities had also changed. For any high-ranking official, the mandatory alternate attendance at the city of Edo had created a growing affinity for urban living. Kyōto, once regarded as the city to end all cities, was now regarded as something of a quaint backwater, still the residence of the emperors but offering little competition with the teahouses, brothels, bookstores and theatres of nearby Osaka and distant Edo. Although Edo was never officially the 'capital' during the Tokugawa period, it had already gained the allure of a city of culture, vice and opportunity.

The theatres, in particular, were centres of entertainment, often attached to restaurants and cafes where the tickets were sold, with each feeding the business of the other. The more staid, old-fashioned Nō theatre was regarded at the beginning of the Tokugawa era as an interest suitable for the ruling class, but tales of the samurai soon devolved into the more populist, garish entertainments of *bunraku* puppet plays and the new kabuki form of lively, melodramatic theatre with a repertoire of classic set-piece tableaux or action sequences. These not only came to entertain the samurai as well as the merchants, but also came to define the samurai, with powerful fictions and enduring legends about key moments in samurai history.

A glance down the listing of the most popular kabuki plays of the Tokugawa era shows a gradual change in the position of the samurai. The victors in the civil war are still respected, even feared in the cities, but their standards and traditions often seem ill-suited to the growing urbanization of Japan. The samurai were creatures of the *jidaimono* ('period pieces') as opposed to the *sewamono* ('worldly pieces') of contemporary comedies and melodramas – the samurai spoke in an old-fashioned way, the drama was more formalized and archaic, and the achievements more fantastical. Many originated in puppet plays that permitted the characters superhuman feats of strength or agility, further increasing the fanciful, legendary sense of the past as another country. Such fictional depictions of the samurai should be regarded with care – they are no more a direct reflection of samurai lifestyle than *Inspector Morse* is of the murder rate in Oxford. Nevertheless, they can point us at certain inner truths about attitudes of the Tokugawa period – are these tales any less 'fictional' than the *Tale of the Heike* or the other war chronicles of earlier eras?

The play *Fuwa* (1680) introduced a common cliché to the vocabulary of samurai stories, with a tale of two warriors who pass in the street, and whose scabbards accidentally touch. The samurai immediately square off, each against the other's perceived 'insult', and are only prevented from cutting each other down by the intercession of a woman, who kneels between them, her hands held out, imploring them to see sense. The scabbard-crossing (*saya-ate*) sequence was originally a mere moment in a larger play, but was excerpted and refashioned as a one-act play in its own right in later years. Today, it is still known simply as *Saya-ate*, and points to the continued tension in everyday actions of the samurai. Succumbing to such bravado might well result in a command to commit *seppuku*, but matters of perceived honour still loomed large for the warrior elite.[6]

Shibaraku (1697) is another iconic moment in the samurai self-image, and began as an accidental moment in another play, five years earlier, when an onstage rivalry between actors led a performer onstage to omit to give a fellow thespian his cue. Instead, the offstage actor yelled out '*Shibaraku*' ('Just a moment!') and barged onto the stage. By the end of the decade, the *Shibaraku* incident had also become a one-act play in its own right. Purportedly an incident from the life of an eleventh-century samurai who fought for the Minamoto during the conquest of the north, it depicts a fight near the temple of Hachiman, broken up by the timely arrival of a burly samurai, who commands the action to halt from the back of the theatre, and then enters through the audience.

With stories well known and well loved, and a setting conveniently far in the past, the Genpei War remained a major source of the most popular plays. *Kagekiyo* (1739) features the titular samurai of the Taira clan, imprisoned by the Minamoto, who keep him in confinement for fifty days, hoping to learn from him the location of other enemies. Instead, his stoicism impresses his captors, and a magical scene where he plays a musical instrument somehow convinces his captors that he knows nothing of value to them. Finally, he breaks free and escapes, swearing vengeance in a spectacular exit. His angry spirit would return in another play prominent in the kabuki repertoire – *The Salvation* (*Gedatsu*, 1744), in which plans by the victorious Minamoto to honour the spirits of their dead Taira enemies are thwarted when the great bell of the Tōdaiji temple refuses to toll. The 'salvation' of the title is Kagekiyo's own, when his spirit is appeased and exorcised with the silk garment of a Buddhist saint.

Stories of Yoshitsune were never far from the Japanese theatre. The first of many variants about his legendary first meeting with his giant henchman, *Benkei on the Bridge* (*Hashi Benkei*), was performed in 1744. *Yoshitsune and the Thousand Cherry Trees* (*Yoshitsune Senbon Zakura*) first appeared as a puppet show in 1747, and was remade for kabuki only a year later. It features a fanciful retelling of the Battle of Yashima (in fact, confusing its events with those of the later Dannoura) and allusions to Yoshitsune's flight to the north, but largely concerns itself with the actions of a transforming fox, who swears allegiance to Yoshitsune's mistress in order to be close to her drum, which has been fashioned using the skins of the fox's parents. Such a fanciful tale was easier to sell to the authorities than *Yoshitsune's Koshigoe Conditions* (*Yoshitsune Koshigoejō*), a play that first appeared in 1754. It also featured Yoshitsune on the run, but contained a controversial scene in which a former retainer of the Minamoto clan, fallen on hard times and forced to become a maker of sword accessories, is rehabilitated as a samurai of principle when he sets out to kill Yoshitsune's enemy, the Shōgun. The victim is, of course, the long-dead Yoritomo, although the government censor did not see things in quite the same way, and refused to permit the act in question to be performed for fear it would encourage similar thoughts about the current incumbent.

Most famous of all was *Kanjinchō* (*The Subscription List*), which is first recorded in 1702. It concentrated on a single apocryphal incident in the later life of Yoshitsune, when he and the last few of his faithful followers are fleeing north from the predations of Yoritomo. Disguised as wandering monks, they slip through a checkpoint at Ataka only after an intense interrogation from the guardpost commandant, whom the warrior monk Benkei fools by pretending to read out a list of pre-agreed donations. When the guards display suspicion about the appearance of the lowliest monk (Yoshitsune), Benkei maintains their cover by beating him as if he is a humble porter. The deception works, but Benkei must beg for Yoshitsune's forgiveness for the capital offence of striking one's master.

It is intriguing, however, to note how many kabuki plays do not concern themselves with the samurai. While the samurai remained a constant presence within society, the concerns of kabuki playwrights and audiences were not limited exclusively to them. Many other plays from the repertoire revolved around star-crossed lovers, pedlars and medicine sellers, and tall tales of legendary courtiers. For many of the samurai class, the samurai lifestyle was now a daily grind of bureaucracy and administration – something for which the theatre was not a reflection, but an escape.

Theatrical elements even crept into the everyday world of the samurai. By the late eighteenth century, many lower-ranking samurai had divested themselves of all but the most conspicuous symbols of their rank. Despite the strict rules on a samurai's military obligations, many simply did not bother to keep the mandated number of retainers as full-time employees, resorting to temporary hired help on those few occasions where protocol required that a samurai have his squires in attendance. In particular, New Year's ceremonies became notorious for sudden spates of enlistment of samurai henchmen, and for the sights of samurai bigwigs accompanied by alleged servants to whom they were clearly strangers. A poem of the day lampooned the practice:

> New Year's, when ready-made samurai are sold out.
> New Year's, when the price of day-laborer attendants goes up.[7]

Similar theatricalities accompanied the samurai even in death. Should a samurai commit a crime or transgression thought to warrant the death penalty, in the Tokugawa era he was accorded the traditional right of dying not like a common criminal with a public execution, but by committing *seppuku* in private. However, *seppuku* was often not what it once was. Instead of the mandated, painful disembowelment of tradition, *seppuku* in the Tokugawa period was more commonly a simple beheading. The victim went through the motions of composing his death poem and kneeling on the tatami mat in preparation, but the dagger he was expected to use was now little more than a wooden sword. Reaching for it was not the commencement of his disembowelment, but a signal to the executioner to cut off his head. For most samurai, this must have been a welcome relief to the alternative, but for some hardliners it was yet another sign of the decline of samurai virtues.[8]

Yamamoto Tsunetomo (1659–1719) was another member of the ruling class who keenly felt the contradictions between the traditions of the samurai and the changing world around them. A loyal servant of the Nabeshima clan since his teens, he had planned to commit *seppuku* in 1700 on the death of his lord. Instead, his dying master forbade him from following him in death, and Yamamoto found himself working for a less likeable heir. Diplomatically taking early retirement, Yamamoto spent the last decade of his life in a remote mountain hermitage, writing down his personal perspective on samurai ethics, mainly in reference to the words and deeds of the two preceding generations of the Yamamoto family. The resultant compilation, published after Yamamoto's death as *In the Shadow of the Leaves* (usually known by its Japanese title, *Hagakure*), was one of hundreds of books of samurai philosophy. However, it would gradually grow in stature over the centuries that followed, until it was one of the cornerstones of samurai belief. Most infamously, Yamamoto boldy restated a truth that had been slowly slipping away from the ruling elite in times of peace: 'The way of the samurai is death.'

Yamamoto's aphorisms reflected a deep knowledge of Japan's military history. He alluded to giving 'seven lives' for the Nabeshima clan in oblique reference to the last words of Kusunoki Masashige, and his writings reflected a mild apprehension that, in banning retainers from following their lord in death, the shōgunate had somehow lost touch. Ironically, the Nabeshima clan itself had banned such suicides in 1661, two years before the shōgunate had done so, seemingly in reaction to several acts of disturbing fanaticism among its retainers. Most notoriously, in 1635, a retainer of the Nabeshima clan had judiciously hacked off three of his own fingers, one by one, in an attempt to buy a magical cure for his lord's mortal bout of smallpox. For Yamamoto, such displays were not fanatical folly, but sign of true loyalty. Yamamoto regarded the true way of the samurai as one of a perpetual state of readiness for death in the service of his lord, as a lifetime spent ready for immediate action. Not for him the two-year plot of the

Forty-Seven Rōnin – instead, Yamamoto believed that a true samurai would have drawn his sword, settle the matter of honour on the spot, and then kill himself to ensure that no blame fell upon his superiors. Far from upholding samurai ideals, Yamamoto bemoaned the decline of the samurai in crotchety, curmudgeonly terms:

> Times have changed in the last thirty years. When young samurai get together they talk of money, of profit and loss, how to run a household efficiently, how to judge the value of clothing, and they exchange stories about sex. If any other topic is mentioned, the atmosphere is spoiled and everyone present feels vaguely uncomfortable. What a distressing pass things have come to![9]

The words of a dying and perhaps rather bitter man, Yamamoto's very personal appreciation of a samurai's duty would gradually transform into a textbook for later generations with no experience of war. In years to come, it would become a dangerous manifestation of samurai fictions as samurai fact.

Meanwhile, actual samurai facts were less palatable. After the golden age of the reign of the 'Rice Shōgun' Yoshimune, his son and grandson were far less competent. Variously described as distracted, disabled or just plain lazy, the ninth and tenth shōguns Ieshige and Ieharu left power largely to their chamberlains. The late eighteenth century saw signs of simmering discontent with the Tokugawa clan, although the checks and balances set in place by Ieyasu kept it from manifesting as open revolution. It was widely understood that the Bakufu was not what it had been in the days of the earliest shōguns, but no outlying lord dared voice this thought, as he could still be summarily dismissed. For commoners without a domain to lose, discontent was in a sense easier to express. Takenouchi Shikenobu, a doctor's son and hence not of the samurai class, openly espoused a doctrine of 'Loyalty to the emperor' (*Shinnō Ron*), pointedly not to the shōgun, which caused a flurry of interest in the court at Kyōto, before he was arrested in 1759.

A couple of years later, a teacher of military science in Edo was ousted from his post by rivals who claimed that he had been preaching a gospel of resistance to the Shōgun. In fact, he was merely critical of the government's need to maintain authority by force, but had inadvisedly alluded to a more peaceable solution with the term 'Kingly Way' (*Ō-dō*). This was taken to be a statement in support of a restoration of the Emperor's direct rule, for which the teacher was sentenced to death. Rumours of opposition persisted, too, among the peasantry, particularly after an agrarian protest in 1764 in Kōtsuke and Musashi swelled to include 200,000 angry farmers. Such numbers, to the shōgunate, represented a disturbing repeat of the unrest of the Shimabara Rebellion in 1637. Although the disturbance was quelled, it was a cause of some embarrassment that it had occurred not in an outlying island or fractious province, but within a couple of days' travel of Edo itself. In an effort to nip future protests in the bud, the shōgunate offered incentives to informers if they tipped off the authorities before any unrest could occur. Furthermore, the rules on lords sending forces out of their domains were relaxed, so that one lord could call on a neighbour for help in suppressing a riot, without having to first wait for authorisation from Edo. There was one condition – such movements of troops could not involve firearms; the Shōgunate was determined to keep the peasants in line with swords and pikes.[10]

We can also see a growing sense of dissatisfaction in the

stories and plays of the period, although such dissent is often allegorised, concealed or otherwise referred to only obliquely. We must also remember that for many of the audiences and gossips of the time, dissatisfaction was not necessarily with the samurai class itself, but with its current masters, the Tokugawa clan. Particularly among the domains whose members had been on the losing side at the Battle of Sekigahara – such as the southern regions of Satsuma and Chōshū – it was whispered that what was required was not so much a change in the system, but merely a change in the regime.

Urban myths of the late eighteenth century suggested that Tokugawa Ieyasu had been troubled by the constant recurrence of the name of one particular swordsmith among his enemies. Late in life, he developed a superstition that blades made by the sixteenth-century school of Muramasa had been specifically cursed to do damage to the Tokugawa family. The reasoning for this, at least as far as the rumours went, was that Ieyasu's grandfather had been killed by one, his father had been stabbed by one, and Ieyasu injured himself with one when he was a child. His worries only increased when he discovered that in the case of two executions, that of his adulterous wife and supposedly treacherous adopted son, the executioner's blade had been a Muramasa, too. Over time, Ieyasu came to believe that every one of the generals who had opposed him had wielded a Muramasa blade, including Sanada Yukimura, who had supposedly dealt him a troublesome wound at the Battle of Tennōji in 1615. The attentive reader may note that sources from the time report that, if Ieyasu was wounded at all by Sanada, he was wounded with a *spear*, but no matter – the fiction was already more alluring than the already shaky facts.

Muramasa blades were highly prized, so it should have

come as no surprise that they were in the possession of wealthy members of the aristocracy. Nor should it have been a mystery why aristocrats facing death would insist on their executioner using the sharpest, highest-performance blade available – a single clean cut being vastly preferable to the three painful hacks that were required to behead Augustin Konishi. But the stories about the 'Curse of the Muramasa' seem to have served another purpose in eighteenth-century Japan: delivering a chilling frisson to audiences with the reminder that there was a time when someone stood against the shōgun, and that their legacy lived on, hidden within clans, buried in storehouses, and traded among sword-dealers.

Muramasa blades, it was said, were cursed. Their creator was half-mad, and the weapons he made could impel their wielders into murderous rages. One story tells of a young samurai, Gentarō, up in Edo as part of his obligatory domain service, who sees a Muramasa hanging among the other swords on a dealer's rack:

> Trembling, he withdrew it from its scabbard, and he forgot to breathe. The sword had hidden depths, like morning mist welling up within the metal. Light danced off the blade in the colours of the rainbow ... Just by holding it in his hand, he could tell it was a masterpiece ... an artefact suitable for a lord's treasure house, fated never to come into the hands of a common samurai ...[11]

The samurai is even happier when the dealer offers to sell him the blade for a fraction of its true value, although he will not say why. Cheerfully, Gentarō brings the sword back with him to his home domain, where he shows it off to his fellow officers at the monthly sword club. Despite everyone's gasps of awe, the club chairman tells him the sword is worthless. Suspecting that the chairman merely wants to buy it from him cheaply, Gentarō seeks a second opinion, and is told the whole sorry story of the cursed blades. In a spate of demises that prefigure the calamities of a modern horror film, most people involved in the story are dead within a week, as is the family servant told to throw the sword in a river, who unwisely plans to keep it for himself.

The legend achieved a wider audience in 1797 when it gained a prominent mention in a popular kabuki play *Oblique Reflections of Brothel Lives* (*Satokotoba Awasekagami*). Revived in 1815 and again in 1860 with slight variations, the story became a recurring staple of the Japanese theatre. The main narrative concerned a missing girl in the pleasure quarter, and an impoverished son of a merchant desperate to raise the money to buy his lover out of indentured servitude in a brothel. Mixed in with these basic plots are shadows of the Muramasa legend – a cursed Muramasa blade is sold by a hapless sword-dealer, who is soon murdered; it falls into the hands of one of the leading characters, and drives him into a serial-killing spree. As so often happened with kabuki theatre, real-world reportage is hidden within the melodrama. It drew inspirations from the collapse of an Edo bridge in 1807, and the 1820 murder of a capricious geisha by the man who had bankrupted himself to buy her freedom. By the nineteenth century, Muramasa swords were associated with a whole series of half-remembered macabre tales of murder and betrayal, and had come to be linked in the popular mind with the decline of samurai honour into bloody, inconsequential vendettas, and fights over bar-girls or petty debts.[12]

Despite the superior quality of Muramasa blades, they became impossible to sell, and there are cases of some swords on which the smith's name was doctored,

Muramasa becoming altered to Masamune – another smith but without a tainted reputation. In fact, the anti-Tokugawa reputation of the Muramasa blades gave them an unexpected *value* among those who despised the government. Those few that survived the Tokugawa era, hidden in family vaults, are now worth millions.[13]

As the Tokugawa era wore on, the strains on the samurai class became more obvious. Among the most unfortunate, there was a difficult choice – of clinging to a class status that they could not afford, or recognizing that they had dropped out of the social bracket that had been won for them at the point of a sword by their ancestors.

Takizawa Okuni (1767–1848) grew up in a poverty-stricken samurai family typical of the fading fortunes of the warrior class. The fifth of seven children, he saw his two elder brothers die before reaching adulthood. His father, a low-ranking samurai in the Matsudaira clan, drank himself to death before Takizawa was nine, and it was not long before the family's rice stipend was cut in half. Both Takizawa and his brother went to work for the Matsudaira clan in their father's footsteps, but the brother hated the service so much that he resigned and spent some time as a rōnin. Takizawa, meanwhile, ran away from the Matsudaira's service at the age of fourteen. His hard-luck story continued in adulthood, and he eventually took a step that would have been unthinkable to former generations – he resigned his samurai status and voluntarily joined the merchant class. Although a great dishonour to his family, it did at least allow him to ply a trade for a living wage, and Takizawa became an author, under the pen name Kyokutei Bakin. He specialized in long, serialized *gesaku* – cheaply printed, luridly illustrated popular novels, full of derring-do and adventure. It was in this role, as a *former* samurai, attempting to instil samurai virtues in a son and then a grandson who only knew him as the author of penny-dreadful novels, that Bakin created modern fictions of the samurai, to which the samurai themselves began to aspire. It was always Takizawa's hope that his descendants would somehow be able to buy their way back into the samurai class, but it was not to be. He ended his days a blind author, dictating to his daughter-in-law, and championing the cause and ideals of a class that no longer accepted him as a member.

Paramount among his works is the *Hakkenden*, 'Eight Dog Story', serialized roughly thrice yearly in a twenty-eight-year period from 1814 to 1842 – a fantasy set vaguely during the civil wars of the Muromachi period in the late fifteenth century, and based to some extent on stories of the semi-historical Satomi clan that are now lost. It was Takizawa's intention to write something to rival the Chinese classic *The Water Margin*, although he reduced the 108 heroes of his inspiration to a more manageable eight.

In the story, a samurai leader rashly promises that whoever brings him the head of his enemy shall have the hand of his daughter in marriage, only to have the head brought to him by the family dog. Forced to stay true to his word, the lord hands her over. A discreet veil is drawn over what happens next in all but the most lurid and pornographic retellings of the tale. Suffice to say that a generation later, after the reluctant bride kills herself and eight 'pearls of virtue' drip from her wounds and fly into the sky, eight warriors appear who are the 'spiritual' children of the noblewoman and her dog. Their problems are textbook knots of Duty versus Emotion. One must deliver a magic sword to a nobleman, another is sworn to stop him. One is a disgraced guardsman in chains, another is the man he has to kill to secure his freedom. One is searching for his lost sister, whom he accidentally kills, another is the sister's betrothed, determined to avenge the death of his sibling. Each of the warriors has a lowly background and a Herculean problem, but each embodies one of the eight samurai virtues, at least insofar as Takizawa could work them out: Benevolence, Righteousness, Courtesy, Wisdom, Fidelity, Loyalty, Filial Piety and Care for the Aged.

Takizawa's definition of what the eight samurai virtues *should be* was at odds with many other authorities. In debates since the Middle Ages, occasional theorists and thinkers had agreed on a nebulous cloud of virtues, largely distilled from Chinese thinkers such as Confucius. The samurai variant seemed to quibble about certain definitions – Filial Piety and Care for the Aged, to the Chinese, are different sides of the same coin, and so it almost seems as if a cantankerous old samurai is making a point to his ungrateful descendants. Other samurai thinkers added Bravery, a rather obvious martial virtue missing from the works of Chinese philosophers, although implicit in several Chinese definitions of 'Loyalty'. Wisdom itself is a bizarrely broad virtue on which some samurai insisted. Would a samurai be wise if he followed the martial precepts of Sun Tzu's *Art of War*? If he did so, and Wisdom called for retreat, would that mean he could no longer aspire to Bravery? If it were Wise to attack an opponent by stealth, would that wipe out any claims of Honesty? It is easy to see how such debates fuelled an entire publishing industry of tormented heroes driven to despair by their conflicting instructions.

Between 1854 and 1869, Okanoye Shigezane serialized 192 biographies of famous samurai, under the title of *The Words and Actions of Great Commanders* (*Meishō Genkō Roku*). In establishing a canon of the greatest, most estimable samurai of days gone by, he pointedly included many who had been enemies of the Tokugawa order, on the understanding that they had been noble opponents. Okanoye also allowed popular myth and superstition to creep into his work as reported 'facts', ingraining many fictional samurai stories into the late nineteenth century's idea of historical truth. Post-Okanoye, for example, it was widely understood not only that the samurai leader Sanada Yukimura had deliberately carried one of the infamously cursed Muramasa blades, but that he had done so *because it brought bad luck to the Tokugawa clan*, imposing later beliefs upon the actions of figures in the past. His wounding of Tokugawa Ieyasu at the Siege of Osaka Castle now took on a reversal of the true progression of events. Whereas Ieyasu had supposedly once come to believe that Muramasa blades were cursed against him because one had wounded him, audiences were now led to believe that a Muramasa blade had wounded Ieyasu *because* of the curse it bore against him. Such retrofitting of fiction to fact created new samurai fads all of its own. The late ninteenth century saw a spate of fake Muramasa blades on the Japanese sword market, as wily entrepreneurs sought to cash in on an underground market for anti-establishment artifacts.

All the while, Japan continued in its self-imposed isolation, although there were many tests of its strength by both accidental foreign arrivals and deliberate attempts to establish trade. In fact, in the seventy-five years before 1853, some seventy-two foreign vessels entered Japanese waters under one pretext or another, and another thirty-six set down anchors in the grey legal area of the Ryūkyū Islands. Although it is the Americans who were the most famous of the arrivals in Japanese waters, the closing years of the Tokugawa shōgunate saw twenty-five approaches from the Russians, fifteen from Britain, other ships from

France and Denmark, and even one from Romania. Russian explorers reached Siberia and the Amur River, and then came across the narrow strait to Sakhalin, and south into Ezo, where they were brusquely ordered to leave. American ships poked at the defences around Japan, and were similarly shooed away. Some returned, cunningly flying the Dutch flag, and were permitted to set down in Nagasaki at the Dutch ghetto-quarantine island of Dejima.

Outside Japan, the land of the shōgun was regarded as a mysterious, fantastical island, with a strong warrior tradition that would not welcome any uninvited guests. Extant sources about the island were limited largely to Marco Polo's awestruck account of the repulse of the Mongol invasions, and the bloodstained chronicles of the persecution of the Christians. Occasional writings by those who had been permitted onto Dejima suggested that Japan was a vibrant but deeply odd society, ruled by a warrior elite. However, as the decades passed, evidence of the decline of the samurai began to mount.

In 1811, a party of Russian explorers in the Kurile Islands were taken prisoner and held in northern Japan for two years. Their captain, Vassily Golovnin regarded the shore batteries at Hakodate to be 'so foolishly constructed that it appears not only that they understand nothing of the rules of the art, but that they are probably wholly deficient in experience.'[14]

An American vessel, the *Morrison*, was fired upon when she tried to land some Japanese castaways in 1837, leading to protests from some quarters that by continuing to pursue such a draconian policy, the Japanese would ultimately kill a foreign visitor and hence provoke the very conflict that they were hoping to prevent.

By the 1840s, not a year went by without a challenge to the Sakoku 'Closed Country' policy. Missionaries, whalers and military vessels were often found poking around Japanese waters, and sternly ordered to leave and not come back. But since the *Morrison* incident, the Japanese had not been placed in a position where their orders were disobeyed to such an extent that they were obliged to open fire. Far from maintaining their ability to repulse invaders, some samurai appear to have been forced by cost cutting or pragmatism into outright trickery. In 1846, the American whaler George Howe and his crew were shipwrecked in northern Ezo, and sought refuge on the island of Eterofu. They walked towards what they presumed was a government fort:

> As we approached it, we saw what appeared to be a fort, but on coming nearer we found it was a piece of cloth extended about three-quarters of a mile, and painted so as to resemble a fort with guns. Here, as we landed, about sixty men armed with swords and spears ran towards us.[15]

In 1844, King William II of the Netherlands sent a diplomatically worded account of the changes that the world outside Japan had seen since the seventeenth century, and urged Japan to shake off its 'closed' society. 'Distance', he warned sagely, 'is being overcome by the invention of the steamship.'[16]

His words fell on deaf ears, although there were plenty of signs that foreign races apart from the Dutch were approaching ever closer to Japanese territory. The British survey vessel *Samarang* was politely asked to leave when she put in at Nagasaki in 1845. A French warship was found selling arms to the Ryūkyū Islands in 1848, but since the archipelago enjoyed a peculiar status as a vassal of the Shimazu clan but not of the Shōgunate, it escaped severe punishment.

The world was getting smaller. Japan was not a remote, mythical idea at the edge of the world as it had been in the time of Marco Polo, but a tantalizing harbour close to one of the world's richest whaling grounds. Herman Melville, in *Moby Dick* (1851) summarized the frustration felt by American whalers about the proximity of coal, food and water in a country that they were forbidden from entering:

If that double-bolted land, Japan, is ever to become hospitable, it is the whale-ship alone to whom the credit will be due; for already she is on the threshold.[17]

10

THE LAST HURRAH
RESTORATION AND REVOLT

The last and most famously insurmountable challenge to Sakoku came in July 1853. As the twelfth Tokugawa Shōgun, Ieyoshi, lay dying in Edo, fishermen in Uraga at the edge of Edo Bay heard a strange thrumming noise from far in the distance. Before long, the distant hum was matched by the sight of thick black smoke on the horizon, and then the ominous bulk of two giant frigates, their steam-powered paddle-wheels churning relentlessly against the wind. Each of the vessels towed another, so that as the four 'Black Ships' drew near, the Japanese were terrified by the sight of 'veritable castles that move freely on the water,' twenty times larger than any ship the Japanese had ever seen before.[1]

Frantic reports back to headquarters alluded to alien vessels as 'large as mountains' and 'as swift as birds', which had brusquely ignored the French-language warning sign on the coast that forbade foreigners from dropping anchor. The new arrival was Commodore Matthew Calbraith Perry (1794–1858) of the US Navy, who was under clear instructions to put an end to Japan's self-imposed isolation for the benefit of American traders and whalers in the area.

Perry's previous service had been in the Mexican War and in the suppression of the Barbary pirates. He was not the sort of captain to be fobbed off with excuses, and he was determined to make a show of force to prevent the usual Japanese prevarications. He eschewed going through the correct channels by dropping anchor in Nagasaki, and went straight for the entrance to Edo Bay, determined to have his audience not with the powerless representatives of the figurehead Emperor, but with the de facto ruler of Japan, the Shōgun. Perry was also in a hurry – he knew that the British and the Russians were sure to be making overtures of their own soon. He refused to negotiate with mere underlings, and insisted that the Shōgun himself accept a letter from the American president Millard Fillmore. While he waited for a more welcome response than the standard request to come back later, Perry put his men to work surveying Edo Bay, possibly quite aware of the damage it was doing to the Shōgun's reputation to have foreign vessels openly punting up and down the coast.

The ships alone were enough to persuade the Shōgun's men that the Japanese could offer no resistance. On the first night that Commodore Perry's mission was anchored off the coast of Japan, the Japanese tried to scare them off by unrolling a fake fortress, made of black canvas. They had not counted on the Americans' possession of binoculars, with which the deception was swiftly scrutinized. 'These diversions were repeated so often during our stay', wrote the master's mate Baynard Taylor, 'that at last we ceased to regard them; but it was amusing to hear some of our old quarter-masters now and then gravely report to Captain Buchanan: "Another dungaree fort thrown up, sir!"[2]

Eventually, Perry was persuaded to leave and return the following year. He steamed back out of sight, leaving the samurai shaken and confused, and lurked in the eastern seas for several months, calling in on the Ryūkyū Islands, Shanghai and Macao. But ironically, Perry's 'surprise' arrival was no such thing. The Shōgun had been tipped off more than a year earlier, in a letter from the governor of the Dutch East Indies, which had set out a detailed account of an impending American mission to Japan, and the demands it was likely to make. The Shōgun's chancellor, in office for eight years, had had ample time to prepare but seemed to have been hobbled by the practices and traditions of the Tokugawa state. Tokugawa Japan had been designed to cope with and hold off incursions by seventeenth-century foreign powers, not by such weapons and vessels as had suddenly been presented. Despite hesitant efforts in 'Dutch studies' over the years, the samurai appeared to have fallen grossly far behind in terms of the technology of warfare. Perry's ships had effectively arrived from 200 years in the future.

Not everyone regarded Perry's infamous Black Ships as a sign of the end of the world. The chancellor himself meekly pointed out that the Black Ships were not invading: they were only asking for trade and harbour facilities, a request which made them little different from the Dutch who were already suffered to drop anchor in Nagasaki. Even as the Shōgun's officials debated their next act, there was news from Nagasaki of yet another foreign incursion, this time by the Russian admiral Evfimy Vasilyevich Putiatin, who had similarly arrived with four ships and a polite request for trade and diplomatic relations.[3]

Suggestions for dealing with the foreign arrivals were laughably tragic. Some samurai suggested suicide squads who could overrun enemy ships with explosives. Others opined that planting more bamboo forests on the coasts would help the villages endure inevitable foreign artillery bombardments. When Perry returned in 1854, his nation was granted trading posts in the ports of Shimoda and Hakodate – the latter seemingly chosen because it was on distant Ezo Island, and hence barely on Japanese territory at all. The Russians, returning the same year, got access to the same ports, as well as a bonus dispensation to drop anchor alongside the Dutch in Nagasaki. By 1858, America's consul in Shimoda had hammered out a Treaty of Amity and Commerce, opening five more ports, allowing American citizens to live in them, and granting them the freedom to be tried by their own courts. This concept – extraterritoriality – supposedly removed the foreigners from Japanese legal jurisdiction, and was an additional challenge to the Shōgun's wavering authority. Before long, other foreign powers had grabbed similar concessions for themselves, and the shōgunate was obliged to countenance the presence not only of 'barbarians' on Japanese soil, but also their virtual immunity from prosecution, at least at the hands of Japanese law enforcers. These foreigners were not only openly Christian, still a capital offence for the Japanese, but often behaved as if they regarded the Japanese themselves as inferior beings.

It was, of course, only a matter of time before an incident would test the efficacy of the piece of paper that supposedly protected arrogant Europeans from thousands of resentful men with swords. The most infamous case came in 1862, at the small village of Namamugi, when the British trader Charles Lennox Richardson found his horse's path blocked by the seemingly endless procession of samurai retainers accompanying Shimazu Hisamitsu, the father and regent to the young ruler of the powerful southern Satsuma clan. Shimazu was returning to his home domain, for what was probably the last time, as the system of alternate attendance was abolished in the same year, and samurai lords were no longer required to either attend on the discredited Shōgun or, crucially, to leave family hostages with him when absent in order to ensure their compliance. Whether this left Shimazu's men feeling overly bullish or victorious, it is difficult to say, but they were marching along on a sunny September day, with weeks of walking ahead of them, carrying not only the father of their lord, but presumably many valuable goods and treasures from their Edo residence.

Richardson was riding with two trading colleagues and a European lady friend, and surely witnessed the Shimazu outriders galloping ahead of the procession, ordering all in its path to stand aside and bow to the ground. But instead of dismounting, which would have been respectful at least, or moving to the side of the road, Richardson decided to ride through the procession. Richardson had formerly lived among the Chinese, still cowed by the British predations of the Opium War, and would brook no delay from a bunch of men in sandals.

With the famous last words 'I know how to deal with these people', Richardson rode straight into the procession, whereupon he and his associates were set upon by angry samurai. All three men were seriously wounded, and the lady, Margaret Borodaille, cryptically escaped with only 'the loss of her hair'. As the riders pelted for safety, Richardson fell, dying, from his horse, and Shimazu Hisamitsu ordered for him to be put out of his misery.

The murder of Charles Richardson was by no means the only incident, but it occurred at a critical moment when the Shōgun had lost one of his last remaining tools for controlling the lords of distant domains. Following British demands for reparations, the Shōgun demanded that the Satsuma domain make amends. With no hostages in Edo, and no sense of wrongdoing, the Satsuma domain not only refused to do so, but did so with the clear implication that not only was it in the right but it was loyally obeying the commands of the Emperor, whereas the Shōgun was cravenly bowing and scraping to the demands of barbarians.

Nor were the Satsuma samurai alone in this. They were caught up, along with many other samurai spoiling for a fight, in a new movement that enjoyed as its slogan the phrase: 'Revere the Emperor, Expel the Barbarians' – *son-nō jō-i*. 'The subjugation of the hated foreigner', noted the 121st Emperor, Kōmei, 'is the greatest of the national tasks facing Us.'[4]

It was a blunt reminder to the Shōgun of the precise wording of his job description – which the Emperor re-inforced at an audience that placed the Shōgun in an inferior position, as court protocol demanded, but on which no Emperor in living memory had dared to insist. In March 1863, the Emperor went even further, decreeing an Order to Expel Barbarians, demanding that all foreigners were to leave Japanese soil within sixty days.

The Shōgun, fully aware of the realities of foreign power, could not comply, although there were incidents scattered all over Japan of intimidation and aggression. Most notably, the domain of Chōshū, which sat by the Shimonoseki Strait, began firing on foreign shipping, to which foreign navies soon replied with retaliatory bombardment.

In August 1863, having waited many months for a resolution, the British government sent a navy flotilla to chastise Satsuma. The warships did so by steaming up to Kagoshima, the capital of Satsuma, and shelling it, starting a catastrophic fire in the largely wooden town. Loss of life was minimal – just five dead in Kagoshima, as the town had been largely evacuated. The British suffered worse, losing thirteen dead, including one of the captains, decapitated by a lucky shot from one of the antiquated coastal batteries. At the end of the brief exchange of fire, the British ships steamed back to sea, while the angry Satsuma samurai stood calf-deep in the water on the shoreline, waving their swords and protesting that the *real* battle – hand-to-hand combat – had yet to begin.

In the aftermath, both sides claimed victory. 'In respect of the Prince of Satsuma, after long forebearance, his capital is in ashes,' claimed the trigger-happy Admiral Kuper. The British got a cash indemnity, although Satsuma borrowed the money from the shōgunate, and never actually paid it back. The Satsuma domain got the chance to boast that Richardson's killers were never actually handed over, and that the British had 'retreated' because they had left without really fighting. The bombardment of Kagoshima, as an attack on a civilian target, became an international cause célèbre, with one observer pointing out: 'when an outcry is made by England about the inhumanity of other nations, we must stop her mouth by the one word "Kagoshima".'[5]

Admiral Kuper, however, was eventually knighted for his actions, and British industry had cause to thank him, too. Determined to meet enemies on more equal terms in future, the samurai of Satsuma enthusiastically embraced modern shipping technology, and spent much more than the value of their indemnity on orders to British shipyards. In years to come, the men of Satsuma would form the core of the modern Japanese navy. One teenage Satsuma youth, who had faced the British navy on the day with two swords and antique armour, would grow up to become Admiral Tōgō, the first Japanese mariner to defeat a European navy.

Far from making things more secure, the Emperor's meddling had only made the Shōgun's position more impossible. The aftermath of the skirmishes in Shimonoseki and Kagoshima led to further foreign demands for reparation and indemnity, which the increasingly impoverished Shōgun was obliged to pay in kind with further concessions. Meanwhile, Emperor Kōmei's behaviour had made Kyōto the centre of activity in an unprecedented way. Troops were seen drilling in the imperial palace, and the imperial capital was soon home to large, boisterous crowds of samurai. Some were 'loyal', disaffected with the Shōunate for its dereliction of duty. Others were rōnin, outcasts and outlaws, laid off from their home domains due to budget cuts, or banished for unspecified misdemeanours. All had one thing in common – they believed that life would be better for them if the Shōgun were removed.

However, this simple principle masked a large number of factions. Most believed that the Shōgun should simply be replaced, perhaps with a more progressive candidate from Satsuma or Chōshū. There was strong disagreement as to whether this would then mean further modernization in Japan, or a return to isolation. A strong faction believed the way to effect any change was to put the emperor back in charge, so that he could dismiss the current shōgun and appoint a new one. Yet another faction believed that there was no need for a shōgun at all, and that the best way to 'Revere' the emperor was to *Restore* him.

The most infamous faction in Kyōto was the Shinsengumi ('New Selected Corps'), a group of over 200 rōnin who had been rounded up by the Shōgun Tokugawa Iemochi and hired to guard him on his embarrassingly ignominious trip to Kyōto to plead with the Emperor to stop making decrees that could not be humanly enforced.

They remained in Kyōto, fanatically loyal to the Shōgun, and terrorized anyone whose behaviour implied that they opposed him. This soon led to lynchings and brawls between samurai with strongly held opinions on how best to 'Revere the emperor' – as ever, a debate on the nature of loyalty. Some of the Shinsengumi were undoubtedly committed, fanatical supporters of the political orders. Others were undoubtedly thugs looking for a fight – a difference of attitude that led to a feud within the Shinsengumi itself, and a purge of many of the worse offenders.

The Shinsengumi achieved the height of their fame in July 1864, when one of their leaders, Hijikata Toshizō (1835–69) kidnapped and tortured a Chōshū samurai in Kyōto. The victim revealed that there was a Chōshū plot to set fire to the capital, and to kidnap not only the city's chief constable, but also Emperor Kōmei himself. The Emperor would then be spirited away to Chōshū, where he would become a mouthpiece for a new Chōshū-led government. A raid on a conspirator's house uncovered guns and documents that seemed to support the accusations. The Shinsengumi descended on the alleged conspirators at the Ikedaya Inn in Kyōto, in a prolonged two-hour fight. The rebels came at them 'like cornered rats', in a dramatic bloodbath, according to the surviving participants' own memoirs. One man was stabbed hiding in a latrine, another fell through the ceiling, reinitiating hostilities downstairs just as others were about to surrender. By the time the dust settled, seven rebels were dead, four were dying (one from *seppuku*) and twenty-three had been captured. Hundreds of samurai loyal to the Shōgun had surrounded the humble tavern, as the Shinsengumi emerged, battered but triumphant.[6]

In the weeks that followed, the Shinsengumi became a

new agency of law enforcement in Kyōto, charged with hunting down other conspirators, kicking down the doors of rival rōnin, to proclaim the inhabitants of each house as more Chōshū conspirators. Many of their suspicions were well founded, although they also managed to initiate several new vendettas by accusing innocent men and, on one occasion, wounding a high-ranking official on the incorrect assumption that he was a Chōshū sympathizer. Nonetheless, the Shinsengumi continued to grow in power and status, with many new recruits flocking to their banner, which bore the single stark character *makoto* – 'Sincerity'.

However, the fight at the Ikedaya Inn had galvanized Chōshū itself. Whereas the remote domain's rulers had previously been divided as to a plan of action, they now unanimously supported vengeance against the powers that persecuted them. A fighting force began the long march from Chōshū towards Kyōto, with the expressed intention of hunting down the murderers of Chōshū samurai, and if that was not possible, to take on the samurai who protected them. This was recognized by both sides as a threat to the Tokugawa loyalists who even now guarded the imperial palace. The shōgunate responded with an order for Chōshū samurai to leave Kyōto, and set a time limit: 19 July 1864.

The Chōshū answer came on the night before the deadline, with a march not out of, but *into* Kyōto. A small group of heavily outnumbered Chōshū samurai attacked the Hamamuri Gate of the imperial palace at dawn. Within the palace, courtiers began a desperate plot to evacuate the Emperor in a covered palanquin – a quaintly old-fashioned escape, recalling the intrigues of the Genpei War. It was the more modernist members of the court who pointed out the unfortunate truth – the Chōshū samurai were armed with guns, with bullets sure to riddle any unidentified palanquin and kill its passenger.[7]

Fires broke out in the avenues near the imperial palace, as the fighting between Tokugawa loyalists and Chōshū loyalists spread across the city. Superior Tokugawa numbers eventually overpowered the Chōshū group, who fled from the city late in the day. The Tokugawa official Katsu Kaishū recalled seeing three of them in a boat, heading downstream on the Yodo River, away from the fighting. But no true samurai could be caught retreating. The boat came to shore and the men clambered out, while the terror-stricken Kaishū waited uneasily for death: the men had identified him as a Tokugawa man, and said so. When Kaishū acknowledged that they were correct, two of the men stabbed each other right before his eyes. The third then knifed himself in the throat, and Kaishū was left alone on the riverbank with a pile of corpses.[8]

The fight at the Hamamuri Gate made the Chōshū public enemy number one. An imperial army set out to chastise the domain on its home ground, joined, with unbridled glee, by samurai from the Satsuma clan, who greatly enjoyed the prospect of showing their 'loyalty' to the Emperor and Shōgun by taking out their long-standing rivals. Chōshū was initially 'softened up' by foreign vessels, who shelled the coastal fortifications in punishment for the domain's preying on foreign shipping, and only inadvertently helping the Shōgunal faction's cause.

Ironically, Chōshū had united both the Emperor and Shōgun, although the expedition against Chōshū only served to distract the samurai from the real issue – the presence of the foreigners. However, the expedition against Chōshū ended bloodlessly, thanks to the machinations of Saigō Takamori (1827–77), a Satsuma samurai who appreciated that if he aided in the destruction of Chōshū, his own domain would be next on the Shōgun's hitlist. In a deal brokered by a fellow anti-Tokugawa agitator, Sakamoto Ryōma (1836–67), Satsuma and Chōshū not only settled their differences, but also formed a powerful new alliance. Each agreed to come to the other's aid if a third party attacked. Tantamount to an alliance against the Tokugawa Shōgun, who was sure to attack one of them soon enough, it also ironically evoked the battle lines of Sekigahara some 250 years earlier. The two most powerful of the Outer Lords, forced to acquiesce to the first Tokugawa Shōgun, now effectively agreed to unite against his distant descendant.

Admittedly, Chōshū was a different place. The pressures of the expedition's advance had caused a new, progressive faction to come to power within the domain, and wiped out all the old conservatives who might have counselled continued support of the shōgunate. Meanwhile, there were ominous signs that the Shōgun feared for his life within his own domains. While the Shinsengumi continued to terrorize Kyōto, the Shōgun cancelled a trip to one of his territories, seemingly out of fear that his own lieutenants might use the opportunity to make an attempt on his life. There were also several suspicious 'fires' on Tokugawa property, which the likes of Saigō Takamori took to be signs of unrest in the ranks.

Loyalty, as ever, was the key. Determined to 'restore' the Emperor, Chōshū samurai began buying arms illegally from Thomas Glover, a Scottish shipping magnate based in Nagasaki. In doing so, they undoubtedly came to the notice of the British authorities, who failed to inform the Shōgun of such behaviour. Behind the scenes, it would seem that foreign powers were now actively drawing their own lines of support, with French military 'advisers' joining the Shōgun's forces, and the quiet complicity of the British with the would-be restorationists.

By the time the Shōgun attempted a second expedition against Chōshū, in summer 1866, the samurai forces they faced were very different. The officers still wore swords and spoke of a warrior's code, but the men were wielding modern guns, and were trained in modern warfare. Satsuma, which refused to come to the Shōgun's aid, now possessed a steam-powered industrial plant, smelting works, a distillery and a chemical factory. It also had infantry regiments with muzzle- and breech-loading rifles and cannons. Satsuma had entertained the British ambassador, Harry Parkes, as if it were an independent power, and indeed, in Europe, Satsuma's agents were often behaving as though it were.[9]

The Shōgun died of natural causes only a couple of weeks after the failure of the second expedition to chastise Kyōto. Emperor Kōmei himself did not live to see the end of the year, dying soon after appointing Tokugawa Yoshinobu (1837–1913) as the new Shōgun. Yoshinobu would be the fifteenth Tokugawa Shōgun, and the last. The new Emperor would be the 113th, Kōmei's son, Meiji.

As preparations began for the new Emperor's enthronement, further threats and sabotages persuaded Tokugawa Yoshinobu to tender his official resignation as Shōgun. He seems to have done so under the impression that the previous organization would be replaced with a council of leading lords – which he would have seen as the ideal opportunity to spread the responsibility for the continued failure of the anti-foreign programme. But Yoshinobu was to be disappointed. Not only were the Satsuma and Chōshū in stern opposition to certain lords on the putative council, but their agents were clearly responsible for the continued unrest. This was never clearer than in the middle of winter 1867–8, when a fire burned down the women's quarters in Edo Castle, and one of Yoshinobu's lieutenants was fired upon by unknown gunmen. When samurai gave chase, the gunmen fled to a mansion owned by the Shimazu clan of Satsuma.

Angry that he had been steered into resigning under false pretences, Tokugawa Yoshinobu protested to the young Emperor that he was being misled by the agents of Satsuma and Chōshū, who were even now perpetrating 'violence and banditry in Edo'. His enemies, meanwhile, promulgated a forged imperial edict calling for him to be executed. Apparently revoking his resignation, Yoshinobu demanded that the perpetrators be brought to justice, and stated that since nobody else would do so, he would take them on himself. It was tantamount to a declaration of open war, with Satsuma and Chōshū and their allies on one side, and the Tokugawa and their allies on the others. Notably, both sides claimed to be fighting out of loyalty to the Emperor himself.[10]

The two sides came to blows in a four-day battle at Toba-Fushimi on the outskirts of Kyōto. Saigō Takamori, leading the Satsuma forces, was outnumbered at least two to one by the Shōgun's men, and seemed as surprised as them by the victory of his modernized troops. But swords played their part, too – samurai armed with medieval weaponry made several suicidal charges against Saigō's riflemen, talking colossal losses in order to put a vital few survivors amidst their enemies with swords in hand. Initally, battle seemed to go in favour of the numerically superior Tokugawa forces, but the troops seemed disheartened and undermotivated, and failed to make advances that capitalized on their advantage. Just as at Sekigahara in 1600, the battle was settled by turncoats, as artillery from the domain of Tsu suddenly decided to fire upon its former Tokugawa allies.

On hearing of the Tsu's sudden switch in sides, Yoshinobu fled for the north. On hearing that their own commander had deserted them, his soldiers stopped fighting. Yoshinobu gave up in Edo, where his castle was handed over to the victorious imperial forces. However, many of his retainers continued north. This was the effective end of the military action now known as the Meiji Restoration, with the Emperor enthroned and rewards duly handed out to his loyal Satsuma and Chōshū vassals. The remainder of the conflict, known as the Boshin War ('War of the [Year of the] Earth Dragon'), comprised the few months between the middle of 1868 and the beginning of 1869 as the new 'imperial' forces gradually advanced north to root out the samurai rebels. A 'Northern Alliance' (Ōetsu Reppan Domei) briefly laid claim to most of northern Japan, encompassing the old provinces of Mutsu and Dewa, but was forced to gradually pull back.

In many places, local defenders were shamed into submission by the appearance of their enemies carrying the Emperor's banner – a stern message of where true Loyalty should rest. This psychological assault became the subject of a popular song by Ōmura Masujirō and Shinagawa Yajirō.

> Noble Prince, Noble Prince
> What is that which flutters
> Before Your Highness's horse?
>
> Know you not?
> It is the Imperial brocade
> Signifying punishment for rebels.[11]

The first verse, usually known by its opening line, 'Miya-sama, Miya-sama', somehow made it to Great Britain, where ten years later it appeared in garbled but still recognisable form accompanying the Emperor's entrance in Gilbert and Sullivan's *The Mikado* (1885).

Many standoffs of the civil war came close to blows, but ended with surrender before a local potentate dared attack the imperial banner. Although not every group of rebels surrendered so easily: fighting in several northern towns was fierce. A group called the White Tiger Corps (*Byakkotai*) achieved lasting fame during the war, not so much for their military prowess as their adherence to samurai ideals. Largely comprising teenage sons of the Aizu-Wakamatsu domain, and intended to be held in reserve, a group of the White Tigers mistakenly believed that smoke in the distance was a sign that their castle had fallen, and committed suicide en masse. When the castle did eventually fall, the samurai resistance lost its best foothold in the north of the country, and retreated even further.

The last of the old-school samurai installed themselves at the southern end of Ezo Island, in the vast star-shaped fortress of Goryōkaku ('The Pentagon'). There, they hoped to salvage some semblance of their dignity by proclaiming themselves to be a samurai nation, the Republic of Ezo, which still proclaimed loyalty to the Emperor, but regarded itself as a state independent from Meiji Japan.

If the last of the samurai had hoped for foreign aid, it proved to be unforthcoming. Foreign ships watched the conflict unfold, and the French military advisers controversially resigned their native commissions in order to lead the Republic of Ezo's armies, but the Boshin War was a mop-up operation against a dwindling foe.

The Republic of Ezo began with limited resources – a mere handful of ships in its fleet, and whatever supplies could be scraped up in Hakodate, the treaty port close to Goryōkaku. The French mounted a daring operation to the south, where they intended to steal an ironclad warship, the *Kōtetsu*, newly delivered from America. Ships from the Republic of Ezo, flying the American and Russian flags as camouflage, got near enough to the *Kōtetsu* to board her, with some of the Shinsengumi forming the suicidally brave raiding party, leaping from the high deck of the Republic's ship to the low-lying *Kōtetsu*, directly into the path of the *Kōtetsu*'s deck-mounted machine guns.

The mission to steal the *Kōtetsu* was a failure, and before long, the imperial forces had pursued the samurai rebels to Hakodate itself. Hijikata Toshizō led the last remnants of the Shinsengumi in the defence of one of the outlying strongpoints, but was forced to recognize that the Republic of Ezo was doomed, and that its hastily selected president was sure to make a deal with the imperial forces. Announcing that he should have already been dead, Hijikata left a death poem that reiterated his faith to the deposed Shōgun:

Though my body may decay on the isle of Ezo
My spirit guards my lord in the east.[12]

He died soon afterwards, not by *seppuku*, but from a bullet wound received while leading a doomed charge against the imperial forces.

In the years that followed the fall of the Republic of Ezo, the samurai lost much of what had defined them as a class. The Emperor left Kyōto and moved to take up residence at the former palace of the Shōgun in Edo, now renamed *Tōkyō* – 'East Capital'. The Kantō region was hence finally officially recognized as the centre of Japanese power. In 1871, the old feudal domains were abolished and reorganized into prefectures. Many of the old feudal lords were given new titles cognate with European nobility, counts, dukes and princes, but they lost their warrior retainers. By 1873, the Meiji government had established a modern army, removing the need for a separate warrior elite. Hairstyles and clothing were already changing, and the standard dress and appearance of the samurai was fading from view. The very word samurai fell out of use, with the last rebranded as *shizoku*, 'warrior clansmen'. With military matters in the hands of a new group, there was not even any reason to see men with edged weapons on the street. The right of the samurai to carry swords in public, long seen as the quintessential trait that defined them, was abolished, as was the right to execute non-samurai who offended them. In 1877, they lost their right to the rice stipend with which they had been paid for centuries. The last of the samurai were unemployed.

Such changes were deeply unpopular with many of those who had fought to put the new regime in power. While some accepted that times had changed, a small hardcore of fanatics regarded the dismantling of the samurai class as a betrayal. Although it seems to have been widely understood by many of the prime movers in the Meiji Restoration that Japan would modernize, some hardliners protested that they had fought for the appointment of a competent shōgun. Paramount among these brokenhearted old soldiers was Saigō Takamori, who had fought so bravely to establish the new order.

Establishing several private 'academies' of swordsmanship in 1874, Saigō spent three years preparing for an insurrection. After the capture of several government agents sent to observe his academies, Saigō went on the offensive, claiming that one of these 'spies' had confessed that he had orders to kill Saigō before he could cause any trouble. Saigō responded in 1877 with the last attack of the samurai, the Satsuma Rebellion, in which he led some 20,000 sympathizers against government forces in his native Kyūshū. Eventually, with his forces worn down to a mere handful of men, Saigō either committed suicide in a mountain hideaway or died from a bullet wound – his head then being removed by a lieutenant in order to imply a warrior's death and hence save face. The 'last samurai' was posthumously pardoned for his misguided insurrection as early as 1889, but the samurai were gone.

11

RETURN OF THE JIDAI
THE SAMURAI AS SYMBOL

Their memory lived on. Historical battles, wily tactics, winning strategies from Japanese history were imparted to the officers of the new army and navy. Martial fervour was certainly not diminished, and those who had rejected the swords and topknot in favour of modern uniforms and weaponry were at the forefront of Japan's expansion overseas.

Japan retained an exotic, erotic frisson for foreign countries. The impoverished samurai clans of the late nineteenth century unloaded priceless heirlooms on the international arts market, creating new vogues abroad for *japonisme*. The idea of a medieval, martial society, awakened from a time warp like something in a fairytale, gave Japan a peculiar fascination to western observers, aided by the whimsical writings of authors like Lafcadio

Hearn, who mourned Japan's rapid modernization, and almost seemed to prefer it when Japan was medieval – beautiful and dangerous.

Among such writers, one in particular helped preserve stories of the samurai in a new century. Nitobe Inazō (1862–1933) did much to popularize Japanese culture abroad, but will probably be best remembered for *Bushidō: The Soul of Japan*. Written in English in 1900, Nitobe's book was snatched up by a readership eager to understand the exotic Japanese. Soon translated into Japanese from its original English, it formed a component of the Japanese self-image in the early twentieth century. Nitobe does not seem to have realized how his work would be received. He stated himself that there was 'no written creed' for Bushidō, and yet in publishing an entire book on the subject, inadvertently created one after the fact. The 'way of the warrior' had always been a matter of some debate, a vague set of principles that varied from domain to domain, sometimes included as guidelines for lordly successors, sometimes made up on the spot. Since not even the Japanese themselves could agree on the nature of a samurai's obligations during the Meiji Restoration, it is ironic indeed that it was a Japanese, writing and lecturing in English, who would codify many of the stereotypes of the samurai worldview:

> This ethical and spiritual legacy we call Bushidō, which literally signifies Fighting-Knight-Ways, or better translated, Teachings of Knightly Behaviour. It was the moral code of the samurai – the class of knights whose badge and privilege it was to wear two swords. Do not imagine that they were only swaggering, bloodthirsty youths. The sword was called the soul of the samurai.[1]

Muddled stories of the end of the samurai drifted westwards, and formed a new subgenre of orientalism. Puccini's *Madame Butterfly* (1904) was a heroine imbued with the samurai spirit. Her story contains shadows of Saigō Takamori's rebellion and of the dying days of the samurai era – a girl from a noble family, fallen on hard times after her father's suicidal participation in an unspecified hardline insurrection. She is sold to a foreign cad, adopts the newly decriminalized Christian faith in his honour, only to be left heartbroken and crushed by his betrayal. In an assertion of her samurai background, she fights back in an iconically samurai way, by killing herself.

It should not surprise anyone that the rhetoric of the samurai era was also soon put to use in Japan's expansion overseas. Ezo Island was renamed Hokkaidō, the 'Northern Seaway', in an attempt to integrate it into other well-known sectors of Japan, such as the 'Western Seaway' (i.e. Kyūshū) and the 'Eastern Seaway' (the road from Kyōto to Tōkyō). Colonial efforts pushed north over the whole island, and into the southern part of Sakhalin beyond. As only the Ainu were there to complain, Japanese expansion proceeded without prominent criticism. Elsewhere, the Chinese soon raised the spectre of Hideyoshi's invasions of the Asian mainland, and referred directly to the spirit of Bushidō in their dealings with the Japanese invaders in the Sino-Japanese War of 1894–5. During the Russo-Japanese War, artists and reporters continually referred to Japan's martial spirit. Admiral Tōgō, the great victor against the Russians in the Battle of Tsushima, famously briefed his commanders in front of a table bearing a samurai blade – the implication being that defeat would require suicidal atonement. When he returned, in triumph, to a hero's welcome in Tōkyō Bay, he chose to fly the ominous words of Tokugawa Ieyasu as a signal from the mast of his flagship: 'At the moment of victory, tighten the straps of your helmet.'

Such a martial spirit attained more ominous trappings as it began to dictate Japanese politics. As had happened so often before in Japan, the 'low' began to dominate the 'high'. Overeager junior officers, often egged on by their superiors, were soon manufacturing disturbances in Asia that required Japanese peacekeeping activities. The thoroughly modernized Japanese army and navy had grabbed toeholds in Taiwan and Korea, and soon Manchuria and China itself. By the time of the First World War, in which Japan fought on the side of the Allies, seizing the Shandong peninsula in China and many German colonial possessions in the South Pacific, there were dire warning signs that the martial proclivities of the Japanese, nurtured through centuries of warfare, made them a danger to the whole world. In 1919, the American diplomat Paul Reinsch put it bluntly:

If this force, with all the methods it is accustomed to apply, remains unopposed, there will be created in the Far East the greatest engine of military oppression and dominance that the world has ever seen.[2]

The suicidal rhetoric of the samurai – born from the last acts of desperate men in the distant past, maintained as a political ideology for 250 years of Tokugawa dominance, and grown to a state religion in the early twentieth century – had its bluff called by the Second World War. With conflict between nations now involving all the participants in those nations, not merely the military class, the government of Japan called upon its people to sacrifice their all in the manner of their soldiers at the front. Conscripts to the imperial army and navy were waved off with funereal cheer, on the understanding that they were 'already dead'. It was but a short step from such rhetoric to the use of suicidal troops, operating human torpedoes, and the most iconic attack of all, the *Shinpū* pilots who were instructed to ram their planes into Allied ships in deadly, one-way attacks. It was translators among the Americans, not the Japanese themselves, who inadvertently gave the characters for *Shinpū* an alternative reading reflecting a classical allusion: 'Divine Wind', or *Kamikaze*. The headbands of the suicide pilots bore suitable slogans: the most popular including 'Certain Victory' and 'Seven Lives for the Fatherland'.

Just as the Divine Winds of legend had wiped the Mongol armada from Japan, now the Japanese Empire placed all its hope in these last-ditch suicide squadrons. As Allied forces drew nearer to the Japanese mainland, they received a taste of of what the Japanese authorities had called 'breaking the jewel' (*gyokusai*): the intention of imparting a samurai's suicidal spirit to the entire population. Savage fighting on Iwo Jima and Okinawa convinced American policy-makers that there would be no simple surrender from a race that, like its hero Yoshitsune, refused to consider preparations for retreat. The Allied victory would need to work like a samurai general's victory of old, with the collusion of the Emperor.

When the atomic bombs were dropped on Hiroshima and Nagasaki, the Japanese were on the verge of starvation. The Shōwa Emperor, better known abroad by his given name of Hirohito, broke with tradition by addressing his people directly, informing them that they must now stoically 'endure the unendurable', and surrender.

After Japan's defeat, Hirohito made an even more infamous speech, the Declaration of Humanity (*ningen sengen*). In it, he disavowed any claims on divine descent, renounced his ancestors' claim to be the children of the Sun Goddess, and essentially proclaimed that he was just a man like any other. Japan itself, in a controversial constitutional change, also officially renounced offensive warfare. At least on paper, there was no such thing as a Japanese army any more, only a 'Self-Defence Force'.

Fictions of the samurai would return to haunt the Japanese through American propaganda. *Know Your Enemy: Japan* (1945), produced by the US Department of War, placed strong emphasis on the swords carried by Japanese officers, using them to tie the modern military to the medieval ethics and concerns of the samurai class.

According to the film that instructed an entire generation of American servicemen about their enemy, the samurai elite were an idle ruling class, distinguished by the right to bear swords, with which they had the mandate to execute any commoner who offended them. Bushidō, according to *Know Your Enemy*, is a code of absolute loyalty to one's superiors, and one that advocated *victory at any cost*, particularly through treachery and deceit. Treatment of the Christians in the seventeenth century is brought right to the fore, with an emphasis on the 'bloodthirsty' spirit of the Japanese people, as opposed to the peace-loving Christians they slaughtered – all very well, but no mention is made of the threats made by the captain of the *San Felipe*, that the Christians were a vanguard of a European invasion that would destroy Japanese society.

As one might expect from a propaganda film, *Know Your Enemy* plays up the concerns of the military elite, and makes no apology for alluding, as did the rulers of wartime Japan themselves, to the samurai past as a precedent for the conflicts of the present. In particular, the sword of the samurai was targeted as the symbol of all that was wrong with Japan – a brutal, medieval instrument, kept in the hands of a corrupt and privileged elite, used to suppress all thought of Christian or democratic values. According to *Know Your Enemy*, it was the sword of the samurai that stopped the twentieth-century Japanese from embracing the values of modern civilization.[3]

Immediately after the war, American policy was similarly steered by the work of the cultural anthropologist Ruth Benedict (1887–1948) who had been commissioned during the war to produce an analysis and guide to the Japanese mind. The resultant work, *The Chrysanthemum and the Sword: Patterns of Japanese Culture* (1946), was written under conditions in which Benedict was unable to enter Japan itself, and instead is based on interviews with Japanese-Americans, and analyses of newspaper clippings and available media. Benedict's book, originally intended for military personnel, was influential in establishing the role of the emperor as a focus of Japanese loyalty, and of explaining some of the vagaries of behaviour of Japanese prisoners of war. In a move that has been criticized ever since, Benedict described the Japanese mind in direct relation to twentieth-century fanatacism of the resurgent samurai ethic. As the title implied, 'the sword' was seen as a crucial component of Japanese culture, and its wielders, the samurai, the masters of Japanese society. Despite being prepared in something of a hurry, for a limited audience, *The Chrysanthemum and the Sword* flourished long after its intended purpose. In the year of its author's death, it was published in Japanese, and contributed to a post-war sense of Japanese uniqueness, even among the Japanese themselves.

It was the opinion of the Occupation forces that the Emperor of Japan, Hirohito, was the ultimate unifying symbol. He should be kept in power, as they could be sure that whatever he did, his people would follow. Just as the

Minamoto had left the imperial line intact, just as the Kamakura Bakufu had let the court ceremonies proceed unabated, just as the Tokugawa shōgunate had ruled in its name for two and a half centuries, the unbroken imperial institution was the key to Japan.

Behind the scenes, there were dissenters. Some, among the British, Australians and New Zealanders in particular, protested that the Shōwa Emperor was a war criminal, and should be tried as such. Meanwhile, as if the situation was not already complicated enough, a taxi arrived at the headquarters of the Supreme Commander for the Allied Powers (SCAP), General Douglas MacArthur, on 17 January 1946. Out of it stepped a man in his fifties, a grocer from Nagoya, controversially wearing the chrysanthemum crest reserved for members of the imperial family. His name was Kumazawa Hiromichi, and he politely presented MacArthur with six kilogrammes of boxed documents outlining his lineage and claim. He was, as the documents persuasively argued, the rightful heir of the Southern Court of the Japanese Emperors, which far from coming to an end in the fourteenth century, had endured as an alternate line of succession all the way to the present day. He took particular pains to point out to MacArthur the political implications – the Southern Court had been the rightful rulers; the Northern Court were widely acknowledged to have been mere puppets of the Ashikaga Shōgunate. His father had even argued the case with the Meiji Emperor, and had been offered a baronetcy if he would just shut up about it.

Kumazawa now presented his credentials to the Occupying powers, offering the inevitable temptation to right a perceived wrong from 500 years in the past, and to do away with the old imperial order in favour of an even older imperial order, albeit one that would have a clean post-Second World War slate. This, however, would ruin MacArthur's plans for Hirohito. Perhaps already learning how to dodge difficult questions in an oriental manner, MacArthur ruled that the question of the Northern and Southern Courts of the fourteenth century was a can of worms best opened by the Japanese judiciary without foreign interference, and the question of the new pretender was left unresolved for several years. Kumazawa was variously described as a crackpot, a Communist stooge or a democratic 'emperor of the people'. He went on the lecture circuit in an attempt to whip up local support, but died in the 1960s. His nominal heir, a bicycle repairman in Osaka, refused to play along, burying the North–South divide once more. But to this day there are people in Yoshino who will claim that a friend of a friend is the new Kumazawa claimant.[4]

It is only natural for a culture's modern media to turn to its past for inspiration – the locations, artefacts and costumes are more accessible, the funding easier to secure, the educational applications more direct. Whereas America turned to the Wild West and Britain to the Victorian age, the Japanese turned to *jidaigeki* – 'period pieces'. There is, on paper, no reason for a *jidaigeki* to be associated solely with the samurai. As the Japanese arts returned in the post-war period, the Occupation authorities were forced to deal with the number of stories in the Japanese repertoire that alluded to the martial past. In November 1945, with Tōkyō still in ruins, two decimated kabuki troupes joined forces to put on a show that included scenes from *Yoshitsune and the Thousand Cherry Trees* in the capital's only surviving theatre. After an informer tipped off the authorities, a clampdown swiftly followed, arguing that the companion piece *Terakoya* (an excerpt from the 1746 play *Sugawara's Secrets of Calligraphy*), placed undue emphasis on discredited 'feudal' loyalty. 'In the case of *Yoshitsune and the Thousand Cherry Trees*,' wrote translator Stanleigh Jones, 'nearly the entire play was proscribed as being undemocratic and promoting ideas of feudalistic loyalty and sacrifice.'[5]

By February 1946, kabuki had found an unexpected champion in the form of Faubion Bowers, an aide to General MacArthur who resigned his post in order to become a theatre censor sympathetic to Japanese drama. Under Bowers' supervision, *Kanjinchō* was back onstage within months, and *Terakoya* within a year. By November 1947, even though film versions of the story of the vengeful Forty-Seven Rōnin were banned in cinemas, Bowers had managed to scrape kabuki versions of it past the censorship authority. In cinemas, it was a different matter, with the censors targeting any film featuring swordplay – even *The Mask of Zorro*.[6]

Instead, the Occupation forces encouraged a number of subjects deemed to be safe for the defeated population. A film that pushed democracy or women's liberation, or encouraged alien, American concepts like baseball or romance would meet with the approval of the censor. Stories of the samurai were strongly discouraged. Kurosawa Akira's *Those Who Step on the Tiger's Tail*, an adaptation of the *Kanjinchō* play of Yoshitsune and Benkei sneaking through the Ataka checkpoint, was completed in 1945 but not released until 1952, falling foul of the censor because of 'the feudalistic idea of loyalty expressed in the film'.[7]

Kurosawa, remembered today as the doyen of samurai films, found samurai subjects to be unapproachable in the post-war era. *Rashōmon*, his famous multiple-viewpoint account of the same event, was sure to appeal to post-war viewers confused over whose propaganda to believe; it is perhaps no surprise that Kurosawa's producers backed out in 1948, and the film did not appear until 1950.

When television arrived, it did so with an assertion of the samurai past. The first official TV transmission by the national broadcaster NHK, on 1 February 1953, was transmitted to a mere 866 television sets, but pointedly contained a scene from the kabuki play *Yoshitsune and the Thousand Cherry Trees*, in which Yoshitsune's mistress walks in the company of a shape-shifting fox. Discouraged by the departed Occupation authorities, its appearance in the first transmission of the new medium might merely have been a recognition that it was one of the few sequences that had been most recently rehearsed. But to many, it amounted to a proclamation that the American occupiers had gone at last, and that the Japanese were back in charge.[8]

A surprising arrival filled the vacuum. With samurai still out of favour, writers and artists, particularly on the left, found a new working-class hero to lionize. Potboiler novels, comics and TV shows began to speak of a heretofore unmentioned underclass of assassins, the ninja. Considering the ubiquity of the ninja in twenty-first-century popular culture, it is remarkable how fast they appear to have sprung out of nowhere in the 1950s and 1960s.

At first, they were imagined in black – the default colour of stagehands and puppeteers, whom traditional theatre-goers were supposed to blank from their sight. Ninja were proletarian heroes, peasants and underlings in the interstices of times past, literally invisible from a military history that had been dominated by the samurai. However, despite the claims of ninja apologists, it is difficult to find any concrete discussion of them long before the novels of Yamada Fūtarō (1922–2001) and the comics of Shirato Sanpei (b.1932). Any attempts to make a scholarly study of ninja lead down a series of false trails, with modern sources that end up only citing each other, and credulous populist works that claim any reference in an old account to *shinobi* (stealth, spies, assassins) was in fact a reference to one of several secret *ninja* societies that stayed in the shadows. This fad achieved global recognition with the appearance of ninja in the James Bond film *You Only Live Twice* (1967) – reaching, by nature of its genre and franchise, a far wider audience than any more reasoned, less fantastic account of Japanese martial traditions.[9]

As colour television took hold in Japan, ninja gained more garish colours, as well as a conveniently rediscovered martial art. The TV series *Ninja Butai Gekkō* (1964, released abroad as *Phantom Agents*) gave them superhuman abilities born from simple camera trickery, and gadgets inspired by James Bond and Cold War espionage. Although ninja were found in some 1960s entertainments for adults, their most enduring legacy has always been in the children's medium, where every generation of little boys seems to have a ninja series to imitate in the playground and the park – *Ninja the Wonderboy* (1964), *Legend of Kamui* (1969), *Battle of the Planets* (1972), *Hattori the Ninja* (1981), *Red Shadow* (1987), or *Naruto* (2002).[10]

While strains of ninja stories flourished and endured, they began to run in parallel with resurgent stories of the samurai. Kurosawa himself most memorably contributed to this with *The Seven Samurai* (1954) a rain-soaked, muddy tale of warriors fighting to save a village of farmers from marauding bandits in the late sixteenth century. And as the character of Kanbei (Shimura Takashi) sagely observes at one point: 'We lose. Those farmers . . . they're the winners.'[11]

The samurai were sure to reassert themselves when the worst of the wartime stigma had passed – there was simply no way to tell most period drama without involving the samurai in some way. In the 1960s, as the Tōkyō Olympics approached, television began to exert a greater hold over the Japanese audience. In 1963, NHK began running annual, year-long mega-serials – or *taiga* dramas in local parlance. In most cases, the underlying objective was typical for a national broadcaster: to offer sumptuous costumes and romance for the female audience, action and adventure for the males, and an educational element for the children.

Although the first was a Meiji-era tale, the story of the Forty-Seven Rōnin featured in 1964, followed by fictionalized biographies of Hideyoshi in 1965 and Yoshitsune in 1966. The years since have often revisited the 700 years of samurai history; to do otherwise would be akin to ignoring everything in British history between the Magna Carta and Queen Victoria, or pretending that the USA had never existed at all. The same period saw a massive, countrywide restoration programme, recreating ruined or derelict castles with concrete replicas to serve as municipal centres and local museums. In some cases, such as Nagoya, this simply restored a local landmark to pre-war glories, often with the aid of reinforced concrete. In others, such as Shimabara, the recreation of the city's lost castle redefined the landscape, turning the local focus from a school, town hall or factory to the towering, martial elegance of the samurai era – in Shimabara's case, the resurrection of a forgotten edifice that had been demolished in 1874.

Remarkably few castles exist in their original state – only a dozen retain their 'original' wooden keeps, and by virtue of the impermanence of wood, even these are usually less than 100 years old. Pointedly, Hara Castle on the Shimabara peninsula, site of the last great massacre of the Christians in 1638, is entirely devoid of the dioramas and reconstructions of other historical sites. It remains in mournful ruins, much of its outer enclosures given over to farmland, a car park at the site where samurai once counted a huge pile of human heads. A large, rusting crucifix sits at its highest point, already partially obscured by young trees. It is somehow a more fitting tribute to the thousands of dead than would be the unwelcome construction of an air-conditioned replica in concrete, complete with gift shop and cafe.

The great castle-building programme of the 1960s is a fascinating symptom of the post-samurai era. Although the warriors are gone and their system dismantled, these symbols of their reign dominate the skyline of dozens of Japanese towns. Most are home to local museums that cling with pride and passion to whatever elements made this particular castle town different to the others – a local hero, an infamous bad guy, a tragic general or a cataclysmic battle.

Mito Kōmon (1969–) runs on the commercial channel TBS, but often seems to aim at fulfilling a brief to foster domestic tourism. Its protagonist is Tokugawa Mitsukuni (1628–1701), uncle of the infamous Dog Shōgun and author of the influential *History of Japan*. In an intriguing confluence of modern concerns with the depiction of Mitsukuni in both early and late Tokugawa-era works, it presents him as a wise old sage who wanders Japan incognito, in the company of samurai bodyguards. Each episode of *Mito Kōmon* thereby combines elements of domestic tourism with the escapades of a samurai-era crime-fighter, a stoic, fatherly figure who sniffs out evildoers, and who then brings them to heel by lurking in stern judgement while his bodyguards whip out the seal of the Tokugawa family and bellow: 'Don't you know who this is?'[12]

One is also tempted to ask *where* this is. The act of telling and retelling stories of the past, either for education or tourism or both, is an industry of its own in Japan. The very homogeneity of Tokugawa Japan counts both for and against it. Many modern TV series are filmed on a single standing film set in Uzumasa outside Kyōto, its eastern end a realistic re-creation of Japan in the ages of civil war, the streets gradually becoming more modern towards the west, until it terminates in a late nineteenth-century Tōkyō town square, trams and all. *Mito Kōmon* might wander the length and breadth of Japan, but since every town he reaches looks suspiciously similar to the one from the previous week, there must be other ways to differentiate them. *Mito Kōmon* and shows like it are responsible for the modern equivalent of the long pilgrimages to and from Edo during the samurai era – a weekly glorification of domestic tourism that highlights some unique attribute of an obscure town or province. In keeping with stories that the original Mitsukuni was something of a gourmet, these assertions of local pride are often culinary: Sapporo noodles have a different broth; the cooks have a particular way with mushrooms; nobody does sponge cake like the people in Nagasaki.

Ironically, those towns in Japan that were once forced open by foreign traders have a whole lot more to talk about. Nineteenth-century foreign contacts in Hakodate, Hirado and Yokohama, be it a 'Chinatown' or a Victorian church, all add to the local tourist trails and the constant hope of dragging in coachloads of out-of-prefecture business. When one spa resort can look very much like another, a famous battlefield or notable castle nearby can be the vital tip of the tourist scales.

The eccentric author Mishima Yukio enjoyed great fame in the 1960s, and ended his life in a media event that proved to be a national embarrassment. Mishima was keen to claim that he was of samurai descent – his father had been the governor of the southern half of Sakhalin, his grandmother a distaff descendant of the Matsudaira clan. Developing an ever-growing obsession with Bushidō as he approached middle age, his formerly intellectual lifestyle became increasingly physical, subsumed in bodybuilding and sword practice while he wrote a commentary on the *Hagakure* and berated modern youth for their lack of loyalty to the Emperor. In November 1970, wearing a headband that bore the last words of the Kusunoki brothers, 'Seven Lives for the Fatherland', he staged an attempted coup at a Tōkyō military base, although his call to revolution seems intended from the start to be seen as a gesture to rival the doomed opposition of Saigō Takamori. The press were present because Mishima had called them himself. The soldiers he exhorted to rise up and 'restore' the Emperor were a hostile audience. He seems to have made no plans for action if his revolutionary call had met with agreement. Instead, he ended his protest as he had always intended, with *seppuku*. True to form, he attempted to commit it in the complete, poetic manner of ancient medieval chronicles, not the stylised, briefer manner of late-Edo custom. In keeping with the minutiae of modern reportage, we have a ghastly, step-by-step account of what really happened, as an understandably inexperienced swordsman hacked several times at the agonized Mishima's neck.

Mishima's death was never a revolution: it was the carefully stage-managed, elaborate suicide of a writer who had been obsessed with death for much of his career – a theatrical gesture designed to add a final, serious coda, a 'poem written in a splash of blood' in his own words, to his many literary works. It was Mishima's intention that he be remembered not as an author, but as a samurai. His suicide ensured him worldwide fame among the non-Japanese, but

crippled his standing in his home country. His unquestionable masterpiece, officially completed on the day he
died, was the *Sea of Fertility*, a chronicle of the decline
of Japanese values from what he regarded as their height
during the militarism of the early twentieth century,
through the arrival of unwelcome foreign influences, to
what Mishima predicted as the sorry state of Japanese
youth by the mid-1970s.[13]

If anything, Mishima's spectacular end only dragged
thoughts of the samurai further into the periphery, as the
last refuge of the far right and associated loonies. Disen-
chantment with the old order and the democrats that had
replaced it would lead in the 1970s to portrayals of the
samurai era that emphasized the old ruling class as a corrupt
and venal authority. As Japan was engulfed in political
protests and industrial corruption scandals, the first famous
samurai of the 1970s was *Monjirō* (1972), a wandering rōnin
who interceded against local bullies only reluctantly, after
wearily intoning: 'It's nothing to do with me'. He shared
the airwaves with the vengeful warriors of the *Sure Death*
series (1972–92), an Edo-period star chamber of samurai
who took the law into their own hands when the
government itself was powerless.

As Japan entered its booming 'bubble economy' of the
1980s, fictional depictions of the samurai reflected the
rising affluence of their audience. Cod-psychology books
and business texts suggested that the samurai ethic was
somehow reborn in the *salaryman* who carried Japanese
business to the world. Ironically, it was foreign money that
boosted the profile of the samurai at home and abroad.
Kurosawa, unable to secure funding for his work from
Japanese sources, found funding for his movies from
George Lucas and Francis Ford Coppola, allowing for the
vast epics *Kagemusha* (1980) and *Ran* (1985). Both were

remotely inspired by real events from the samurai era, but were presented as highly symbolic, unhistorical stories of family conflict and betrayal.

There are hundreds of films, TV shows, novels and comics that could just as easily be used to describe modern samurai. This book lacks the space to include the works of Inagaki Hiroshi, Gosha Hideo, Okamoto Kihachi and dozens of other directors; there is no time to describe the undercover magistrate of *Tōyama no Kinsan*, or the plodding *Onihei the Investigator*. There are, too, action-adventure tales from the twentieth century that pointedly exclude true 'samurai' protagonists. *Zatōichi* is a blind masseur, a member of the underclass because of his disability. *Heiji Zenigata* is a commoner who merely works alongside the samurai ruling class. But even when focusing on characters who are not samurai, their interactions, problems or encounters will invariably cross over into the samurai world.

Institutions and leadership in Japanese history are subject to endless debates over nomenclature, responsibility and interpretation. Unchallenged 'facts' about the samurai are revised and rethought on a generational basis and, of course, often reflect attitudes of their own times. In the twenty-first century, new texts – including this one – are more likely to look beyond the borders of Japan, reflecting the admission of the incumbent 125th Emperor, Heisei, that one of his ancestors was Korean, and hence playing up, for the first time, Japan's prehistoric contacts not with gods, but with other races. Despite being openly mentioned in ancient chronicles, the Korean forebears of the imperial house were never spoken of. The Heisei Emperor's admission is remarkable not only because it took him until 2001 to say it, but also because it cleverly occludes a deeper issue. By acknowledging that Kammu, the fiftieth Emperor mentioned in the ancient chronicles, had a mother of Korean descent the Heisei Emperor deftly twisted the focus of enquiry onto the eighth century, and away from any discussion of Kammu's forty-nine predecessors.

We should also not discount the influence of the mass media on interpretations of the samurai – a historiography of opinions and impressions of the samurai should recognize that modern fads exert a strong influence on what is written and what is read. Miyamoto Musashi (1584–1645), one of thousands of samurai who wrote guides to the warrior's life in old age, achieved worldwide fame centuries after his death, thanks not to his *Book of Five Rings*, but to Yoshikawa Eiji's long-running fictional account of his life, serialized from 1933 to 1939 and published in English in the 1980s. Japan's national broadcaster NHK continues to make the samurai era the frequent subject of its *taiga* dramas, often driving subsidiary publishing trends, and forcing popular reconsiderations of famous figures. So it is that Taira Masakado came back into fashion in 1976, Tokugawa Ieyasu got a new lease of life in 1983, and the fortunes of Hōjō Tokimune were suddenly the subject of late-night discussions in Japanese pubs in 2001. In 2010, Sakamoto Ryōma will be back in fashion among tourists and readers on the Tōkyō subways. In 2011, it is the turn of Tokugawa Hidetada, son of Ieyasu, his story told through the eyes of his wife Gō.

Modern Japan is infested with great snaking crocodiles of bored children on compulsory school trips. They slouch sulkily around the Dejima museum in Nagasaki, they lark about among the temples of Nara when the teachers aren't looking. For such children, the samurai past is a confusing whirl of forgotten clans and renamed domains. In terms of their education at these many sites of the samurai past, generalities of good conduct and obedience are emphasized above the petty politicking of clan conflicts. Despite the push towards Bushidō, Japanese teenagers can zoom in with contrary irreverence to the inconvenient episodes of Japanese history. If the items on sale at tourist concessions throughout Japan are anything to go by, the Shinsengumi, that bunch of deluded, doomed warriors, remain predictably popular with Japanese teenagers, who fixate on the tragic youth and disastrous opposition of the shōgun's last loyalists, and the hopelessness of their resistance. In such a glorification of the 'nobility of failure', we see a resurgence of the sympathy for the underdog that characterized much of the poetry of the Genpei War. Mishima might have been proud, but as ever it is difficult to see where the samurai spirit truly resides.

There are those who still regard the samurai as the blinkered fools who opposed modernization in favour of an impossible, medieval time warp. Perhaps, instead, we might see the samurai spirit as the indomitable will to reform, which led the opponents of the Tokugawa to topple the shōgun, restore the emperor at last, and modernize Japan as his willing 'servants'.

Modern Japanese would prefer to use neither of these politically sensitive, incomplete definitions. They might instead argue that the samurai spirit encapsulates all that is best about Japan – law-abiding citizenry, cleanliness, organization, loyalty, a respect for old ways and traditions. Even dissenters would heartily agree, but would instead cite unquestioning obedience to authority, pointless bureaucracy, authoritarianism and the relentless hammering down of difference. The attitudes of the samurai permeate the very language that the Japanese use. In modern Japanese, the phrase *hara o watte hanasu* – 'opening the belly to speak' – endures as an idiom for forthright honesty. To this day, to 'do one's best' in

Japanese is *isshō kenmei* – literally, to 'give one's all to the feudal domain'.

A warrior elite does not dominate a state for 700 years without leaving a long shadow, for good or ill. However, we should not be surprised if we are unable to precisely classify the nature of the samurai, since even the Japanese have never been able to agree among themselves about the true nature of Bushidō. The 'way of the samurai', whatever it may be, is an integral component of the soul of Japan. Nothing happens in modern Japan that is not in imitation of it, or reaction to it. Loyalty or opposition to the way of the samurai takes as many forms as there were sides in the Meiji Restoration, but it is always there, like the Emperor himself, ancient, unknowable and enduring.

SOURCES AND RECOMMENDED READING

There is a difficult line to walk in accounts of Japanese history. A combination of readable, action-packed, exciting tales of the samurai rarely seems to exist in-between the same covers as a properly referenced, source-critical, accurate and, dare I say it, rather dry account of Japanese historiography, institutions and terminology. This is why I have concentrated so heavily on the Tokugawa era in this book, in order to emphasize how many 'true' stories of the samurai are based on doubtful accounts or embellishments made long after the fact.

As in my earlier *Brief History of the Vikings*, I have endeavoured to keep the text simple and the notes detailed, so that any interested reader may pursue deeper analysis. Most of the primary sources referred to in this book are available in English translation, and indeed online in the original language in places such as the *Nihon Bungaku Denshi Toshokan* (J-Text Online E-Library:

http://j-texts.com/), or the University of Virginia Library's *Japanese Text Initiative*, which afford the modern historian the chance to check the likes of the *Heike Monogatari*, *Taiheiki* and *Ōninki* from anywhere in the world.

With attitudes still in flux, it should come as no surprise that the history of the samurai is similarly subject to massive revisions. There are excellent works in English that assess the recent debates among Japanese authorities, including *Heavenly Warriors* by William Wayne Farris and *Hired Swords* by Karl Friday. Farris and Friday form the epicentre of modern samurai academia in English – their bibliographies present a concise appraisal of recent Japanese-language scholarship, and their analyses offer an excellent roadmap of samurai studies in the early twenty-first century. An honourable mention should also go to Stephen Turnbull, whose many books since *The Samurai: A Military History* have contributed immeasurably to the popularization of the field. Unlike many armchair historians, Turnbull has trudged over many of the battlefields himself, step by thoughtful step, often producing unexpected and trenchant speculations that are no less worthy than the textual analyses of old chronicles favoured by most other authorities.

Joan Piggott's *Emergence of Japanese Kingship* approaches the early period from the point of view of the first historical emperors and proto-emperors, demonstrating the conjoined origins of both the samurai and the imperial system that they would serve and largely supplant. In terms of recent studies, *Tour of Duty* by Constantine Vaporis is a groundbreaking study of life in the Tokugawa era, as seen through the eyes of the lords who were made to commute back and forth to Edo at the pleasure of the shōgun. For a perspective on Japanese history that concentrates less on the samurai than on everyone else, I recommend Farris's

Japan to 1600: A Social and Economic History, which fills in much background detail that is necessarily jettisoned in this compulsorily 'brief' history.

Further Reading

Ackroyd, J. *Lessons from History: The Tokushi Yoron by Arai Hakuseki.* St Lucia: University of Queensland, 1982.

Alden, D. *Charles Boxer: An Uncommon Life.* Lisbon: Fundaçao Oriente, 2001.

anonymous *Heike Monogatari [Tale of the Heike].* Tōkyō: Hōbunkan, 1933.

—— *Gikeiki [Chronicle of Yoshitsune].* Tōkyō: Kokumin Bunko, 1881.

—— *Ōninki [Chronicle of the (war of the) Ōnin Period].* http://homepage1.nifty.com/sira/ouninki/, accessed 25 August 2009.

Aoki, K. (ed.) *Shoku Nihongi [Further Chronicles of Japan].* 5 vols. Tōkyō: Iwanami Shoten, 1989–98.

Arnesen, P. *The Medieval Japanese Daimyō: The Ōuchi Family's Rule of Suō and Nagato.* New Haven: Yale University Press, 1979.

Aston, W. *Nihongi: Chronicles of Japan from the Earliest Times to AD 697.* 2 vols in 1 edn. Clarendon, VT: Charles E. Tuttle, 1972.

Barnes, G. *The Rise of Civilization in East Asia: The Archaeology of China, Korea and Japan.* London: Thames & Hudson, 1999.

Bender, R. 'The Political Meaning of the Hachiman Cult in Ancient and Early Medieval Japan'. PhD thesis, Columbia University, 1980.

Benneville, J. de *Saitō Musashi-bō Benkei (Tales of the Wars of the Gempei) being the story of the Lives and Adventures of Oyo-no-Kami Minamoto Kurō Yoshitsune and Saitō Musashi-bō Benkei the Warrior Monk.* 2 vols. Yokohama: James S. de Benneville, 1910.

Berry, M. *Hideyoshi.* Cambridge, MA: Harvard University Press, 1982.

Best, J. *A History of the Early Korean Kingdom of Paekche together with an annotated translation of the Paekche Annals of the Samguk Sagi*. Cambridge, MA: Harvard University Asia Center, Harvard University Press, 2006.

Bix, H. *Peasant Protest in Japan 1596–1884*. New Haven: Yale University Press, 1986.

Blomberg, C. *The Akō Affair: A Practical Example of Bushidō*. Uppsala: Text Grupper i Uppsala AB, 1977.

Botsman, D. *Punishment and Power in the Making of Modern Japan*. Princeton: Princeton University Press, 2005.

Bottomley, I. and Anthony Hopson. *Arms and Armor of the Samurai: The History of Weaponry in Ancient Japan*. New York: Crescent Books, 1988.

Boxer, C. *The Christian Century in Japan 1549–1650*. Manchester: Carcanet Press, 1993.

—— *Jan Compagnie in Japan*. The Hague: Martinus Nijhoff, 1936.

Brown, D. 'The impact of firearms on Japanese warfare, 1543–98'. *Far Eastern Quarterly*, 7(3): 236–253, May 1948.

Bryant, A. *Sekigahara 1600: The final struggle for power*. Oxford: Osprey Publishing, 1995.

Caron, F. *Le Puissant Royaume du Japon: La description de François Caron (1636)*. Paris: Chandeigne, 2003.

Cleary, T. *The Japanese Art of War: Understanding the Culture of Strategy*. Boston: Shambhala, 1992.

Clements, J. *The Moon in the Pines: Zen Haiku*. London: Frances Lincoln, 2000.

—— *Coxinga and the Fall of the Ming Dynasty*. Stroud: Sutton Publishing, 2004.

—— *A Brief History of the Vikings*. London: Robinson, 2005.

—— *Marco Polo*. London: Haus Publishing, 2006.

—— *Wu: The Chinese Empress Who Schemed, Seduced and Murdered Her Way to Become a Living God*. Stroud: Sutton Publishing, 2007.

—— *Prince Saionji*. London: Haus Publishing, 2008.

—— *Wellington Koo*. London: Haus Publishing, 2008.

—— *Admiral Tōgō: Nelson of the East*. London: Haus Publishing, 2010.

—— and **Tamamuro Motoko**. *The Dorama Encyclopedia: A Guide to Japanese TV Drama Since 1953*. Berkeley: Stone Bridge Press, 2003.

—— and **Helen McCarthy**. *The Anime Encyclopedia: A Guide to Japanese Animation Since 1917*. Revised and expanded edition. Berkeley: Stone Bridge Press, 2006.

Cobbing, A. *Kyūshū: Gateway to Japan – A Concise History*. Folkestone: Global Oriental, 2009.

Collache, E. 'Une Aventure au Japon', in *Le Tour du Monde: Nouveau Journal des Voyages*, no. 77 (1874), pp. 49–64,

Conlan, T. *State of War: The Violent Order of Fourteenth Century Japan*. Ann Arbor: University of Michigan, Center for Japanese Studies, 2003.

—— *In Little Need of Divine Intervention: Takezaki Suenaga's Scrolls of the Mongol Invasion of Japan*. Ithaca: East Asia Program, Cornell University, 2001.

Cooper, M. *Rodrigues the Interpreter: An Early Jesuit in Japan and China*. New York: Weatherhill, 1994.

—— *The Japanese Mission to Europe, 1582–1590*. Folkestone: Global Oriental, 2005.

Cory, R. 'Some Notes on Father Gregorio de Cespedes, Korea's First European Visitor', in *Transactions of the Korea Branch of the Royal Asiatic Society*, 27 (1937), pp. 1–55.

Cranston, E. *A Waka Anthology. Volume One: The Gem-Glistening Cup*. Stanford, CA: Stanford University Press, 1993.

Crasset, J. *The History of the Church of Japan, written originally in French by Monsieur l'Abbé de T, and now translated into English by N.N.* London: (publisher not indicated), 1707.

Deal, W. *Handbook to Life in Medieval and Early Modern Japan*. Oxford: Oxford University Press, 2006.

Delgado, J. *Khubilai Khan's Lost Fleet: History's Greatest Naval Disaster*. London: Bodley Head, 2009.

Elison, G. *Deus Destroyed: The Image of Christianity in Early Modern Japan*. Cambridge, MA: Harvard University Press, 1991.

Farris, W. *Heavenly Warriors: The Evolution of Japan's Military, 500–1300.* Cambridge, MA: Harvard University Press, 1995.

—— *Ancient Japan's Korean Connection.* Durham, NC: Duke University Working Papers in Asian/Pacific Studies, 1995.

—— *Japan's Medieval Population: famine, fertility and warfare in a transformative age.* Honolulu: University of Hawaii Press, 2006.

—— *Daily Life and Demographics in Ancient Japan.* Ann Arbor: Center for Japanese Studies, University of Michigan, 2009.

—— *Japan to 1600: A Social and Economic History.* Honolulu: University of Hawaii Press, 2009.

Feifer, G. *Breaking Open Japan: Commodore Perry, Lord Abe and American Imperialism in 1853.* New York: Harper Collins, 2006.

Field, N. *The Splendor of Longing in the Tale of Genji.* Princeton: Princeton University Press, 1987.

Friday, K. 'Teeth and Claws: Provincial Warriors and the Heian Court', in *Monumenta Nipponica*, 43(2), Summer 1988, pp. 153–85.

—— *Hired Swords: The Rise of Private Warrior Power in Early Japan.* Stanford, CA: Stanford University Press, 1992.

—— *Samurai, Warfare and the State in Early Medieval Japan.* New York: Routledge, 2004.

—— *The First Samurai: The Life and Legend of the Warrior Rebel Taira Masakado.* Hoboken: John Wiley and Sons, 2008.

Friends of Silent Films Association. *The Benshi – Japanese Silent Film Narrators.* Tōkyō: Urban Connections, 2001.

Goble, A. *Kenmu: Go-Daigo's Revolution.* Cambridge, MA: Harvard University Press, 1996.

Goodman, G. *Japan and the Dutch.* Richmond, Surrey: Curzon, 2000.

Graff, D. *Medieval Chinese Warfare, 300–900.* London: Routledge, 2002.

Hall, J. and Toyoda Takeshi (eds). *Japan in the Muromachi Age.* Ithaca: East Asia Program, Cornell University, 2001.

Harris, V. and Ogasawara Nobuo. *Swords of the Samurai.* London: British Museum Publications, 1990.

Hawley, S. *The Imjin War: Japan's Sixteenth Century Invasion of Korea and Attempt to Conquer China.* Seoul/Berkeley: Royal Asiatic Society/University of California, 2005.

Hillsborough, R. *Shinsengumi: The Shōgun's Last Samurai Corps.* North Clarendon, VT: Tuttle, 2005.

Hirano, K. *Mr. Smith Goes to Tokyo: Japanese Cinema Under the American Occupation 1945–1952.* Washington, DC: Smithsonian Institution Press, 1992.

Honda, K. *Ainu Minzoku* [*The Ainu People*]. Tōkyō: Asahi Shinbunsha, 1993.

Hoshi, R. *Sendai Boshin Senshi: Kitahō Seiken o Mezasushita Yūshatachi* [*The History of the Boshin War in Sendai: The Heroes Who Wanted to Rule the North*]. Tōkyō: Sanshusha, 2008.

Howard, B. *Life with the Trans-Siberian Savages.* London: Longmans, Green and Co., 1893.

Howe, C. *The Origins of Japanese Trade Supremacy: Development and Technology in Asia from 1540 to the Pacific War.* London: Hurst & Co., 1999.

Inuzuka, T. (ed.). *Shin Satsumagaku: Satsuma, Amami, Ryūkyū* [*New Satsuma Studies: Satsuma, Amami Islands, Ryūkyū Islands*]. Kagoshima: Nanbō Shinsha, 2004.

Ishida, Y. (ed.). *Minna no Terebi Jidaigeki: Dai Hit-saku kara Chō-cult Sakuhin made* [*Everybody's TV Period Dramas: From the Great Hits to the Super-cult Works*]. Tōkyō: Aspect, 1998.

Jansen, M. *China in the Tokugawa World.* Cambridge, MA: Harvard University Press, 1992.

—— (ed.). *The Emergence of Meiji Japan.* Cambridge: Cambridge University Press, 1995.

Johnston, E. 'Buried Treasure: The Mysteries and Majesty of Nara', in the *Japan Times*, web edition, 6 July 2003, http://search.japantimes.co.jp/cgi-bin/fl20030706a1.html, accessed 30 July 2009.

Jones, S. *Yoshitsune and the Thousand Cherry Trees: A Masterpiece of the Eighteenth Century Japanese Puppet Theater.* New York: Columbia University Press, 1993.

Kanda, C. *Shimabara no Ran: Kirishitan Shinkō to Busō Hōki* [*The Shimabara Rebellion: Christian Belief and Armed Uprising*]. Tōkyō: Chūōkōron Shinsha, 2005.

Kazusa, H. *Gracia Hosokawa no Subete* [*All About Gracia Hosokawa*]. Tōkyō: Shin Jinbutsu Ōraisha, 1994.

Keene, D. *Emperor of Japan: Meiji and His World, 1852–1912.* New York: Columbia University Press, 2002.

Keith, M. 'The Logistics of Power: Tokugawa Responses to the Shimabara Rebellion and power projection in 17th-century Japan'. PhD thesis, Ohio State University, 2006.

Kerr, A. *Dogs and Demons: The Fall of Modern Japan.* Harmondsworth: Penguin, 2002.

Kerr, G. *Okinawa: The History of an Island People.* Rutland, VT: Tuttle, 2000.

Kimura, K. *Konishi Yukinaga Den* [*Biography of Augustin Konishi*]. Tōkyō: Chōeisha, 2005.

Kitabatake, C. *A Chronicle of Gods and Sovereigns: Jinnō Shōtōki of Kitabatake Chikafusa,* trans. Paul Varley. New York: Columbia University Press, 1980.

Kitagawa, T. 'The Conversion of Hideyoshi's Daughter Gō', in *The Japanese Journal of Religious Studies,* 34/1, pp. 9–25.

Kitajima, M. *Katō Kiyomasa: Chōsen Shinryaku no Jitsuzō* [*Katō Kiyomasa: A True Image of the Korean Invasion*]. Tōkyō: Yoshikawa Hirobumi-kan, 2007.

Kitamichi, K. *Ainu Gochina de Tabi Suru Hokkaidō* [*Travels Among Ainu Place-names in Hokkaidō*]. Tōkyō: Asahi Shinsho, 2008.

Knutsen, R. *Sun Tzu and the Art of Medieval Japanese Warfare.* Folkestone: Global Oriental, 2006.

Kumar, A. *Globalizing the Prehistory of Japan: Language, Genes and Civilization.* London: Routledge, 2009.

Kuno, Y. *Japanese Expansion on the Asiatic Continent: a study in the history of Japan with special reference to her international relations with China, Korea and Russia.* 2 vols. Berkeley: University of California, 1937.

Kusaka, T. *Gunkimono-shu* [*Collection of War Tales*]. Tōkyō: Waseda Daigaku Shuppan-bu, 1990.

Leiter, S. *New Kabuki Encyclopedia: A Revised Adaptation of Kabuki Jiten*. Westport: CT: Greenwood Press, 1997.

Leupp, G. *Servants, Shophands, and Laborers in the Cities of Tokugawa Japan*. Princeton: Princeton University Press, 1992.

Lu, D. *Japan: A Documentary History*. Armonk, NY: M.E. Sharpe, 1996.

Maltarich, B. *Samurai and Supermen: National Socialist Views of Japan*. Oxford: Peter Lang, 2005.

Mass, J. *Yoritomo and the Founding of the First Bakufu: The Origins of Dual Government in Japan*. Stanford, CA: Stanford University Press, 1999.

—— **and William B. Hauser** (eds). *The Bakufu in Japanese History*. Stanford, CA: Stanford University Press, 1985.

Matsuno, T. *Wives of the Samurai: Their Eventful Lives During the Period of Civil Wars*. New York: Vantage Press, 1989.

McCullough, H. *Taiheiki: A Chronicle of Medieval Japan*. New York: Columbia University Press, 1959.

—— *Yoshitsune: A Fifteenth Century Japanese Chronicle*. Stanford, CA: Stanford University Press, 1966.

—— 'A Tale of Mutsu', in *Harvard Journal of Asiatic Studies*, no. 25 (1967–68), pp. 178–211.

—— *The Tale of the Heike*. Stanford, CA: Stanford University Press, 1988.

Melville, H. *Moby Dick*. London: CRW Collector's Library, 2004, reprint of 1851 edition.

Mishima, Y. *On Hagakure: The Samurai Ethic and Modern Japan*. Harmondsworth: Penguin, 1977.

Mitani, H. *Escape from Impasse: The Decision to Open Japan*. Tōkyō: International House of Japan, 2006.

Miyamoto, K. *Vikings of the Far East*. New York: Vantage, 1975.

Miyamoto, M. *A Book of Five Rings*. London: Allison and Busby, 1974.

Miyazaki, S. *The Story of Building the Shimabara Castle*. Nagasaki: Dejima Bunko, 2003.

Morris, I. *The Nobility of Failure: Tragic Heroes in the History of Japan*. London: Secker & Warburg, 1975.

—— *The World of the Shining Prince: Court Life in Ancient Japan*. Harmondsworth: Penguin, 1979.

Mulhern, C. (ed.). *Heroic With Grace: Legendary Women of Japan*. Armonk, NY: M.E. Sharpe, 1991.

Muramatsu, T. *Westerners in the Modernzation of Japan*. Tōkyō: Hitachi, 1995.

Murdoch, J. *A History of Japan*. 3 vols. Yokohama: Asiatic Society of Japan, 1910.

Najita, T. *Japan: The Intellectual Foundations of Modern Japanese Politics*. Chicago: University of Chicago Press, 1974.

Nathan, J. *Mishima: A Biography*. Tōkyō: Charles Tuttle, 1975.

Nawa, Y. *Yōtō Muramasa: Mukashibanishi Kisho Hikae* [*The Cursed Sword Muramasa: Notes on a Popular Myth*]. Tōkyō: Kawade Shobō Shinsha, 2001.

Nitobe, I. *Bushidō: The Soul of Japan – an exposition of Japanese thought*. Tōkyō: Kenkyūsha, 1936.

—— *The Japanese Nation: Its Land, Its People and Its Life*. London: Kegan Paul, 2006.

Nomura, Y. *Jitsuroku: Terebi Jidaigeki-shi – Chanbara Chronicle 1953–1998* [*Veritable Record: A History of TV Period Dramas – Swordfighting Chronicle 1953–1998*]. Tōkyō: Tokyo Shinbun Shuppansho, 1999.

Okada, A. *Amakusa Tokisada*. Tōkyō: Yoshikawa Hirobumi-kan, 1960.

Ōmori, K. *Shakushain Senki* [*Chronicle of Shakushain*]. Tōkyō: Shin Jinbutsu Ōraisha, 2002.

Omoto, K. and Francis Macouin. *Nihon no Kaikoku: Émile Guimet, Aru Furansu-jin no Mita Meiji* [*The Opening of Japan: Émile Guimet, Meiji as Seen by a Frenchman*]. Osaka: Sōgensha, 2004. Japanese translation of *Quand Japon s'ouvrit au monde*.

Ōyama, K. 'Historical Drama', in Sata, M. and Hirahara Hideo (eds), *A History of Japanese Television Drama*. Tōkyō: Japan Association of Broadcasting Art, 1991, pp. 147–66.

Paske-Smith, M. *Japanese Traditions of Christianity, Being some old translations from the Japanese, with British Consular Reports of the Persecutions of 1868–1872.* Kōbe: J.L. Thompson et al., 1930.

Perrin, N. *Giving Up the Gun: Japan's Reversion to the Sword, 1543–1879.* Boston: David R. Godine, 1979.

Piggott, J. *The Emergence of Japanese Kingship.* Stanford, CA: Stanford University Press, 1997.

Rabinovitch, J. *Shōmonki: The Story of Masakado's Rebellion.* Tōkyō: Sophia University Monumenta Nipponica, 1986.

Ravina, M. *The Last Samurai: The Life and Battles of Saigō Takamori.* Hoboken: John Wiley & Sons, 2004.

Richie, D. *The Films of Akira Kurosawa.* Berkeley: University of California Press, 1996.

Rossabi, M. *Khubilai Khan: His Life and Times.* Berkeley: University of California Press, 1988.

Sadler, A. *The Maker of Modern Japan: The Life of Tokugawa Ieyasu.* London: George Allen and Unwin,1937.

Sansom, G. *Japan: A Short Cultural History.* London: The Cresset Library, 1987.

—— *A History of Japan 1615–1867.* Folkestone: Dawson, 1978.

Sato, H. *Legends of the Samurai.* Woodstock: Overlook Press, 1995.

Satow, E. *A Diplomat in Japan: The Inner History of the Critical Years in the Evolution of Japan When the Ports Were Opened and the Monarchy Restored.* San Francisco: Stone Bridge Press, 2006.

Scott-Stokes, H. *The Life and Death of Yukio Mishima.* London: Peter Owen, 1975.

Screech, T. *The Shogun's Painted Culture: Fear and Creativity in the Japanese States 1760–1829.* London: Reaktion Books, 2000.

Seeley, P. 'The Japanese March in "The Mikado"', in *The Musical Times,* 126 (1985), pp. 454–6.

Seidensticker, E. (ed./trans.). *The Tale of Genji.* Harmondsworth: Penguin, 1981.

Snelling, J. 'Shoku Nihongi (Chronicles of Japan)', in *Transactions of the Asiatic Society of Japan*, 2nd series, vol. XI, 1934, pp. 151–240.

So, K. *Japanese Piracy in Ming China During the 16th Century.* East Lansing, MI: Michigan State University Press, 1975.

Sonoda, N. *Agostino Konishi Settsunokami Yukinaga Kaisōjō [Augustin Konishi Memorial Notes].* Chūōkōron Jigyōsha, 2004.

Steichen, M. *The Christian Daimyos: A Century of Religious and Political History in Japan (1549–1650).* Tōkyō: Rikkyo Gakuin Press, c.1900.

Sugawara, M. *The Ancient Samurai.* Tōkyō: The East Publications, 1986.

Tamamuro, F. 'Local Society and the Temple-Parishioner Relationship within the Bakufu's Governance Structure', in the *Japanese Journal of Religious Studies*, vol. XXVIII (2001), pp. 262–92.

Takahashi, T. *Emishi.* Tōkyō: Chūōkōron, 1986.

Thornton, S. *The Japanese Period Film: A Critical Analysis.* Jefferson: McFarland and Company, 2008.

Tsuruta, K. *Tsushima kara Mita Nitchō Kankei [Japanese–Korean Relations as Seen from Tsushima].* Tōkyō: Yamagawa Shuppansha, 2006.

Turnbull, S. *The Samurai: A Military History.* London: Osprey Publishing, 1977.

—— *Battles of the Samurai.* London: Arms and Armour Press, 1987.

—— *The Samurai Sourcebook.* London: Cassell & Co., 2000.

—— *Nagashino 1575: Slaughter at the Barricades.* Oxford: Osprey Publishing, 2000.

—— *Ashigaru 1467–1649.* Oxford: Osprey Publishing, 2001.

—— *Samurai Invasion: Japan's Korean War 1592–98.* London: Cassell & Co., 2002.

—— *Japanese Castles 1540–1640.* Oxford: Osprey Publishing, 2003.

—— *Pirate of the Far East 811–1639.* Oxford: Osprey Publishing, 2007.

—— (ed.). *The Samurai Tradition*. 2 vols. Richmond, VA: Japan Library, 2000.

Vaporis, C. *Tour of Duty: Samurai Military Service in Edo, and the Culture of Early Modern Japan*. Honolulu: University of Hawaii Press, 2008.

Varley, P. *Warriors of Japan as Portrayed in the War Tales*. Honolulu: University of Hawaii Press, 1992.

—— with Ivan and Nobuko Morris. *The Samurai*. London: Weidenfeld and Nicolson, 1970.

von Verschuer, C. *Across the Perilous Sea: Japanese Trade with China and Korea from the Seventh to the Sixteenth Centuries*. Ithaca: Cornell University East Asia Program, 2006.

Vlastos, S. *Peasant Protests and Uprisings in Tokugawa Japan*. Berkeley: California University Press, 1986.

Walker, B. *The Conquest of Ainu Lands: Ecology and Culture in Japanese Expansion 1590–1800*. Berkeley: University of California Press, 2001.

Walthall, A. *Peasant Uprisings in Japan: A Critical Anthology of Peasant Histories*. Chicago: University of Chicago Press, 1991.

Wang, Z. *Ambassadors from the Islands of Immortals: China–Japan Relations in the Han-Tang Period*. Honolulu: Association for Asian Studies and University of Hawaii Press, 2005.

Watanabe, N. *Date Masamune*. Tōkyō: Kawade Shobō Shinsha/ Sendai City Museum, 1986.

Watanabe, T. and Junichi Iwata, *The Love of the Samurai: A Thousand Years of Japanese Homosexuality*. London: Gay Men's Press, 1989.

Watts, J. 'The emperor's new roots: the Japanese emperor has finally laid to rest rumours that he has Korean blood, by admitting that it is true', in the *Guardian*, 28 December 2001.

Webb, H. 'What is the *Dai Nihon Shi*?', in the *Journal of Asian Studies*, vol. 19 (1960), no. 2, pp. 135–49.

Wilson, W. *Ideals of the Samurai: Writings of Japanese Warriors*. Burbank, CA: Ohara Publications, 1982.

—— *The Lone Samurai: The Life of Miyamoto Musashi*. Tōkyō: Kōdansha, 2004.

Woodson, Y. *Lords of the Samurai: Legacy of a Daimyō Family.* San Francisco: Asian Art Museum, 2009.

Xiong, V. *Emperor Yang of the Sui Dynasty: His Life, Times and Legacy.* Albany: State University of New York Press, 2006.

Yamada, N. *Ghenkō: The Mongol Invasion of Japan.* London: Smith, Elder and Co., 1916.

Yamamoto, H. *Tsushima-han Edo Karō: Kinsei Nitchō Gaikō o Saseta Hitobito* [*Tsushima Domain, Edo House Elder: The Men Who Ran Recent Japanese–Korean Diplomacy*]. Tōkyō: Kōdansha, 2002.

——— *Edojō no Kyūtei Seiji: Kumamoto-ban Hosokawa Tadaoki Hosokawa Tadatoshi Oyako no Seifuku Shojō* [*The Imperial Politics of Edo Castle: Military Dispatches of the Heads of House Hosokawa, Hosokawa Tadaoki and His Son Hosokawa Tadatoshi*]. Tōkyō: Kōdansha, 2004.

Yamamoto, T. *Hagakure: The Book of the Samurai.* Tōkyō: Kōdansha, 2002.

Yanagida, K. (ed.), *Shimabara Hantō Mukashibanashi Shū* [*Legends of the Shimabara Peninsula*]. Tōkyō: Sanseidō, 1943.

NOTES AND REFERENCES

Chapter 1: Strong Fellows

1. Aston, *Nihongi*, vol. I, p. 123.
2. Farris, *Heavenly Warriors*, p. 41.
3. Xiong, *Emperor Yang of the Sui Dynasty*, pp. 202–3.
4. Piggott, *The Emergence of Japanese Kingship*, p. 117.
5. Best, *A History of the Early Korean Kingdom of Paekche*, p. 407. Life is too short in a book about Japan to give alternate Korean readings in the main text, but the Kum river is also known as the Geum. Baekje is also known as Paekche. The battle is known as the Battle of Paek river, or *Baekgang*, (white river) in Korean sources, or *Baicunjiang* (white village river) in Chinese. Those same characters are read *Hakusonkō* in Japanese.
6. Farris, *Heavenly Warriors*, p. 39.
7. Clements, *Wu*, pp. 84–6; Wang, *Ambassadors from the Islands of Immortals*, p. 231.
8. Friday, *Samurai, Warfare and the State in Early Modern Japan*, p. 70. Earlier accounts of Japanese archery often

assume that the asymmetric bow was adopted in order to permit use of bows by horsemen. As Friday persuasively argues, Chinese accounts as early as the third century AD were already commenting on the Japanese bow's distinctive shape, long before the rise in Japan of mounted archers.

9. Piggott, *The Emergence of Japanese Kingship*, p. 127. As Piggott notes, it is also possible that Temmu's widow and successor, Jitō, was truly the first to use the title of Tennō while regnant, and that Temmu himself, like his ancestors, only had his imperial status conferred after his death.

10. Aston, *Nihongi*, vol. II, p. 363.

11. Bender, 'The Political Meaning of the Hachiman Cult in Ancient and Early Medieval Japan.' p. 30.

12. Takahashi, *Emishi*, pp. 22–7. The Emishi were also called the Ebisu.

13. Farris, *Heavenly Warriors*, p. 85.

14. *Shoku Nihongi*, quoted in Farris, *Heavenly Warriors*, p. 92.

15. *Shoku Nihongi*, quoted in Farris, *Heavenly Warriors*, p. 93.

16. Farris, *Heavenly Warriors*, pp. 102–3.

17. In later periods with different design concerns, the very top of the helmet became a notorious weak spot.

18. Farris, *Heavenly Warriors*, pp. 114–15; Friday, *Hired Swords*, pp. 42–3. The Chinese character for *ōyumi* is written with components that mean 'slave bow'. The pronunciation, however, is Japanese for 'great bow'. Friday suggests that the *ōyumi* may have fired multiple bolts, but only has the stock chronicler's phrase 'arrows fell like rain' to support this claim. The cliché occurs throughout Chinese and Japanese history, and should not be taken to imply anything more than many arrows – a situation one gets when one has many *ōyumi*! The crossbow gets a mention in the Genpei wars, tellingly in the north, but seems to have been forgotten by the Japanese by the time of the Mongol invasions, where its use by a new foe caught the Japanese by surprise; see Bottomley and Hopson, *Arms and Armor of the Samurai*, p. 48.

Chapter 2: The First Samurai

1. Sugawara, *The Ancient Samurai*, pp. 82–3. Sugawara identifies the origin of the Taira name as the character *Hei* from the name of the capital, Heian-kyō. The precise inspiration for the name Minamoto remains unclear.

2. *Shōmonki*, quoted in Friday, *The First Samurai*, p. 45.

3. Friday, *The First Samurai*, pp. 130–1.

4. Friday, *The First Samurai*, pp. 3–6. For other gruesome tales of Masakado in the afterlife, see Leiter, *New Kabuki Encyclopedia*, pp. 387–8.

5. Friday, *The First Samurai*, p. 153.

6. Farris, *Heavenly Warriors*, p. 132.

7. The *Shōmonki* is merely the best known of over forty-five medieval tales about Masakado. See Friday, *The First Samurai*, p. 7.

8. Bottomley and Hopson, *Arms and Armor of the Samurai*, p. 32.

9. Friday, *The First Samurai*, p. 145. The method of buying peace from pirates, effectively paying poachers to turn gamekeeper, was not unknown in the East. It was also a common strategy to offer the same government position to rival pirates, in the hope that each would annihilate the other in the struggle for supremacy. See, for example, Clements, *Coxinga and the Fall of the Ming Dynasty*, p. 57.

10. Morris, *The World of the Shining Prince*, p. 93.

11. Farris, *Heavenly Warriors*, p. 225; Sugawara, *The Ancient Samurai*, p. 87. Varley, *Warriors of Japan*, p. 223, notes that this is usually referred to in Japanese as the Former Nine Years' War, despite spanning *twelve* years from the initial arrival of Yoriyoshi in 1051 to the last stand of the Abe in 1062.

12. McCullough, 'A Tale of Mutsu,' p. 191. Sugawara, *The Ancient Samurai*, p. 110, suggests that 'Hachiman Tarō' may have already been a childhood nickname of Yoshiie, and that attributing its coinage to awestruck enemies was merely dramatic licence. In fact, it seems to be a mere coincidence –

each of his brothers was similarly named after a god's temple; Yoshiie was merely 'lucky' enough to be named after that of the God of War.

13. In Japanese: '*Koromo no tate wa hokorobinikeri/toshi o heishi ito no midare no kurushisa ni.*'

14. Varley, *Warriors of Japan*, p. 39.

15. Sugawara, *The Ancient Samurai*, p. 106.

Chapter 3: The Latter Days of the Law

1. The imperial reign period Hōgen spanned the years 1156–9.

2. Varley, *Warriors of Japan*, p. 52; Farris, *Heavenly Warriors*, p. 270.

3. Sugawara, *The Ancient Samurai*, p. 158.

4. '*Akaji no nishiki no hitatare ni/sakaomodaka no yoroi/chō no maru no suso kanamono shigeuttaruga/kurenai no horo massō ni fukasete ...*', *Hōgen Monogatari*, quoted in Sugawara, *The Ancient Samurai*, p. 158. The 'stars' are the rivets – see Varley, *Warriors of Japan*, p. 74.

5. Reputedly, one arm was dislocated in order to prevent him using a bow again, although legend suggests that having a left arm six inches longer than his right only made him an even better archer. However, this, like many other stories of Tametomo interpolated into the *Hōgen Monogatari*, seems very doubtful.

6. Varley, *Warriors of Japan*, p. 65.

7. Sugawara, *The Ancient Samurai*, p. 178.

8. *Azuma Kagami*, quoted in Varley, *Warriors of Japan*, p. 79.

9. Sugawara, *The Ancient Samurai*, p. 206. There are several variant versions of the proclamation, and indeed, considering the infelicities of copying by hand, perhaps all are genuine. Sugawara argues that (a) a proclamation of some sort was certainly written, and (b) the version in the *Azuma Kagami* is probably the most accurate.

10. Sugawara, *The Ancient Samurai*, p. 208.

11. *Heike Monogatari*, IV: 5.

12. Farris, *Heavenly Warriors*, p. 301.

13. *Heike Monogatari*, IV: 12.
14. *Umoregi no/Hana saku koto mo/Nakarishi ni/Mi no naru hate zo/Kanashi karikeru*. Sugawara, *The Ancient Samurai*, p. 213.
15. *Heike Monogatari*, IV: 16.
16. *Heike Monogatari*, V: 3.
17. *Heike Monogatari*, VI: 7. Notably, the term Kiyomori uses for Yoritomo is rōnin, here meant as a true exile rather than the 'internal' exiles of Tokugawa-era vagabonds.

Chapter 4: The Proud Do Not Endure

1. Farris, *Heavenly Warriors*, p. 293.
2. The *Gen* are the Minamoto, the *Hei* are the Taira, with an initial letter that converts to p when formed as a compound word. Farris, *Heavenly Warriors*, p. 289, justifiably calls it 'the Japanese version of the Peloponnesian Wars,' both for its far-reaching effects and the polar divisions it engendered.
3. *Heike Monogatari*, I: 1.
4. *Heike Monogatari*, VII: 6. Sugawara, *The Ancient Samurai*, p. 248, puts the number of dead at a smaller but still impressive 40,000.
5. *Heike Monogatari*, VIII: 6.
6. Sugawara, *The Ancient Samurai*, p. 251.
7. *Heike Monogatari*, VII: 20.
8. *Heike Monogatari*, VII: 20.
9. Sugawara, *The Ancient Samurai*, p. 258.
10. McCullough, *Yoshitsune*, pp. 41–2. See also Leiter, *New Kabuki Encyclopedia*, pp. 154–5.
11. *Heike Monogatari*, IX: 2.
12. *Heike Monogatari*, IX: 2. See also Varley, *Warriors of Japan*, p. 95. The fact that there were two Battles of the Uji River, one in 1180 and another in 1184 (and yet another later on), has confused many authorities. Sugawara, *The Ancient Samurai*, p. 259, for example, claims that the river in February 1184 is flooded with 'snowmelt', which is surely a description more befitting it in July 1180.

13. See, for example, Varley, *Warriors of Japan*, p. 144, where Yoshitsune deliberately claims not to be the leader of the Minamoto at the Battle of Dannoura, in order to allow him to lead from the front.

14. *Heike Monogatari*, IX: 4. Tomoe is described first as a female attendant (*binjo*), then as a front-line captain (*ippō no taishō*). Some texts describe her as a beautiful woman (*bijo*), suggesting perhaps that either *bijo* or *binjo* might have been misheard by scribes when the tale was set down.

15. Varley, *Warriors of Japan*, p. 104 and p. 235, n.112.

16. *Heike Monogatari*, IX: 4.

17. The police appointment was the origin of Yoshitsune's title 'lieutenant' (*hōgan*), crucial because *hōgan-biiki*, or 'sympathy for the lieutenant', would evolve into a Japanese idiom for supporting an underdog.

18. *Heike Monogatari*, IX: 8.

19. *Heike Monogatari*, IX: 9.

20. *Heike Monogatari*, IX: 9 – the tale specifically notes that Yoshihisa is at Yoshitsune's side at the time of his death in 1189.

21. *Heike Monogatari*, IX: 16.

22. *Heike Monogatari*, XI: 4.

23. Although there is no reason to doubt the veracity of the archery-based stories that have accreted around the Battle of Yashima, *ya* is a homophone for 'arrow' in Japanese, and we may hence be witnessing several centuries of additions by storytellers who believed themselves to be recounting the 'Battle of Arrow Island'. For yet more archery stories of the Minamoto, see Varley, *Warriors of Japan*, p. 141.

24. Quite accidentally, this scene has become one of the most widely heard traditional Japanese songs in the world outside Japan. A snatch from the song *Ogi no Mato* ('The Folding Fan as a Target') forms the background of a scene in Ridley Scott's film *Blade Runner* (1982).

25. Varley, *Warriors of Japan*, p. 141 and p. 225, n.26.

26. *Heike Monogatari*, XI: 11.

Chapter 5: The Divine Wind

1. McCullough, *Yoshitsune*, p. 289.
2. Turnbull, *The Samurai: A Military History*, p. 87; Rossabi, *Khubilai Khan*, p. 100. Conlan, *In Little Need of Divine Intervention*, p. 256, notes that Khubilai's communiqué is 'remarkably cordial' by Mongol standards.
3. Yamada, *Ghenkō: The Mongol Invasion of Japan*, p. 108. Note, however, the prevalence of bird-arson tales in sources elsewhere, e.g. Clements, *A Brief History of the Vikings*, pp. 111 and 192.
4. Yamada, *Ghenkō: The Mongol Invasion of Japan*, pp. 114–15.
5. For example, Sugawara, *The Ancient Samurai*, p. 458, cites Tokimune's 'lack of a policy'.
6. Turnbull, *The Samurai: A Military History*, p. 91.
7. Yamada, *Ghenkō: The Mongol Invasion of Japan*, p. 145.
8. Delgado, *Khubilai Khan's Lost Fleet*, p. 97.
9. Kadenokōji Kanenaka, quoted in Conlan, *In Little Need of Divine Intervention*, p. 266.
10. Conlan, *In Little Need of Divine Intervention*, p. 266.
11. Yamada, *Ghenkō: The Mongol Invasion of Japan*, p. 162.
12. Clements, *Marco Polo*, p. 93.
13. Yamada, *Ghenkō: The Mongol Invasion of Japan*, pp. 193–4.
14. Conlan, *In Little Need of Divine Intervention*, p. 272.
15. Clements, *Marco Polo*, p. 96.
16. Delgado, *Khubilai Khan's Lost Fleet*, pp. 149–50.
17. Conlan, *In Little Need of Divine Intervention*, p. 260.
18. Conlan, *In Little Need of Divine Intervention*, p. 274. Sugawara, *The Ancient Samurai*, pp. 452–3, goes even further, and suggests that there was no second Kamikaze either. His evidence for this, however, is circumstantial reportings of *20th century* weather conditions in Hakata Bay, which even he admits is 'unscientific'.
19. Farris, *Heavenly Warriors*, p. 334.
20. Conlan, *In Little Need of Divine Intervention*, p. 255.
21. Varley, *Warriors of Japan*, p. 162.

Chapter 6: Two Suns in the Sky

1. Sugawara, *The Ancient Samurai*, p. 462.

2. Sugawara, *The Ancient Samurai*, p. 473, notes that Go-Daigo based his reign name on that of a restored dynasty in China. Unquestionably, he was thinking of the Han dynasty, which was briefly usurped by the Regent Wang Mang, before being violently restored in AD 25. The first-era title of the 'Later Han' was *Jianwu* (in Japanese pronunciation, *Kenmu*), and Go-Daigo clearly meant to draw historical parallels, not only with his enemy's unwelcome grab for power, but with the fact that the Han dynasty endured for two more centuries after the troubles.

3. Varley, *Warriors of Japan*, p. 173. McCullough, *Taiheiki*, p. xvi, notes that 'More than two thirds [of the *Taiheiki*] is devoted to episodic, disorganized accounts of fighting in local areas; the sort of things one finds in certain Icelandic sagas, where stories of particular interest to a certain family . . . have been added haphazardly over the years.'

4. Varley, *Warriors of Japan*, pp. 187–8. I do not agree, however, with the twentieth-century commentators cited by Varley who believe that Kusunoki was a 'student of the art of the ninja' simply because he was not above stabbing people in the back. See the final chapter for my assessment of this strangely pervasive modern fad.

5. Turnbull, *The Samurai: A Military History*, p. 98.

6. So, at least, claims the *Taiheiki*. See Varley, *Warriors of Japan*, p. 176. I am ready to believe that the legions of Hōjō dead were 'helped' along by their attackers in a massacre that has been carefully retold as a mass suicide. The number is also open to debate. According to Sugawara, *The Ancient Samurai*, p. 473, archaeologists excavated a mass grave in Kamakura dating from the defeat, and estimated that they had found the bones of around 910 individuals, mainly young men.

7. *Saigenin-bon Taiheiki*, quoted in Varley, *Warriors of Japan*, p. 195.

8. Varley, *Warriors of Japan*, p. 198. Seven, in classical Chinese, is not intended as an exact number but as a signifier of multitudes. Similarly, modern Japanese department stores are purveyors of '100 articles', and Ali Baba fought '40 thieves'.

9. Murdoch, *History of Japan*, vol. 1, p. 565.

10. Turnbull, *The Samurai: A Military History*, pp. 107–11, has a long series of documentation showing the Shibuya clansmen milking the Ashikaga shōgunate for all they could get.

11. *Ōninki*, XLVII, http://homepage1.nifty.com/sira/ouninki/

12. Brown, 'The impact of firearms on Japanese warfare, 1543–98', p. 239.

13. Berry, *Hideyoshi*, p. 42. See also Leiter, *New Kabuki Encyclopedia*, p. 10, for a précis of the uses of Akechi's story in the theatre after 1702.

14. Turnbull, *The Samurai: A Military History*, p. 164.

Chapter 7: The Far West

1. The man credited with coining the term 'Japan's Christian Century' was the historian Charles Boxer, with his seminal 1951 book on the subject. However, he later complained that the title was foisted on him without consultation by his publishers, and he never much liked it or its implications. See Alden, *Charles Boxer: An Uncommon Life*, p. 29.

2. Hawley, *The Imjin War*, pp. 80–1. The concerns of this necessarily brief history require me to ignore much of the fascinating story of the Korean defence, for which Hawley's *Imjin War* offers much detail. See also Turnbull, *The Samurai Sourcebook*, pp. 241–50.

3. Hawley, *The Imjin War*, p. 88.

4. Nomenclature has been deliberately simplified here. Karatsu was known in Hideyoshi's time as Nagoya. Modern Nagoya did not then exist, but was known as the village of Nakamura – the hometown of both Hideyoshi himself and his leading general Katō Kiyomasa. 'Katō Kiyomasa built Nagoya castle' is not only a true statement, but true in two separate places!

5. Wilson, *Ideals of the Samurai*, p. 130. Damian Kuroda Nagamasa (here erroneously assigned his father's Christian name of Simeon) follows on p. 134, *passim*. I note with interest the distinctive shape of Katō's helmet. When approaching Nagoya Castle in 2007, I was able to identify his statue at a distance of half a kilometre, largely because of the distinctive headgear. It was sure to have served a similar function on the battlefield – impractical in single combat, but invaluable for leading large bodies of men.

6. Wilson, *Ideals of the Samurai*, p. 134, *passim*, although in this source Damian Kuroda Nagamasa is erroneously assigned his father's Christian name of Simeon.

7. Sonoda, *Agostino Konishi Settsunokami Yukinaga Kaisōchō*, p. 430. Sources vary as to Konishi's date of birth. I trust Sonoda the most.

8. Hawley, *The Imjin War*, p. 99.

9. Turnbull, *The Samurai: A Military History*, p. 206, observes: 'If [Hideyoshi] had wished to sap the strength of likely opponents, he would have made sure that men such as Date Masamune and Tokugawa Ieyasu were the first to step on enemy soil. As it was, it was these who, owing to the distance of their domains from Kyūshū, found it easiest to refuse.'

10. Turnbull, *Samurai Invasion*, p. 51.

11. Hawley, *The Imjin War*, p. 155, notes that 'fighting with a river to one's back' was an approved strategy in Sun Tzu's *Art of War*, for precisely such a reason.

12. Turnbull, *The Samurai Sourcebook*, p. 245, questions whether the use of noses as substitutes for heads truly originated in the Korean War, and suspects that it was already an acceptable practice in some earlier Japanese campaigns.

13. Kimura, *Konishi Yukinaga Den*, pp. 251–2.

14. Hawley, *The Imjin War*, p. 166, makes this bold but not impossible claim. The impression one certainly gets from Seoul tourist sites is that any damage is the fault of the Japanese, whereas Hawley notes that Korean sources often simply mention that the damage was done at the *time* of the

Japanese invasion, and leave readers to infer that this must therefore be the work of foreign invaders.

15. Hawley, *The Imjin War*, pp. 184–206. I am sticking to Hawley's dates; many older sources, translated uncritically from Japanese or Korean documents, erroneously convert lunar months directly to solar months, and hence mis-date Yi's counter-attack by several weeks.

16. Turnbull, *Samurai Invasion*, pp. 67–8.

17. *Chingbirok*, quoted in Hawley, *The Imjin War*, p. 232.

18. Hawley, *The Imjin War*, pp. 287–8.

19. Kitajima, *Katō Kiyomasa: Chōsen Shinryaku no Jitsuzō*, pp. 65–70.

20. Kuno, *Japanese Expansion in the Asiatic Continent*, vol. 1, p. 333.

21. Crasset, *History of the Church of Japan*, vol. 2, pp. 14–15.

22. Cooper, *Rodrigues the Interpreter*, p. 116.

23. Hawley, *The Imjin War*, pp. 441–524.

Chapter 8: No More Wars

1. Crasset, *History of the Church of Japan*, vol. 2. p. 22.

2. Hawley, *The Imjin War*, pp. 563–4.

3. Bryant, *Sekigahara 1600*, p. 64.

4. Turnbull, *The Samurai: A Military History*, p. 245.

5. Crasset, *History of the Church of Japan*, vol. 2, p. 88.

6. Turnbull, *The Samurai: A Military History*, p. 244.

7. Crasset, *The History of the Church of Japan*, vol. 2, pp. 96–7. See also Kimura, *Konishi Yukinaga Den*, p. 544, which has the same letter in Japanese, but clearly translated from a European source. Was the piety of Augustin Konishi a late addition by Jesuit chroniclers?

8. Kimura, *Konishi Yukinaga Den*, p. 546. Father Mancio Konishi (*c*.1600–44), born in Tsushima, educated at a Jesuit seminary in Macao, and eventually ordained in Rome, is presumed by some sources to be the son of Maria Konishi and Dario Sō. He sneaked back into Japan in 1644 and was martyred, becoming the last confirmed Jesuit on Japanese soil

until the Meiji Restoration. See also Sonoda, *Agostino Konishi Settsunokami Yukinaga Kaisōjō*, p. 424, for more details of Konishi's distant descendants, not the least Konishi Kiyohira and Konishi Toshiko, who contribute essays to the book.

9. Crasset, *History of the Church of Japan*, vol. 2, p. 258: '[Ieyasu] complained that the Prince his Master had engrav'd several characters on the great bell of the Daybut, much to his Prejudice.'

10. Turnbull, *The Samurai: A Military History*, p. 250.

11. Crasset, *History of the Church of Japan*, vol. 2, p. 259.

12. Miyazaki, *The Story of the Building of Shimabara Castle*, p. 66.

13. Hosokawa Tadatoshi, quoted in Kanda, *Shimabara no Ran*, p. 34.

14. Paske-Smith, *Japanese Traditions of Christianity*, pp. 55–6, names the men as Oye Matsuemon, Chizuka Zanzaemon, Oye Genemon, Mori Soiken and Yama Zenzaimon. However, compare this list with that offered in Yanagida, *Shimabara Hantō Mukashibanashi Shū*, p. 162: Tsukaru of Koruba, Churen of Amiba, Hikoren of Enoura, Tokichi of Chijiwa and Naokichi of Ono Island.

15. Correa, quoted in Okada, *Amakusa Tokisada*, p. 19.

16. *Kirishitan Monogatari*, quoted in Elison, *Deus Destroyed*, p. 364.

17. *Hosokawa-ke Ki*, quoted in Okada, *Amakusa Tokisada*, p. 252–3.

18. Paske-Smith, *Japanese Traditions of Christianity*, p. 91.

19. Jansen, *China in the Tokugawa World*, p. 33.

20. See, for example, Clements, *Coxinga and the Fall of the Ming Dynasty*, pp. 291–2.

21. Turnbull, *The Samurai: A Military History*, p. 269.

22. Webb, 'What is the *Dai Nihon Shi*?', p. 135.

23. Blomberg, *The Akō Affair*, p. 19.

24. Yamamoto, *Hagakure*, p. 26.

25. Clements, *Moon in the Pines*, pp. 40 and 87–8.

Chapter 9: Twilight of the Samurai

1. See, for example, Howard, *Life with the Trans-Siberian Savages*, p. 59, which notes that Ainu women were 'all over the body nearly as hairy as the men'.

2. Walker, *The Conquest of Ainu Lands*, p. 57.

3. Walker, *The Conquest of Ainu Lands*, p. 66. In fact, the Ming resistance, led by the 'pirate king' Coxinga, had unsuccessfully sought Japan's help against the Manchus. As with the earlier Mongol invasion of Korea, the Japanese preferred to hedge their bets and stayed clear. Jansen, *China in the Tokugawa World*, p. 27.

4. Sansom, *A History of Japan 1615–1867*, pp. 164–5.

5. The arrival of the sweet potato in Japan in 1734, and the overjoyed reaction of the populace to this new alternative to rice, mirrors the vegetable's arrival in China in 1594 under similar circumstances. See Clements, *Coxinga and the Fall of the Ming Dynasty*, p. 15.

6. Leiter, *New Kabuki Encyclopedia*, pp. 106–7.

7. Leupp, *Servants, Shophands and Laborers in the Cities of Tokugawa Japan*, p. 33. '*Dekiai no bushi urikireru matsu no uchi/Hiyatoi no tomo neagari no matsu no uchi.*'

8. Botsman, *Punishment and Power in the Making of Modern Japan*, p. 71.

9. Yamamoto, quoted in Mishima, *On Hagakure*, pp. 24–5.

10. Sansom, *A History of Japan 1615–1867*, pp. 178–80.

11. Nawa, *Yōtō Muramasa: Mukashibanishi Kisho Hikae*, pp. 192–3. Gentarō ... assesses the blade at a value of 100 gold *ryō* (400,000 copper coins). It is offered for sale at a mere 30 *ryō*.

12. See Leiter, *New Kabuki Encyclopedia*, pp. 139, 261 and 397–8 for some of the best-known variants.

13. Harris and Ogasawara, *Swords of the Samurai*, p. 66. It is this alteration that has led to the apocryphal story that Muramasa was a pupil of Masamune, even though their dates do not overlap.

14. Perrin, *Giving Up the Gun*, p. 71.

15. Perrin, *Giving Up the Gun*, p. 71.
16. Feifer, *Breaking Open Japan*, p. 42.
17. Melville, *Moby Dick*, p. 169.

Chapter 10: The Last Hurrah

1. Peifer, *Breaking Open Japan*, p. 5.
2. Taylor, *A Visit to India, China and Japan in the Year 1853*, quoted in Perrin, *Giving Up the Gun*, pp. 106–7.
3. Clements, *Prince Saionji*, pp. 19–20.
4. Clements, *Prince Saionji*, p. 28.
5. Hansard, H.C. Deb., 09 February 1864, vol. 173, cols 335–6.
6. Hillsborough, *Shinsengumi*, pp. 77–9.
7. Clements, *Prince Saionji*, p. 27.
8. Hillsborough, *Shinsengumi*, p. 90; Ravia, *The Last Samurai*, p. 117.
9. See, for example, Clements, *Prince Saionji*, p. 44.
10. Ravina, *The Last Samurai*, p. 149.
11. Seeley, 'The Japanese March in The Mikado'. *Miya-sama, Miya-sama/On-uma no mae ni/Pirapira suru no wa/Nan ja na . . .?* The 'prince' referred to is Arisugawa Taruhito (1835–95), the Meiji Emperor's uncle by adoption, who was the leader of the imperial forces in both the Boshin War and during the suppression of the Satsuma Rebellion. A statue of him, appropriately mounted on a horse, can be found in today's Arisugawa Memorial Park in Tōkyō.
12. Hillsborough, *Shinsengumi*, p. 173.

Chapter 11: Return of the Jidai

1. Nitobe, *The Japanese Nation*, p. 155.
2. Clements, *Wellington Koo*, p. 89.
3. Hirano, *Mr. Smith Goes to Tokyo*, p. 68.
4. Johnston, 'Buried Treasure'. Although the visit of Kumazawa was reported in the *Stars & Stripes* at the time, the fact that he was taken seriously was not properly appreciated until the declassification of SCAP documents in the 1970s.

5. Jones, *Yoshitsune and the Thousand Cherry Trees*, p. 2. For further details of *Terakoya*, see Leiter, *New Kabuki Encyclopedia*, pp. 615–18.

6. Hirano, *Mr. Smith Goes to Tokyo*, pp. 66–9.

7. Richie, *The Films of Akira Kurosawa*, p. 32.

8. Clements and Tamamuro, *The Dorama Encyclopedia*, p. xi.

9. Both terms, *ninja* and *shinobi-mono*, are written with the same characters, a fudge that has allowed some authorities to claim an entirely undeserved provenance. I invite any doubting reader to trace the references back themselves, until they find themselves in a misty world of misattributed paintings, misread characters and optimistic reinterpretations of historical events. The earliest verifiable mention of ninja is that in the book *Sarutobi Sasuke* (1913), as mentioned in Thornton, *The Japanese Period Film*, p. 96.However, even then, Thornton's account conflates indisputable ninja films such as *Shinobi no Mono* (1962) with earlier appearances in fiction of the same *characters*, such as Ishikawa Goemon. Merely because the same characters appear in earlier works does not make those works ninja stories. Ishikawa, as Leiter's *New Kabuki Encyclopedia* (pp. 224–5) notes, has been a staple of Japanese drama since the 1680s, but only as a rogue, thief and outlaw. His co-option into the lore of ninja is a twentieth-century development, not unlike suddenly being told that Robin Hood was also a vampire. In fact, the word 'ninja' does not occur even once in the whole 800-plus pages of Leiter's kabuki reference guide – you would think that something so supposedly well known would have cropped up in the last 300 years of the Japanese theatre. To me, at least, this is further proof that they only became a subject of discussion in Japan in the twentieth century. 'But I've seen the places where they hid!' a man once protested to me in a pub, citing his visit to an 'old castle' in Japan that turned out to have been built in 1965.

10. Clements and McCarthy, *The Anime Encyclopedia*, passim.

11. Richie, *The Films of Akira Kurosawa*, p. 103.

12. Clements and Tamamuro, *The Dorama Encyclopedia*, p. 195. *Mito Kōmon's* genesis is fiendishly complex. Apocryphal stories of Mitsukuni's disguised wanderings already flourished in the late Edo period, and *Mito Kōmon* was not even the first TV show to be based on his life.

13. I refuse to get involved in the polarized opposition between fans of the two great Mishima biographies, and instead recommend them both: Nathan's *Mishima: A Biography*, and Scott-Stokes' *The Life and Death of Yukio Mishima*. *The Sea of Fertility* was actually completed many weeks before Mishima's death, but the choice of its official completion date was all part of the theatre of his suicide.

INDEX

Note: Where more than one page number is listed against a heading, page numbers in bold indicate significant treatment of a subject. Abbreviations used: bro. – brother; neph. – nephew; s. – son